SYMPHONIES
AND THEIR MEANING

SECOND SERIES

SYMPHONIES
AND THEIR MEANING
SECOND SERIES

BY PHILIP H. GOEPP

PHILADELPHIA & LONDON
J. B. LIPPINCOTT COMPANY

COPYRIGHT, 1902
BY
J. B. LIPPINCOTT COMPANY

PRINTED IN UNITED STATES OF AMERICA

Res severa verum gaudium

PREFATORY

THIS book completes the whole survey of classic symphonies. The aim of the first volume was to find the mystery of symphonies,—not here, nor there, but of the ideal type; to see what tonal meaning really *means*, and, quite as clearly, what it does not mean. The quaint confusion ever will intrude that only that is definite that finds a term in common speech. And so the lay-world seldom dreams that music, pure and simple, in highest form of art, will tell a message clearer far and richer, nobler and more human, too (in its own field), than one may hope of prose or even verse.

In this design the special symphonies described were the mere proof and evidence. A later thought, helped by the kind response to the first volume, was to test these hidden truths in other classic symphonies that varied in their plan and quality, and lastly to survey the whole field of the great tonal works of art.

PREFATORY

In thus returning to the earlier masters, the third of Mozart's group of masterworks remained to be included. With Haydn the problem is a special one. The long list of his symphonies implies two consequences, really two in one. First, they are all much alike in inner content,—in that which here is sought to bring to clearer light. Then, for the same reason, this very message is a lesser one, does not so well invite or quite deserve, nor does it surely need the verbal sketch. The aim was to amuse and cheer in highest sense. While they do cheer, each in a novel way, they do not vary in significant degree within the original mood of merry humor.

Of Beethoven's symphonies all are here discussed except the three of volume one. The question there must face us of Beethoven's earlier art,—the true degree of independence, the share of Mozart (and of Haydn) in the younger master's thought. And this must touch the other problem, ever rising new to view, of highest rank.

In face of warning proverb of odious comparisons, there are some questions that will never down. You cannot cure the world of having

PREFATORY

its greatest—poet or soldier. It does not want a democracy of genius; it tends, however wrong, to feel with Odysseus: "One must be foremost." The later Beethoven compels two subjects of profoundest interest and moment, where reasoning may well confirm the test of great experiment. In the "Pastoral" we wonder at the bounds of tonal art, in actual graphic copying of nature; in the Ninth we are aroused to take sides as to the highest ultimate effect of instruments alone, or of joint orchestra and chorus.

The works of Raff bring a new phase of titled symphonies; and here the "Scotch" of Mendelssohn belongs. And so the whole field of programme music opened forth with Berlioz's Fantastic Symphony, the literal story of an artist's woes. Liszt's "Faust" must show the touches of the great dramatic school; Tschaikowsky's Pathétique is here in line of clear descent. At the same time, the symphonies of Schumann and of Brahms preserved the standard of highest tonal epic, of pure subjective quality.

The raging quarrel of the two great modern schools can somehow not be all ignored. There the new word of latest instrumental poet

PREFATORY

must surely shed a ray of brilliant light on coming lines. And so, though Richard Strauss has not as yet chosen the strict symphony, his broadest, latest work, *Ein Heldenleben*, could not be resisted.

At this point came a certain strong desire to include in all this view each individual symphony that has uttered its new note of sincere poetic message. As there must doubtless be dispute in such a list of those composers whose final laurels are not yet secure, at least one work of each is treated. So, in appended note, Gade and Goetz disclose a narrower vein, though still of truest art. The charming " Country Wedding" of Goldmark shows well the limits of the symphony. Another work, by Gilchrist, is an instance of the form transplanted in a newer field.*

The description is really all symbolic, and must be taken as such, for any value whatever. We might, in a sense, have printed in the inside of our book on the meaning of symphonies,—

---

* There is a group of American symphonies, by such composers as Paine and Chadwick, that would well repay an exposition. Lack of space forbids the choice of more than one.

PREFATORY

nothing. It would be true in a way. Music means nothing that can definitely be put in words. It means so much to the musician, indeed it seems often to hold all truth, that he could talk about it indefinitely in more than one sense.

And it is certainly worth helping others to the same joy of intelligence, even though he can only eagerly point to the glorious beauties, anxious for responsive agreement, as at sight of fleeting clouds in waning light of sunset one would catch at this figure and that to fix it to the eye of a friend. So if ordered beauty as well as delight of golden touches can be brought in some measure to fellow ears and minds, it will be the main object,—at least of the descriptions.

But, somehow, there is a little more than mere chance imagery; for there is real truth in the symbolism of the moral strife of individual, of debate and dispute, drawing truth from the dregs, rising to final enlightenment. Every phase of life is here idealized. Again, the symbol has real truth. Beauty, strength, each have their figures. The moral, not the external life of man finds in music its full play and mirror. The true essence of life is in its emotions, and

PREFATORY

these play in tones as do fish in the waters. The highest problems are ethical, emotional, of experience; science is but a lesser helpmeet. In music their utterance is so real that they seem to be there themselves in the life of the tonal stream.

Given the type of pleading, of defiance, of plaint, of dim foreboding akin to objective omen, of prayerful trust, of triumphant joy,—given all these, together with the full play of dispute and strife,—and you have all the resources, unconscious and therefore the more genuine and convincing, for the utterance of man's most vital thought. So you have in the Fifth Symphony actually as stirring a refrain of the same high truth as in the book of Job.

The elements of rhythm, pace, and melody, of single song and polyphonic or mere hymnal chorus, the lesser, of orchestral color, are all quickly caught; they need no technical account. Even the element of form, the highest in the mastery of the art, can be suggested in recurrence of the themes. One phase there is that seems more difficult to show in direct meaning. The schoolmen call it modulation, the change of tonality. The latter we have agreed is scene

PREFATORY

or tonal residence. The key may thus be said in simplest truth to be the home of a tune,—where it begins and ends, whence it may wander for a long or shorter journey. It were, indeed, idle to speak of tunes or lesser figures without this sense of residence. They would be as shadowy as the spirits of the unreal world. It is the tonal color that gives the living hue.

If a key is the home of a tune, what then is the grateful change? Whether you regard yourself as going about subjectively, wandering tonally from scene to scene with conclusion in each, returning finally home to the first, or whether you are resting and it all passes before you, is of no moment of difference. If we were to sit still and have the planets fly past us, it would be as much of a journey as if we were flying ourselves. In any case we are taking a tonal journey; that is as near the true state as a symbol will take us. All the motion is there of voyage,—all the incident, main and lesser, of the change.

So a modulation is literally change of scene, and it may be graded or sudden, as in wandering through a plain or over a mountain. Indeed, the quick surprise of new turn of view is just

PREFATORY

the same sort of pleasure as the charm of sudden shift of key. The symbol for us will be our own journey, or of picture moving before our eyes. We may even leave quite vague the figure each one chooses for himself. But we shall hope for ready response of the reader without need of literal fulness.

Suppose the symbol is of action, what then of the key? Where the first theme is type of energy, the second may be of passive apprehension, the state of joyous perception; in any case, under whatever guise, you must have a dual quality, not merely of tune but of tone. Contrast there must be in outer garb and colors as well as in actual lineaments of theme. Else, if the second follows in the same tone, there is no progress, no relation, no sequence, no contrast. One is mere continuation of the other, like a building all in one dimension. One figure belongs in one line and light, the second in another. The tonal color of melodic subjects is one of the main elements of musical enjoyment; it marks the difference of old fugue and new earthly sonata. What the tunes stand for, what they do, where they are aiming, none of it is more important than where they come from

PREFATORY

tonally, in what tonal quarter do they sing, what is the change of tonal scene from one tune to the other. It may, to be sure, be possible to stress too far this matter of the scene or light. It is the nearest word that comes for the idea. There may be a better that may fit in certain other symbols of the whole.

In all the discussion of the meaning and potency of musical works of art this cannot be lost. It is of first moment, though so intimate a matter that it is hard to separate from the nature of the melody itself. In the symbols of scene or journey it is all clear enough, and needs no further light. In the profounder figures of actual or moral struggle the matter is deeper and more difficult; it cannot be dismissed so easily. In any case the tonal shift serves as in lighter symbols to mark the change. Change there must be in garb, guise, point of entrance; in strife there is the more need of opposite directions in the fighters, complete separation of residence, even of origin. So the change may approach almost to realism of stage shifting, so as to give the new direction. The villain must enter on the other side.

But the music must show it all. Nevertheless

PREFATORY

in all symbols it will be yielded that tone or key stands ever for residence; carried to mathematics, for orientation or location. So whether tunes are lines of picture, or the traveller himself is moving about making his own scenes, or whether they are types of action and of strife, they must have each their quarter where they dwell, whence they emerge and advance. For music is a very real sort of human process. It is no shadowy, abstract allegory. It is all genuine, real existence and enjoyment. These musical figures must have their entity, their real being, and so their place. Further, music is all astir with living, thrilling beauty that ever transcends. So this residence is not of mathematics or topography, but rich in color,—beauty is again its main designation. And thus, as every bit of music has a home where it begins and where it ends, every melodic figure has its own nook or niche, and every idea, of whatever symbolic guise, has its own tonal vine and fig-tree.

The best excuse, it must be here admitted, for treating more than one of the included symphonies, was their strong evidence, in converse proof, by negative example. There is no truth more

PREFATORY

urgently to be proclaimed than the absolute connection between a clear and honest art and a high moral tone. Here music can be shown to be the truest record of man's best intuition; thus it becomes the strongest power for moral inculcation. And so the author, with all desire to give a fair account of every work, can somehow not restrain the hope that the reader will subtly feel how, where the whole poem lacks in true organic growth, the strong pervading moral tone is absent, the impulse of display, of less sincere poetic message, finds a special channel. For here we see most clearly how the pure type of symphony has won pre-eminence of all the forms as the evangel of the highest truth.

No doubt there is most gain in positive approval. Disparaging attacks are on much lower plane. Ring out the praise of all the best in the world, and that which stands opposed, must meet its own deserved fate, by its own force, that needs no outer aid.

And yet no other field of human intellect, not all dramatic poetry nor varying lines of other arts do seem to hold so tense a moment and concern as just this double question: the meaning of the greatest tonal works, as it has worked

PREFATORY

its own solution through the century just passed, and as it must prove in that which has begun. For music is the art of latest age; it is the present self-expression of the race, the only channel where a creative vein runs still unchecked.

But music has a double power not merely for the good. The quality that brings the message home in warmest living tones may easily run riot in sensuous effect or meretricious sentiment. And so the question, What is good and what is permanently great? yields to no other in ultimate importance. It must affect the whole thought and ethics of the race. It has a greater urgency than the latest problems of theology. For here, in music, seems to lie the true creed and religion that has a common language clear to all.

CONTENTS

	PAGE
PREFATORY	7
CHAPTER I.—*Mozart*	13
Symphony in E Flat.	
CHAPTER II.—*Beethoven*	34
First Symphony.	
CHAPTER III.—*Beethoven* (Continued).	
Second Symphony	59
CHAPTER IV.—*Beethoven* (Continued).	
Fourth Symphony. (The Poet of Pathos and Humor)	87
CHAPTER V.—*Beethoven* (Continued).	
Eighth Symphony. (An Epic of Humor) . .	111
CHAPTER VI.—*Beethoven* (Continued).	
Sixth (Pastoral) Symphony. (Tonal Depiction)	233
CHAPTER VII.—*Beethoven* (Concluded).	
Ninth (Choral) Symphony. (The Final Need of Words)	153
CHAPTER VIII.—*Schumann*	195
First Symphony, in B Flat	195
Fourth Symphony, in D Minor	210

CONTENTS

Chapter IX.—*Mendelssohn and Raff.* PAGE
   Programme Music 230
   "Scotch" Symphony 231
   "Im Walde" Symphony 241
   "Lenore" Symphony 257
   "Winter" Symphony 267

Chapter X.—*Brahms* 282
   First Symphony.

Chapter XI.—*Brahms* (Continued).
   Third Symphony 323

Chapter XII.—*Brahms* (Concluded).
   Fourth Symphony 361

Chapter XIII.—*Liszt, Tschaikowsky, Strauss* . . 401
   "Faust" Symphony 408
   Symphony Pathétique 420
   Heldenleben 435

Appendix 457
   Berlioz 457
      Fantastic Symphony.
   Gade 463
      Symphony No. 4, in B Flat.
   Goetz 468
      Symphony in F Major.
   Gilchrist 477
      Symphony in C Major.
   Goldmark 483
      Country Wedding Symphony.

I

MOZART'S SYMPHONY IN E FLAT

IT is ever an old question, like that of the lost tribes of Israel, and some others that are never settled, on which the world's judgment stays poised. There are always people who believe that Mozart reached an absolute pinnacle of Parnassus,—that Beethoven marked a descent. The problem is incapable of solution. Both views are true, in a way. One thing is certain: every man has a right, in more than legal sense, to think Mozart the greatest. Von Ambros, prince of historians, says of the group of Mozart's symphonies in C, E Flat, and G Minor: "They are the *ne plus ultra* of art." Thus it becomes a question whether there was more gain or loss in a dominance of the emotional over the purely æsthetic. It may belong to the dualism of human things that both have their opposite, correlative, eternal positions; that each must come in its phase; that each is greatest in independence. One is inclined to think that you cannot com-

MOZART'S SYMPHONY IN E FLAT

pare Mozart and Beethoven any more than a lake and a mountain. One turns from the cold, smooth perfection of the elder with eagerness to the fire and wealth of sympathy of the younger master, and again from the wild, ruthless abandon and harshness of the latter with delight to the sane serenity and limpid art of the former. Perhaps each is needed in his time. Perhaps it were a better world if there were no cause for the fiery wrath of a Beethoven,—a perpetual Nirvana, where Mozart sings the theme of constant blessedness. But then, we might say, a world without the stress of moral strife very like is no world at all,—a state of non-existence. The chief business of the world, after all, is the moral strife and onward, upward course; we know no other and conceive of none. The angelic note of eternal praise fails of sustaining interest, suggests a lack of dignity, a somewhat pointless task for all the ages.

Of such a world of moral strife Beethoven is the great prophet; he is, therefore, the most human of all the tone poets.

But ought there to be a content at all? Is it a lowering of pure art when that begins? There is no reason for this fear. For, if the poet is not

MOZART'S SYMPHONY IN E FLAT

self-conscious in his special mood, absorption and concentration are more perfect. The beauty is used as means. There is less of material enjoyment. A wonderful wedding of joy and truth is this of art. To be sure, there is an immediate descent on the other side, where music has constant label in graphic account of detailed event or scene.

It is a simple problem, almost algebraic. If there is no emotional hue, there is too little absorption. If there is such a coloring, there must be a projection of subjective spirit, which immediately assumes a moral (or immoral) quality.

There is a constructive phase of art forms, where the tinkering is conscious,—is all there is. It seems to be a needed link; it has no other reason for existence; it is not interesting in itself. The consciousness of form forbids spontaneity. Then comes the phase of perfected form, where the facile master goes roving freely in the prepared pastures, plucking the flowers that are blossoming for him.

A period arrives when there is a certain relish of the perfect dwelling, when one eyes and touches the panels and pillars with a delight in the new design. But it is not as yet the sense

MOZART'S SYMPHONY IN E FLAT

of home, the quality of human association. In music, so long as consciousness of outer design is there, the high point is not reached. On the other hand, in the dwelling, association and special quality enter unwatched and unushered, one knows not when. So in the very master who has the sense of outer perfection, a strong quality of emotion, of sympathy, and secret moral spur may exist unreckoned by himself. Here we reach the three great symphonies of Mozart. He combines both phases. On the other hand, when the master gets wind of his own power of special utterance, comes the temptation wittingly to paint certain feelings. Here is Beethoven's design in the Sixth and Ninth. Thus broadly in the curve of the symphony we trace the formal growth to sudden height, to overbold experiment across the bounds of tonal art to absolute depiction. We see a gentler later journey in the realms of more defined emotion, where intimate fragrance is gained with loss of primal truth. And at the latest do we have the brave return to biggest view, that reaps all gain of earlier experience and best contains the present message of the world, pointing the way and form of utterance of even greater, deeper thought.

MOZART'S SYMPHONY IN E FLAT

Mozart's Symphony in E Flat connects Haydn and the earlier Beethoven. The absolute innocence of purpose strikes us first. *Adagio* here in the beginning meant no mood, merely a decent suppression of spirits for ceremony's sake. It was a tradition in line with the old French overtures. Haydn follows it much of the time. It was the feeling of Gluck, Cimarosa, Paer, those worthies of the stiffer school. It has something in common, too, with the old prelude before the fugue. In a way it utters the sense of gravity of the coming epic,—an invocation for the right spirit. So these Adagios seem to be cast in the same mould. Yet this did not prevent a structure of solemn beauty with clear tracery of lesser figures; there are no eminent themes, no main ideas. There is a free-flowing sequence, and again,

FLUTES, VIOLINS & FAGOT.

CELLOS AND BASSES.
(See page 18, line 4.)

MOZART'S SYMPHONY IN E FLAT

towards the end, a bold, clashing modern discord, all done in the polyphonic process. At the end the voices enter in turn (of canon) on a placid theme, which seems to have something of prophecy, and thence hurries instantly into one of those dancing melodies that were first conceived in Haydn's humor, but here with Mozart have an added inevitable quality. They cannot be imagined otherwise by smallest note. Yet they lie not in that voice or this, but consist in the interplay and imitation of several, mostly in strings:

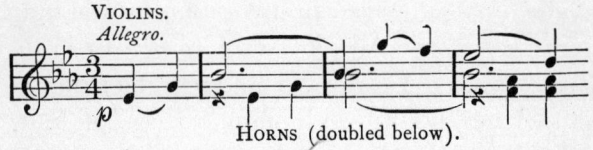

The second verse has the tune all in the bass, much in the later Beethoven fashion, with new phrases to suit in the upper voices. Wonderful, too, how the bass follows it out, even in the answer. The upper voices seem to lead, but merely suit the song of original melody below. All this has been lightest drollery, almost whispering. Now breaks in the full chorus at the loudest, very much in Gluck's old martial effect, —pure, childlike pomp.

MOZART'S SYMPHONY IN E FLAT

(Lower strings in rhythmic $\frac{1}{8}$ notes.)

Next follows a period in livelier strumming motion; still the play of simplest sort of phrases, mere runs of strings and blasts of woodwind. But the sequence is charming, running gradually to neighboring tonal mooring, with jolly cadence

(See page 20, line 4.)

MOZART'S SYMPHONY IN E FLAT

in cheery chirp of smaller figures. Then, on still lighter trip of foot, a prettily moving duet in strings is given a pert response in low cellos, with assenting chorus in the wood.

A new strain, more thoughtfully serene, just escaping sadness, moves in the strings.

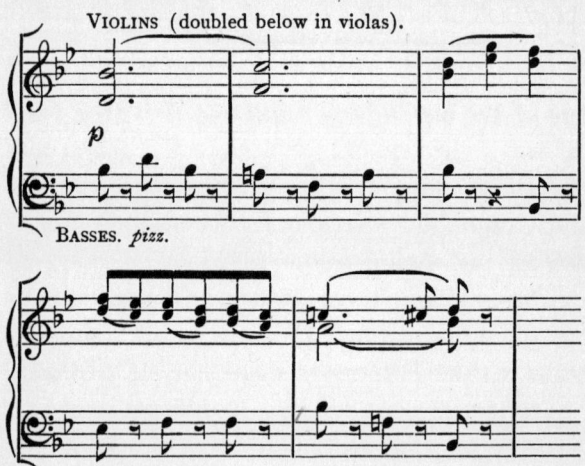

Most charmingly, right against the expressive answer, woodwind follow (in canon) with the theme. A return to general tripping and trilling merriment ends the repeated statement. It all shows how in music the big man can ever be a child,—need never be ashamed to dance about

MOZART'S SYMPHONY IN E FLAT

in all his corpulence like any schoolboy or tot.

After the rehearsing, the discussion begins on

one of the last lightest figures, as if with a "by-the-way," then quickly returns to the graver second theme sung in the earlier manner,—a real and thorough discussion, too, though short, driving the theme home by logical process to cadence of conclusive beauty. When the serious question is thus disposed of, we naturally return to the lighter,—a mere line of retorts in two former phrases, of skipping motion in strings (that began the discussion) and blows of the wind; or rather the retort is of the former alone in trebles and basses of strings, the latter chiming in with general lack of importance. But the whole is ever moving tonally, shifting the scene and light until it enters the original region with scampering figures. A pause, a few touches of the thoughtful vein, bring us back to the original

MOZART'S SYMPHONY IN E FLAT

song of themes, which follows in the old lines. But, of course, the second melody plays in the home tone, and Mozart's wit never fails of a new way of saying old things. The ending is true to the pervading spirit of noisy mirth. It seems that in the very artisan perfection of the whole and of detail, that, least of all music, suggests verbal translation, lies the magic one vainly tries to utter in words.

The second movement, *Andante*, suggests how simplest utterance may be profoundest. It has the melody here of lyric pathos nearest akin (of all of Mozart's) to the great Beethoven type.

One must not forget to trace the origin to Mozart. The whole first period, repeated, too, is all given to the song of the reigning melody; not least is the moving sequence, against steady strum of viola, of the first phrase, with strange

MOZART'S SYMPHONY IN E FLAT

taste of harmony, returning in free, almost playful, descent to the strict theme.

Now, after two bars that seemed irrelevant preface,

that quaint pompous effect breaks out in full chorus with no particular tune,—mere short

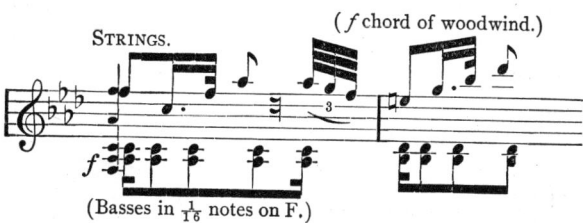

phrases that lend themselves easily to the play of sequence and imitation. The whole is, frankly, nothing but foil to the principal melody, a short relief from the sustained strain of its pathos, though to us it seems to have no great burden of grief; there is a very sure undertone of con-

MOZART'S SYMPHONY IN E FLAT

tentment. In those days the main business of music was to cheer and amuse. To us this loud striding and shouting seems like a sort of stage device,—a sudden change to rouse the mood from pathos, to prepare the better for its return. It is, it must be confessed, the least real of Mozart. It came from a tradition abounding in Haydn and vanishing entirely in Beethoven. It is a symptom that marks the evolution of music from workmanship, from conscious external effect, to emotional utterance. But very beautifully the gentle ascent on strain of first theme in the wood returns to the old strum of violas, this time answered in basses. As the phase repeats, a graceful curve of melody is suited above to the constant ascent of the former below:

(In 8ves of violins; rhythmic $\frac{1}{8}$ note chords in woodwind.)

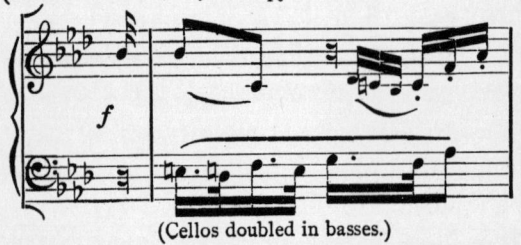

(Cellos doubled in basses.)

Strange, this Mozart genius! In our modern sensational way we are just smiling despisingly at

MOZART'S SYMPHONY IN E FLAT

his triteness, when here he does a bolder stroke, all with the innocence of a child playing with blocks. Right in the last free cadence on strain of first theme, in its very midst, a canon begins

(that is, a game of follow the leader) on a strange motive,—strange till we force our memory back to that irrelevant preface of second subject. Most curiously is blended the ending of one episode and the formal beginning of another, and on the same tone. And the almost ominous ring of the theme is repeated at each successive entrance of new voices. But in the end all is resolved on most primitive, nay, homely cadence, with a special touch of humor.

Sometimes it seems that music must be true to the old adage: "Still waters run deep." Where there is most blatant noise there is least thought. Again comes the quaint, serious canon leading in liveliest cadence back to original theme. Now

MOZART'S SYMPHONY IN E FLAT

(Violins with lower 8ve.)

(Woodwind with lower 8ve;
Basses of strings sustaining harmony.)

a full-fledged phrase grows over the lower subject, and other figures are coursing about the former ascending strain. The whole song of main melody sings with new fulness, here in sombre minor, now in bright change of light, followed by the second theme, pompous as before, but more brilliant in its shifting hues, with now a most modern flourish. So magnificent is this prismatic round of colors that the tune finds here a new reason and a new beauty. And there is little to add, save that in this recurring round there is ever a greater richness of surrounding figures, so that the whole is almost transformed in mood. Indeed the lesser phrase threatens to o'ermaster the theme in outer emphasis and in humor. That might be, save that, after a return of the canon, the main melody sings in original simplicity, and the air of sincerity is heightened as the theme, refusing to close in the usual way,

MOZART'S SYMPHONY IN E FLAT

puts off the farewell in a few ingenuous words of extension.

For once the Minuet is a true minuet; there is no disguise nor idealized Platonic form with the original quality distilled away, but very frankly the old dance, though in magnificent equipment.

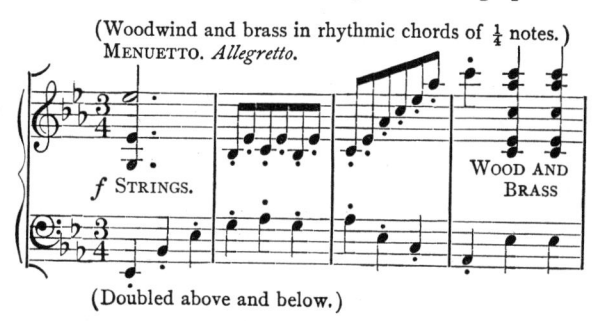

(Woodwind and brass in rhythmic chords of ¼ notes.)
MENUETTO. *Allegretto.*

f STRINGS.   WOOD AND BRASS

(Doubled above and below.)

There is no "meaning" whatever here beyond just this joy and sense of the dance; but it is a nobler movement than its lesser descendant the waltz. Assured strength there is in the slow, restrained swing, which is not merely a single skip, but three measured steps, the first being strongest. The grace is consummate, stately and ever brilliantly resplendent with full martial accoutrement,—brass, drums, and all. But this does not prevent a sudden soft gliding phrase in answer, as if soothing after the awe of the first.

MOZART'S SYMPHONY IN E FLAT

Repeats come with due precision; there is absolutely no yielding to a modern spirit of extension and exception. On goes the dance with full military stride on new phrase, gotten from the first,

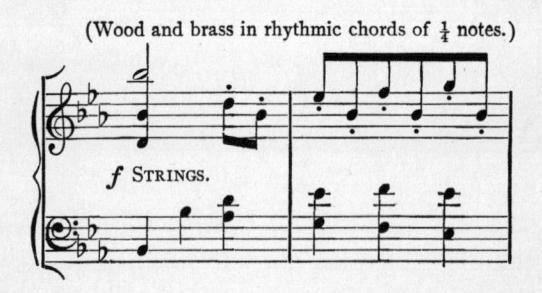

with a certain relentless attack of step, sweeping a splendid curve back to main theme. Again comes the full ceremonial of rehearsal.

The Trio is very different. It does approach our later waltz. But there is a blended sort of cradle song and dance in the rocking of clarinets and skipping of strings. Woodwind sing the tune in pretty echo of cadence. Here, too,

MOZART'S SYMPHONY IN E FLAT

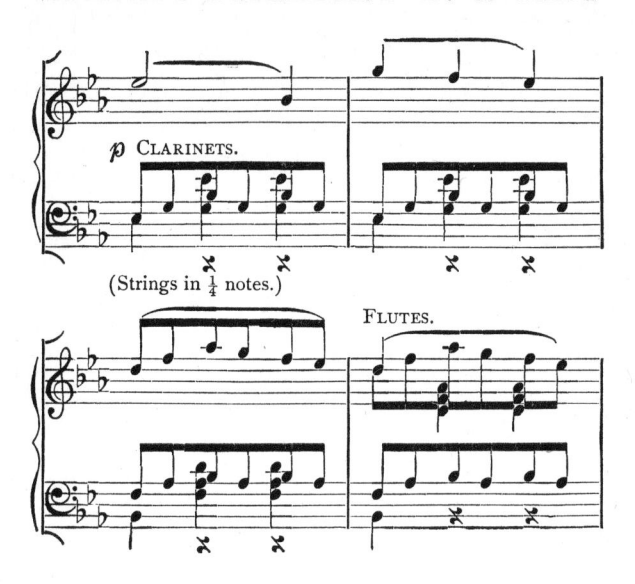

reigns the strict rule of repeat. Then the song winds along in freest phrase,—all trick of movement gone for once, in naïve discussion of the new melody. Thence we are led with greater formality to the main tune with due rehearsing, and back once more to the full pomp of majestic minuet. Again the absolute innocence of early symphony is surely proved.

Finale : Allegro. Sportiveness is the mood of this vehement chorusing of merry round dance, given out first by timidly jaunty strings. The

MOZART'S SYMPHONY IN E FLAT

whole band almost frighten you with its mirth; perhaps they intend it. There is another charm in the way the jolly jingle begins, not on strict

bass note, as a respectable melody ought to do, but high in careless inverted chord at the very beginning, like the informal word that betrays friendly feeling. There is again something of the holiday from school in these final rondos,—of the gay feeling that the task is nearly done and well done, and the rest is merry-making. For, after the melody has sung twice, the band merely prance about in almost infantile glee, with not a sign of articulate theme, a kind of prolonged musical laughter,—anything to keep the jingle going. But, looking deeper, it is significant and curious how this Mozart *finale* sets the pace for

MOZART'S SYMPHONY IN E FLAT

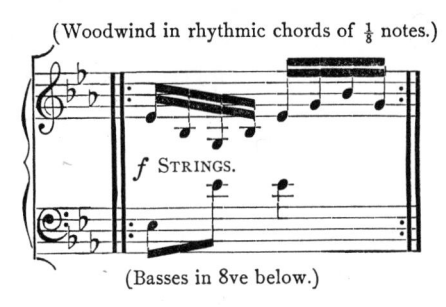

(Woodwind in rhythmic chords of $\frac{1}{8}$ notes.)

f STRINGS.

(Basses in 8ve below.)

the later Beethoven, even of profoundest symphony, as the Third and Seventh. It is the perfect link between earliest Haydn and latest Beethoven. For the childlike is ever an element of profoundest art. Without it there is no art; just as there is no ethics, no morals, without clinging to simplest principle.

And all this vacant frolicking is repeated, too, fearlessly. To be sure, these dancing figures do gradually edge away into neighboring scene of tone, whence they come to a full stop and give the main tune a chance again. Now there are new pranks. The highest note of the jingle is put higher by most mischievous, charming touch.*

---

* To be sure, the original note is merely doubled an octave higher. But the boldness of harmonic touch, that was almost lost in the quick flow of first verse, is here daringly and repeatedly emphasized.

MOZART'S SYMPHONY IN E FLAT

Yet, reason it out in modern theory, and you find the boldest harmony implied. And then who but Mozart thought of such a delicious pushing out of the rhythm as the strings mock the wood in the middle of the tune? Later they suddenly shift the scene through darker shades to more brilliant light, where they merely toss back and forth the first running motive.

After a boisterous but ever buoyant climax, the reigning motive is discussed more thoughtfully, to return the more gayly to a close on repeated song of tune.

In the hour of strict discussion, such as it is, the main theme is announced almost defiantly as the text for the evening, and there is a sudden complete pause. Instead of the expected, is a magical change of tone; the tune sings half through; then in another light the first motive above is echoed midway by basses again and again, ever trying a new tonal spot. Later the echo comes much closer on the heels of the call.

Finally the chase grows wilder, and all the voices join in the game, and again there is a stop. The search through varying scenes goes on in a new way; strings will start the reigning motive, and wood will answer in slow groping

MOZART'S SYMPHONY IN E FLAT

chords, though the bass is ever tripping away. Finally, the strings keep eagerly on and the home tone is reached, where the original verse is now sung again, the tune in all its fulness, the chorus shouting the refrain as at first, followed, too, by the merry, simple, inarticulate dance. All the round of tunes and scenes plays here, save that the path is of course homeward, not afield. At the very end the main motive runs down with sudden slam in reckless fun.

The sole prevalence of single theme throughout sonata movement can only be conceived with the blending of fulness and economy, of abandon and restraint, which seems indeed to belong to the highest reaches, the *ne plus ultra* of art.

II

BEETHOVEN'S FIRST SYMPHONY

ONCE more bravely refusing to spy on date of writing, or age of composer, and thus by outer irrelevant aid to compound a view of the probable dominant influence, let us look at the notes themselves and hope thus for truest light.

Adagio molto was the old tradition for the beginning, which Haydn rarely broke. We have seen with him its innocent formality, a harmless ceremony, sometimes plunging into the *Allegro* with almost comic haste, like a hungry diner who cannot wait for grace. Here, with Beethoven, it does seem all free of this tinge of ceremony. The rhythm is so very solemn, the figures of vague outline, though the best is placidly playful in strings, pleasantly answered by a similar one in woodwind.

Finally, the brevity makes most strongly against deep import of the *Adagio*. The beginning and end seem a little obvious of phrase; still, we cannot judge the prelude without the

BEETHOVEN'S FIRST SYMPHONY

(See page 34, line 16.)

whole; we cannot test a chance prophetic strain. Those first chords of simplest cadence (as of Amen), all in neighboring tones,—what can make them worthy of earliest invocation?

The *Allegro* has a theme of unusual nervous dash, that raps its accent on first tone with bold insistence, though in gentle sound of strings:

The theme is carried on in natural sequence of higher pitch, and ends in galloping descent of arpeggio, with big chords, in simplest cadence. Right here we cannot miss, withal, a subtle relation to the first and the last chords of

BEETHOVEN'S FIRST SYMPHONY

Adagio; a brave and vigorous simplicity is thus made to hold sway as far as we have heard. And it is strengthened by the continuing phrase (without change of tone), still in primitive chord of first scene, met by like notes of answer. They are just of the tissue of like Mozart phrases. They mean no more than the hearty greeting, with the inevitable response; they come from the earlier, artisan days of symphony and sonata, when the sound of simple chord was fresh to the ear. Men were like the child of to-day, that delights to find the "new" chord of oldest triad.

This very quality of opposite fitness of two great chords in every bit of music had to be rung and driven home. The older fugue gave no sense of tonal color in the æsthetic toil of its journey. But even to-day there is great doubt whether we feel the full depth of just these two main chords that are like the eternal duality of things, of yea and nay, of black and white, of good and bad.* In the Symphony, above all, this dual nature abounds, where there are two

---

* In England the Sonata is commonly called the "binary" form.

BEETHOVEN'S FIRST SYMPHONY

themes in contrasting tone.* Nothing is clearer than the answer of first chord to the question of the other. The modern view of true basis of many chords of supposed independence has greatly lowered their number. It is a matter of wonder whether they must not narrow to the limits of these two.

Nor was this tonal emphasis the sole purpose. So in those early days of melodic discovery—when the sense was fresh of a tune at home and another abroad—the very clearness of setting needed a separation that was merely formal, a digression purely general of figure. Thus the early Beethoven is timidly roaming to freer fields. By contrast, these simple phrases are surprising in melodic relevance; yet we must not forget that the historical is not the true and final view. A classic must be intrinsically great and beautiful.

---

* Tone is used at least in two big senses: first, of the home key which may change for a time; second, as one of the seven harmonic bases in this key or tonal home. Of these seven, the first and fifth have a striking trait of correspondence, as of question and answer,—finality resting with the original first tone. Their technical names are tonic and dominant. The dominant, throughout this volume, has been called the neighboring or nearest tone.

BEETHOVEN'S FIRST SYMPHONY

And there is no need to eke out here with explanation; these figures, however primitive, have a fresh vigor that will not fade merely because the time has passed for saying them anew. What is at any time a true expression will stay, without regard to later growth and experience.

The text of main theme fits for big, spirited, dashing close in neighboring tone, where the second subject sings a graceful melody in woodwind to a soft dancing step of strings:

It is built on brief motive that is merely passed along the voices of the wood in rising tones, so that the whole gives outline of single tune.

If we have not over-preached the text, the dual idea is still heightened here; for, best of all, it is in their nature that the themes are most opposed. The sense of clear resolution of the first, of restless drive, is met with type of innocent, helpless grace that has a touch of timid appeal. We have seen the full strength of this dual

BEETHOVEN'S FIRST SYMPHONY

meaning in the Fifth Symphony. And the true force must come, not in the first mention, but in the later story.

In its close and climax this feminine trait is quickly lost. And most striking is the quiet, dim passage of second theme far down in murmuring basses, while higher strings keep lightly dancing and oboe far aloft sings a brightening reply:

Striking it is how, with all the gentle volume, the passive hue here has vanished. The sense in lower theme is clear, of a certain masculine stern-

BEETHOVEN'S FIRST SYMPHONY

ness, returning through boisterous close to the dash of first theme, both in refrain of tunes and in the following discussion. But, with all danger of too close a view, we must not forget the clear source of cadence of the song of tunes. The line of slow notes, lengthened from a strain of second

subject, is the same as the main phrase of introduction. And now we see there, too, the simple response of massive chords. The clear unity of the *Adagio* with the *Allegro* is already established.

Strange, now, in these retorts the changed nature of main subject. For its timid phrase is always met with firmer accents of the answer of second theme, and thus the main subject has lost its original temper for the while. We see that

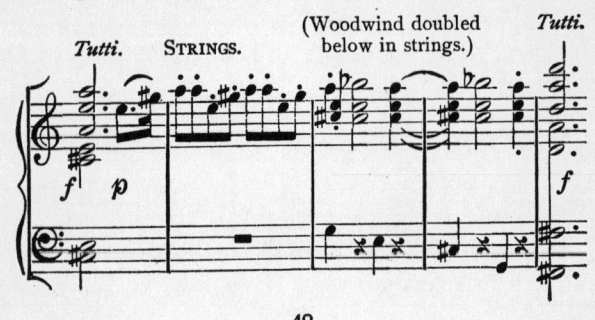

BEETHOVEN'S FIRST SYMPHONY

there is, after all, no final quality in a tune or theme of itself; it is all in the poetic handling. The childlike motive may get the sense of deepest import by a light touch of rhythmic bass.*
Thus it is that, in a master's hands, tunes, as personal figures, may show big drama of experience, of emotion and moral strife; they are not stereotyped. Thus, as symbols, they give, to him who listens, clearest message of the deepest meaning that man may need; and it is not blurred with dogma, but comes with straightest force.

The anxious queries end in a new phrase (the last motive of main theme) that rises from below in sombre minor, with higher echo, curving in constant change of light.

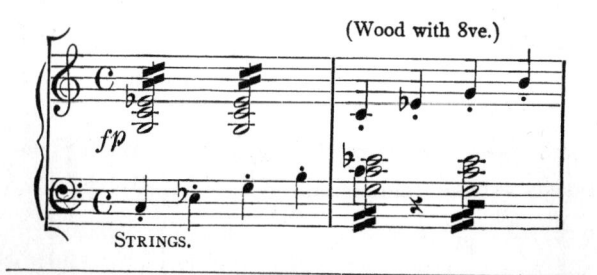

---

* Compare the first theme of Beethoven's Eroica Symphony with a common nursery rhyme, Vol. I.

BEETHOVEN'S FIRST SYMPHONY

Simple though the harmonies be, they are marked with a clear flash that gives them the charm of novel boldness. After all, the inner thought is all, not the means of utterance. If the touch, the true ring of bold idea, be there, who cares how simple be the expression? So throughout this symphony, amid all the simplicity of tonal roaming, there are clear, varying shades of light and mood. Here, in the gloom of minor, there is a shifting between dim earnest and grim sort of playfulness. Through loudest clash of discord we rush into the doubled speed of the last cadent phrase. Up and down, crossing each other in the eager chase, joining in united run, they enter on a lesser function of quick-flitting figure, above which the first motive of theme enters, in turn, in voices all about, of wood and strings. We can, somehow, never be sure that it is play; there is an uneasy kind of undertone throughout. Higher mounts this long phrase, compounded of echoing bits of the theme with nervous trembling of strings. Finally it ends in united motive and coursing run of all strings in loudest unison chorus, while horns and trumpets hold a big blast on the main tone,

BEETHOVEN'S FIRST SYMPHONY

followed by broad, conclusive phrase of the wood. Hearty it would be but for this prevailing cast of minor that ever shuts out the song of cheery hope. In repeated phrase of climax we are led back to the whole round of themes, and though there we return to major, there is still a want of cheer and joy. The main theme goes straightway wandering into higher, cloudier lights, and soon hurries its flight to find the magic spot. There is somehow, too, a hard, fitful rap in the first phrase of subject. The flight through higher tones is, we must confess, almost homely in the singleness of each slow step. The feeling is less of beauty than of relentless climb. At the top the sense of exultation breaks out in unpretending phrase. The beauty of second theme enters

BEETHOVEN'S FIRST SYMPHONY

as before, though now in original tone, and, too, the dim strain in basses, crowned by song of woodwind.

As we near the end, the old rollicking of wood returns and a long stride of arpeggic motive, from end of second theme, that closed the original verse of theme and has its rise in earliest *Adagio*.

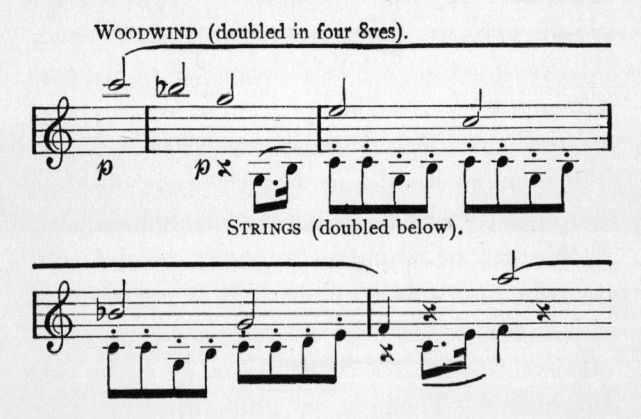

But this is now blended, rather welded, to a nervous song of most of main subject. The duet of contrasts winds its higher journey and ends in final shouts of glee, where the primitive chords of cadence are rung with a certain intent of elemental celebration. The last score of bars are in a single, unvaried tone. The simplicity

BEETHOVEN'S FIRST SYMPHONY

of introduction has thus a bearing on the first *Allegro*.

Andante cantabile con moto. A melody, like a flower, is perfect of its own reason, fulness, and symmetry. The violet does not lack because it has not the warmth and richness of the rose. So there is an organic completeness that proves the beauty of tune, as of flower. However simple the lines, we do not test or compare it herein. All the question is: Is it beautiful of its own agreement? And this perfection never comes by toil, that tinkers at a mere chance phrase. The first idea has the seed of the tune's beauty, and finds thereby its own test of soundness.

We cannot compare the violet to the rose, nor, often, to another violet. It is not size that makes the flower. So we cannot compare our *Andante* either to the Mozart kind or to the later Beethoven. There is, in truth, much temptation here. If we were allowed comparison, we should surely choose the *Andante* of Mozart's G-Minor* Symphony. For the melody begins very like this of Beethoven's; but the fragrance is very different. The Mozart melody is of much

---

* See Vol. I. p. 77, third edition.

BEETHOVEN'S FIRST SYMPHONY

prouder bloom,—has, too, a certain impersonal beauty, almost awful in majestic moments. The Beethoven *Andante* is more modest in garb and dimensions, makes, throughout, a more direct human appeal, above all in the phrase of answer.

Possibly a fanciful question might be asked without impertinence: How would one prefer the first notes of the theme to be treated,—in the Beethoven or Mozart manner? The answer then at best would bring us back to the original problem. We can merely cite differences, not measure the relative rank.*

Instead of the pomp of second theme, here are the briefest bits of timid phrases, yet again answered in broad sympathetic strain, the second time with more of serene assurance:

---

* To follow out this idea, so far as it may be seriously conceived, we have but to trace the course of the Mozart *Andante* of the preceding chapter, especially in the episode of second theme.

BEETHOVEN'S FIRST SYMPHONY

The close here has a sudden joyous step, with a dancing beat of drum and simplest flowing refrain above.

After rehearsing of themes, our timid second melody creeps in, darkly clad, suddenly bursts into big flash of new light, and now, in gentle grace of the new restrained dance, trips along (in strings), while, in the wood above, voices pipe sweetly back and forth on the brief strain. At every two steps of the slow dance there is again a sudden crash of chord that almost frightens. With rare beauty this verse winds through deli-

BEETHOVEN'S FIRST SYMPHONY

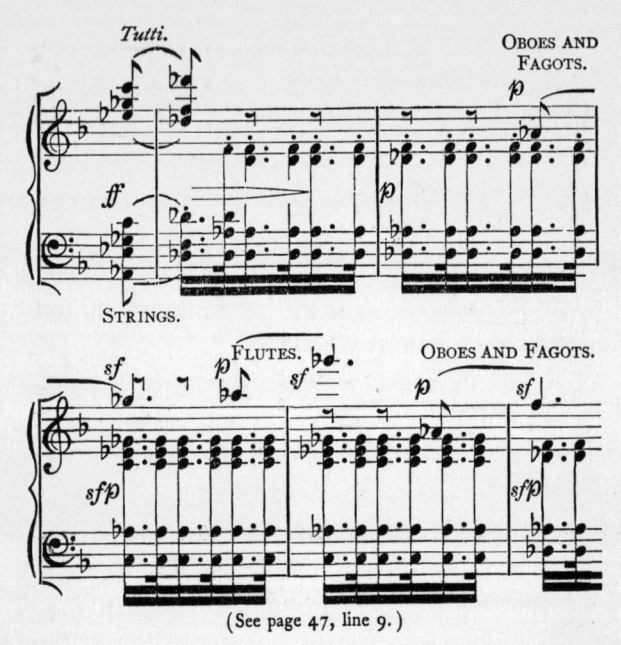

(See page 47, line 9.)

cate tints of shifting shades, ever with a sudden swoop of sound. And that new lilt of slow, jaunty skip has come to stay, or else there is an even quicker pace for most of the song. After final climax it lightly leads the way back to the first verse. In all this rhythmic episode Beethoven has never lost the secret touch of pathos that is part of *andante*. There is here the happiest blending of dance and lyric plaint.

BEETHOVEN'S FIRST SYMPHONY

Again, if we are given leave to take an historic glance, Beethoven has here, in the first instance, wonderfully solved the question of tradition. Where Mozart (even in the *Andante* of G-Minor Symphony) breaks into tumultuous, vacant episode, in formal contrast with the pathos of tune, Beethoven has never lost the pervading vein, though he does not lack the dynamic touch and the sparkle of new rhythm.*

The trait of varied, quickened pace of *andante* became almost a habit with our master. Of course we must not forget that the new step lay all within the line of the original melody. Singing again all the themes with still richer rhythm (which never disturbs the basic mood), the *Andante* ends with almost passionate stress of first answer.

The third movement is called *Menuetto*, but is really *Scherzo*, and the first of its unmistakable kind, freed from the bond of dance,—pure glee, without the least need or heed of aught besides.

For theme, look at the line purely of scale, all

---

* See also the discussion of the *Andante* of Mozart's E-Flat Symphony in the preceding chapter.

BEETHOVEN'S FIRST SYMPHONY

the notes in successive steps, touched with magic wand of rhythm to most expressive song:

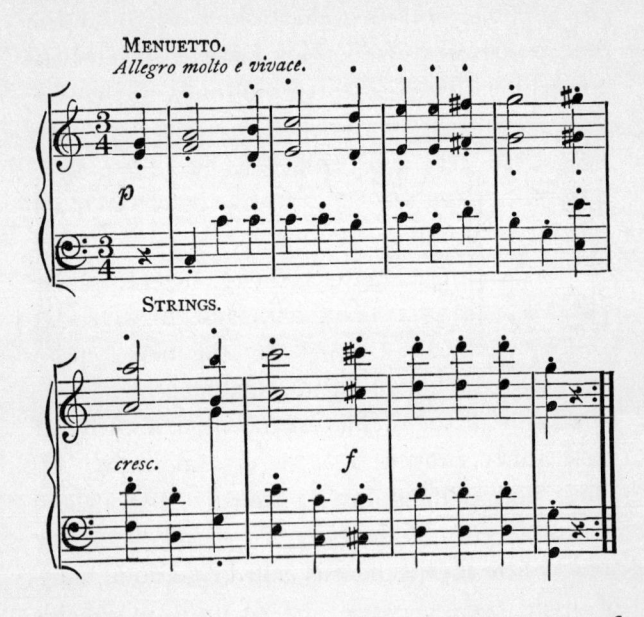

And the second part is really a full discussion of the mere rhythm itself:

BEETHOVEN'S FIRST SYMPHONY

driving along to boldest scenes, ending in full cadence far from familiar ground. Here, as the gay tripping of former bass sings overhead, the tune is down below, dinging away with most sonorous iteration,—all this inversion with the ease

of mature master. The trip now keeps on alone, most softly, broken by a sudden single skip of lower and echoing higher voices. These three in mischievous flight bring us suddenly to first tone, where all the chorus join in the loud song of main theme, carried on to brilliant pranks of tone and rhythm, ending in a step of unison clog.

The *Trio* has, first in Beethoven, the sense of tense, quivering rhythm, in sustained chords of woodwind, too, and clumsy brass, while running phrase of strings ever spurs the restless pulse:

BEETHOVEN'S FIRST SYMPHONY

Almost greater is the hidden motion here, merely implied in the slow gurgling notes of wood and horn,—the finest, subtlest revel, with all economy of motion. In the second verse, on go the throbbing tones of wood and answering pulse of strings, calling back and forth like playing children,

BEETHOVEN'S FIRST SYMPHONY

softer and softer, till the strings are coursing alone. Then the wind dance in again and end in biggest chorus, joined by strings in full career. Almost two motions here there are, if we cared to single the quaintly heavy clog of wind,—like an old person taking long steps to three of the younger. And so, back to the fling of earlier *scherzo*.

The *Finale* shows the capacity for highest exultation, in feeling and expression, which seems part of genius. There is a certain delight in finding all the ear-marks of the older master, and, withal, the freshness of the younger. The method is of Mozart; the bold, big rushing humor of late *Finale* is not dreamt of, yet.

There is no resisting a reminder of the *Finale* of Mozart's E-Flat Symphony.* Nor can the movement here be said to strike a deeper note of glee, nor to wing a broader course. In workmanship, too, there is a feeling of the great *Finale* of the Jupiter Symphony, as short phrases in long notes are combined in close architecture with quick coursing themes. Indeed, there is a likeness of actual phrase.

---

* See the preceding chapter.

BEETHOVEN'S FIRST SYMPHONY

First, after gradual approach from the pace of *Adagio*, comes the quick, flashing, jesting theme in running strings.

Allegro molto e vivace.
STRINGS.

(With low C in the Bass.)

For answer (where fagots aid the cellos) we have, in slower notes, again a new rhythmic guise of scale, presently inverted and sealed in

full cadence. The next phrase has a certain flavor of Jupiter Symphony, indeed a much stronger, to trace farther back, of the *Finale* of

BEETHOVEN'S FIRST SYMPHONY

Haydn's in E-Flat,* where the very theme and part of answer are used. Nevertheless, of actual

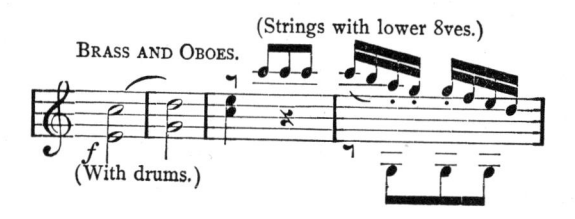

borrowing there is none. For, first of all, it is here mere digressing phrase, which was supposed to consist of commonest figure (as we have shown above), where all the world had equal property. Nor is the answer brought on the heels of theme, as in Haydn with quite different effect. The resemblance does show a common phase of the three masters who guided the career of the Symphony. It shows Beethoven here in obedient suit of the other two. Moreover, the leadership was not, as we might think, with the oldest; for the Jupiter Symphony † preceded Haydn's in E Flat by seven years.

---

* Peters Edition, No. 1. See Vol. I., "Symphonies and Their Meaning."

† It was written with the others of the great trio in 1788.

BEETHOVEN'S FIRST SYMPHONY

The true importance lies in the fact that our poet was not yet free from a touch of formal phrase. Nor does the outward themal likeness prove it, but merely confirms the direct view. The spirit has not roamed far from the humor of Haydn.

This duet of long and short notes soon drops into a sort of canter on the trip of the quicker phrase, and leads to the neighboring tone, in which it closes with a most jovial entrance of answer of main subject in the basses, echoed in almost unison chorus.

The virtue of second verse, now in new tone, lies in the trick of rhythm, of easy stride of basses and constant quicker strum of violas on single note, whereby the tune has a witching sort of leisurely pleasantry:

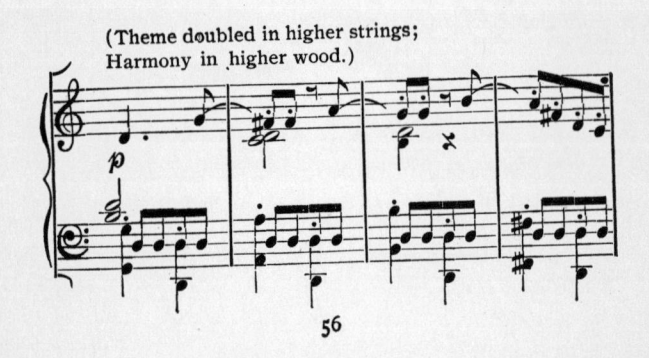

(Theme doubled in higher strings;
Harmony in higher wood.)

BEETHOVEN'S FIRST SYMPHONY

The climax is not overwhelming, and closing figures follow which do not show a strong creative effort. Indeed, the spirit of the whole is mere innocent humor—when a man was frankly glad to near the end of his work.

The themes repeated, the closing phrase is taken up, as if for serious thought, and twice considered in varying lights. But suddenly an unforeseen chorus bursts in with bouncing, heavy gait and unimportant message, leading quickly to a very pretty encounter of two phrases of first subject:

Then the main melody itself is tossed here and there, the upward phrase runs down for answer; all, musical quips and puns, and flashes of wit. There is no earnest intent, no serious mood. There is, too, little sequence; for here, when

BEETHOVEN'S FIRST SYMPHONY

the dispute looks a bit fugal, a gentle dance from the woodwind comes to the relief; the phrases trip along with still gayer abandon, ending in the same jovial song of answer in the basses. Through merry climax we reach the original chain of tunes, the second appearing in the main tone. All the lesser phrases recur with an added verse of theme; the Haydn strain follows in quite a new guise.

The simplicity of first movement is all here in the last, and thus agrees with the introduction. But of the two *Allegros*, the stress is with the first. The *Andante* and even more the *Menuetto* suggest a far maturer stage. The latter seems, indeed, to point to a *Finale* of greater weight. It seemed as if the master here retreated into the safer shell of earlier tradition.

III

BEETHOVEN'S SECOND SYMPHONY

WE must think of the traditions existing: Haydn's playful idea; little real pathos; abundant mock heroics, however unwitting; but, of Mozart, a real Olympian force, even if there be no Promethean fire. The symphony and, with it, music and musicians have gained by degrees a breadth, a dignity, a respect, merging in awe.

A symphony no longer amuses and merely charms; the minstrel doffs the guise of clown; he takes the stand of prophet and of poet.

Hovering in this border-land is much of the second of Beethoven. When the fire appears, it comes unknown to the poet himself. There can never be aught of assumed dignity in the true poet. All his power is won with his own reluctance. He cannot help the greatness of his words; he can only prepare for his own best expression. This period, when an undreamt

BEETHOVEN'S SECOND SYMPHONY

moral force is first evolved in the very servants of outer nobility, is truly dramatic,—the wonderful proof of the greatest kind of hidden truth,—as in Scripture, the "evidence of things not seen."

The full pause at the start, to call for "sacred silence," is almost a formality. It means little in itself; by tradition it may run straight into a

burst of merriment. There follows a placid strain, in the wood, of gently flowing, thoughtful song, hardly the note of pathos. Recurs the pause and the strain, now in strings, with trilling cadences. Climbing to higher perches, it does strike, at the top, a blow of new force and meaning in sudden new light of tone, of a certain stern reality. Through all dreamy haze a new masterful phrase descends in strings, followed

BEETHOVEN'S SECOND SYMPHONY

in fugal chase by other voices, the first returning in slow chords of harp to the heights. Against

Adagio molto.
STRINGS.

ff p
(Basses in lower 8ve.)

(Flutes doubled in fagots two 8ves below.)

sfp
sfp

the nervous quicker strum, the slower figure grows to clearer song on seeming text of first phrase. In the stirring pulse of movement, in the authority of themal utterance, in the growing maze of speaking voices, we see Beethoven taking his prelude more seriously than was the wont. All this profounder episode ends in a big unison tone, descending in notes of minor chord. Then follows another phase, gentle of volume, but ever close-knit in the double canon, the exchange of higher air with lower. The basic

BEETHOVEN'S SECOND SYMPHONY

phrase is in the spirit, if not in the outline of original strain,—a kind of last refrain of its essential notes.

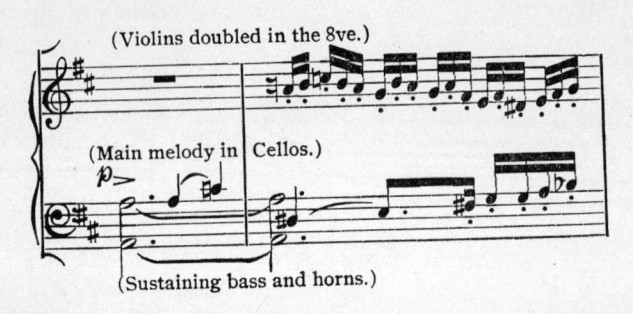

(Violins doubled in the 8ve.)
(Main melody in Cellos.)
(Sustaining bass and horns.)

Thence in vague, trembling chords, answered by trill of flutes with strange accents echoed below in strings, the voices hurry in eager though solemn swell of song to the new speed and dash of the *Allegro*. There is indeed a kind of prophetic quality of big overture in this true prelude, as we shall see clearly far on towards the end of the whole work.

One of those themes is this first of *Allegro*, where motion stands out more than outline. Beginning in basses of strings, the tune lifts the whole structure directly and powerfully on the momentum of its own current. That is the virtue of a melody in the bass: it is not cum-

BEETHOVEN'S SECOND SYMPHONY

bered with the duller weight of mere harmonic and rhythmic harness. There is a great economy and telling force in its whole utterance, rhythmic as well as harmonic,—the two elements of melody.

Strange how certain tunes need a translation through moving mass of cumbrous chords for real effect, while others mark their own harmony in the melodic path and ever bear above the tune the weight of other melodies. It is a little like the natural law, where more power is needed, the nearer it is applied to the basic point; and of course the effect is the more direct. Some such instant result has the melody which lies in its own bass. Were we to call on science, our simile would prove an example of the broad law itself. This basic quality continues, save in lighter phrases of answer (in high strings or wood). In its Titanic manner the tune descends,

BEETHOVEN'S SECOND SYMPHONY

without reck, into bold changes of ever lower tonal base, then swings suddenly off into bustling phrase in high strings and wood, that might

[musical notation marked ff STRINGS.]

be a second tune but for the paling melody that soon sounds in neighboring tone, which has been reached with due formality.

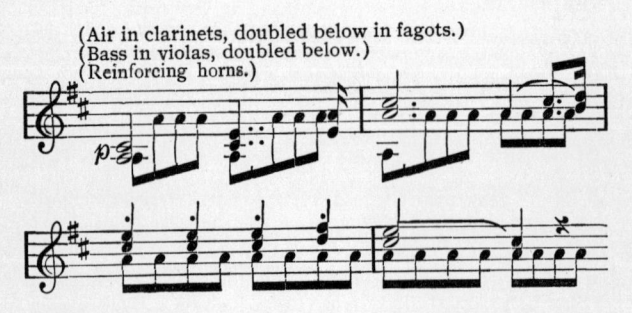

[musical notation with annotations: (Air in clarinets, doubled below in fagots.) (Bass in violas, doubled below.) (Reinforcing horns.)]

In notes of lower wood and horns this hunter song sings brave and blithe, with quivering strings below, acclaimed with full chorus, that ends the

BEETHOVEN'S SECOND SYMPHONY

(repeated) verse in still farther tonal station. Quite a line or two are built on mere chance phrase of the end of last cadence,—just to show how little formal theme is needed if there be a good charge of spurring rhythm. It is indeed rhythm alone that will give to the outline of mildest tune the most heroic figure. With its magnificent torrent of pace, the second melody comes to tumultuous close 'mid big plunging chords.

But, dispensing with formal end, the motive of first theme steals whispering in, far down in strings, on the same feverish pulse and leads in swelling volume to final cadence of still greater power on the tonal quarter of second melody, whence the song of themes is repeated.

Two episodes stand out in the discussion, marking something of the later power of the poet. Beginning in dim minor of strings, the basses growl the strain of main theme with a clash of bold jarring chords against trembling of high violins, as they hold their sure, unyielding course. Presently, out of the lower tune and the high tremolo emerge at the same time two themes of fugal hue and emphasis, which meet and exchange rôles, each standing as answer for the other. A special relevance lies in the close like-

BEETHOVEN'S SECOND SYMPHONY

ness of upper phrase to the one we nearly mistook for second theme; but it has here a much more masculine look. Carried on in several steps of sequence, the whole has a very dogmatic air of stern logic. Later the woodwind, which had been silently watching the dual exposition, join in lighter kind of answers of less serious strain.

For some time the quick motive of main theme holds sway, while first the chords of basses strike lower steps with stern emphasis; later, chords in woodwind descend, through shifting tones, while the motion runs below. There is **a**

BEETHOVEN'S SECOND SYMPHONY

sort of border-land of earnest and humor. Perhaps the serious intent is not quite attained. Now, in nearby tone, the second melody sings light versions of its main phrase. Then, as the climax is reached, comes the second of our episodes upon a basic phrase, strong of tone and active movement, again like the two former whose kinship we have traced. There sounds, above, a phrase in simple though sturdy notes of single chord,

ff STRINGS (the upper tune doubled in 8ve above, the lower below. Sustained octave chords of C sharp in the wood).

rising and descending much like the famous King of France, and, especially in downward motion, showing a clear origin in answer of main theme. The whole is an innocent phase, where the old play does not quite emerge to the later grim earnest, though it shows the tendency. From the resulting crisis the fall is quick to the entrance of main subject, as at first. The whole journey of tunes is much as before, save, of

BEETHOVEN'S SECOND SYMPHONY

course, homeward; but there is an after-thought which marks a third period of mild discussion. A short phrase of quiet reflection, which had served to turn back to repeated song of themes, here sings at the corresponding spot; is taken up

(Strings in 3 octaves.)

with firm emphasis by the basses against bits of main theme; rises in higher and higher steps, doubling soon the speed of its tune, driving the themal phrase before it in eager chase. Before the ending frolic there is a strain of real profundity, when on the spur of main motive, darting into strange shades, in trembling strings and sustaining wood, there rises, in pent tension, through brilliant steps of changing light, the climax of movement, whence the descent is in shifting chords, as a while ago. In the ending frolic, the unofficial (second) tune runs its jolly course in the basses against vague merry phrase above. Later the main motive very simply runs

BEETHOVEN'S SECOND SYMPHONY

up and down, in full career, and ends with the usual harmonic farewell in big chords.

Larghetto. One might say these earlier Beethoven poems are Mozartian; if they are, they by no means measure Mozart; they merely show his influence on a very opposite spirit. We are inclined to think these Mozartian *Andantes* of Beethoven decidedly lower than their great models. Comparison has, here, less of odium, because it depends on the single measure of the elder master's art.

Poets cannot be compared. Even if two poets had the same strength and equipment, all things, in other words, being equal save the individual temper, they would certainly take different views of life and of the world; they would have no common unit of measure. Their supposed equality could never be determined. Now, as no two poets have just such equal endowment, the problem of comparison is so much the more difficult,—in short, is clearly impossible.

The Mozart *Andantes* are complete. The Beethoven *Larghetto* of the Second Symphony lacks something that we feel in the later symphonies. The lack is also in Mozart; but there it has a compensation.

BEETHOVEN'S SECOND SYMPHONY

As yet serenity has not lost its sway. There is no depth of world-woe in our flowing *Larghetto*. But there is a most charming folk-song of appealing pathos. There is no doubt that the glorious melody of the beginning might hold its own with any of the later ones:

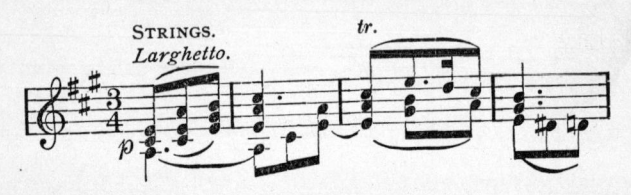

It is really of the same mould of profound sympathy. It is in the rest of the movement that the difference of mood and basic purpose lies. The lowest depths of our *Larghetto* are reached at the beginning, in the first melody; the rest is relief, foil, almost apology for its seriousness. In the later symphonies, the first melody is but the principal figure of a tragedy.

But nothing can gainsay the beauty of our main subject; and it has a generous satisfying reach. After the first half, a full tune in itself, has come to rest in the neighboring tone, the second flows on with sense of anxious questions

BEETHOVEN'S SECOND SYMPHONY

which are answered with rare and deep solace. But immediately, in the original tone, all strain of pathos is lightened in simplest time of ambling to placidly dancing pace, with playful answers, on smallest fragment of melody:

It rises, to be sure, quickly to big height of tone and volume, in stern colors of chord, against reversed motion in the bass, all echoed most lightly, followed by bolts of big, bold harmony. But all this must be half pretence, mock earnest. For, on the tune goes dancing, saucily almost. Immediately afterwards follows the second theme,

BEETHOVEN'S SECOND SYMPHONY

utterly reckless of anything else in the world but its own springing gait.

STRINGS AND FAGOTS.

Later the tune sings in quicker variation, while high wood come piping in, fitly in place. Very soon, of course, against its minor note on high, lower voices press in rising stress with touch of original earnest, to the crisis.

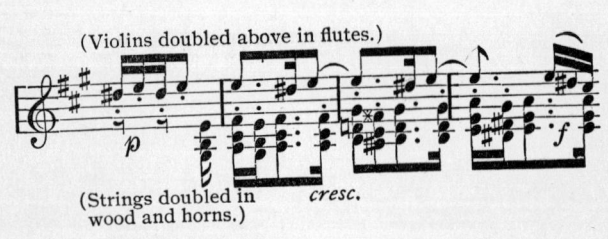

(Violins doubled above in flutes.)

(Strings doubled in wood and horns.)

Quickly the stress is relieved in lightest run, now rises again with more urgency, where the echoes of phrases are less play than emphasis,

BEETHOVEN'S SECOND SYMPHONY

to far bigger climax, awful for the moment. But once again the massed chords dance gently away from the stern height and the tune runs lightly down to lower, harmless plane, repeating all this easy descent in whispers. At the end, much like the coda of first theme, is an after-touch in pleasantest good humor, like a primitive peasant dance. It is evident that our poet will

(Cellos doubled above in violins.)

not harry our feelings in this *Andante*. But in this battledore and shuttlecock of moods we

BEETHOVEN'S SECOND SYMPHONY

are never safe; the end of the dance, comic in its lumbering step, rings again and again, and always louder until it quite frightens us in its full height, when it runs down once more to the level of first tone. Thence the original melody sings in minor, not so much to heighten the pathos,—for this is neither needed nor achieved,—but as a path towards stranger tones, where a new quality of sternness is reached in spite of the light run that ever answers the motive of main theme. Now the lowest fathoms are touched, as always in the discussion, where the dim line of the motive sounds far down in ominous bass, against trembling strings, answered on high by fearsome cries in the wood (in reversed theme), all in tune

(Cellos doubled below.)

of restless gloom. Call and answer ring again and again, and the volume swells to big cadence, still in gloom of minor. Once more sings the sad duet, beginning now on high, answered below.

BEETHOVEN'S SECOND SYMPHONY

Here the swelling volume brings gladder cadence in brighter major, in distant scene, to be sure. Still the sense is most of power and striving, less of joyous triumph, as the treble and bass in eager canon rear big mass in thundrous toil of Titans, on the base of first motive. The hue of minor darkens the struggle for a moment before the big crisis. And no dancing step comes in for relief; instead, the former urging ascent of lower voices against higher note, that followed second theme. Here, too, the stress is sterner than before, and from the height that is reached, no playful skip descends, but a phrase of graver color. From this point we return to the original course of themes, main and lesser, official and incidental. Change there is, first in the richer suite of flowing phrases attending main melody, though they do not add to sense of pathos. The after-phrase, to be sure, attains a greater force in its deeper extension. Else there is no new note or mood. And so the prevalence of lighter dance, as at the beginning, must prevent a final sense of real profundity. The end is in note of main theme—a last word of the speaking solace of original cadence.

Scherzo. Full of childlike playfulness is the

BEETHOVEN'S SECOND SYMPHONY

Scherzo, dashing from loud strokes to light skip, like a game of "frightening:"

Most development is by faintest gradation; there is here nothing of the profound humor of the type of Beethoven *scherzo*. We might call it Haydn-like, but for a certain forcefulness of rhythm, a greater vigor of accent than Haydn cared to assert. Herein, however, it has no advantage over Mozart's great *menuettos* of E-Flat and G-Minor symphonies; and so, if we were

BEETHOVEN'S SECOND SYMPHONY

forced to compare, we should place it thus in intermediate rank.

The second verse of *scherzo*, after a strain or two of first theme, runs in jolly, informal tune in freest abandon, without least serious undertone.

All the more vigorous is the stroke of returning theme. This time, instead of the stop in full chorus, it scampers away on trip of dance, really a very quick waltz. At the faintest, the high oboe sounds gently an unexpected lay, swaying to the broad swing of quicker trip,—answered in

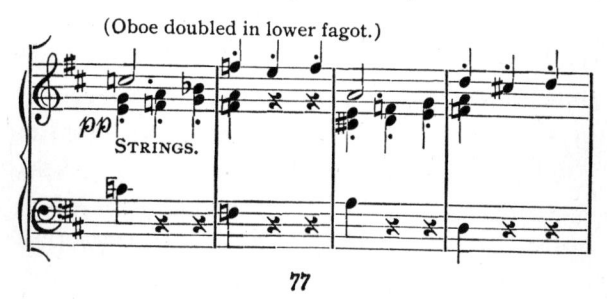

BEETHOVEN'S SECOND SYMPHONY

bustling chords of strings, first up, then down,—that extends to usual spirited close. The theme of Trio, merely a new verse on the same buoyant wing, is a most tuneful roundelay in its narrowest limits:

The second part merely keeps the rhythm humming alone in sustained trill of neighboring tone, or in unison glide up and down the arpeggic chord,—coming with a halt to the first tone and tune of Trio. In the last refrain, the bass is busily running along in quicker trip, and the

BEETHOVEN'S SECOND SYMPHONY

last cadence is sportively rung in constant canonic iteration.

There is little ground for holding these earlier symphonies as lesser because they do not strike the deeper note of sympathy or of humor. To be sure, they are in the Haydn and Mozart tradition; yet they have their own spontaneous quality. Slowly the younger spirit moves to independent utterance; but the growth itself is all of the real Beethoven, and perhaps the Mozart influence means a healthier feeling and art. Who shall say? It is our old question. It is best to be glad of the purely joyous spring of the youthful master, and to take the maturer works with sombrer though profounder hue, as another phase of poetry. We may compare two forms of art that utter the same feeling, not two different kinds of thought.

Allegro molto. The first tune somehow, for right or wrong, carries us back to the prophetic trilling motive (the only phrase of the prelude of which we can find a literal trace in the later symphony).

BEETHOVEN'S SECOND SYMPHONY

It seems to suit with the big breadth of this true overture, more serious in plan than any earlier of symphony. That very first strain of all had a certain width of view, disdaining mere literal foretaste of tune. It did not give a glimpse of the *Andante*, though in similar spirit. It seemed like poetic forecast of the real meaning of the whole. The sense of strife of second phase, returning to quieter thought, ended with nervous figure of trill, spurring to the rush of first *Allegro*.

Unconsciously now the *Finale* returns to this figure for text, and binds the whole with faint semblance of outer theme:

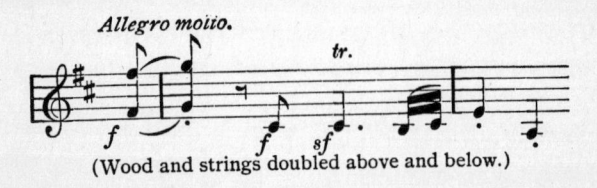

(Wood and strings doubled above and below.)

The timid expectant cry of wondering flutes finds here an assured utterance in the firm, unison phrase of masterful chorus of woodwind and strings.

In answer, strings run lightly in even trip of curve to simple cadence, while the bass moves in big, sweeping tones, almost of melody. After

BEETHOVEN'S SECOND SYMPHONY

repeating, the strings answer the skip of first notes with short, almost comic stride, that soon

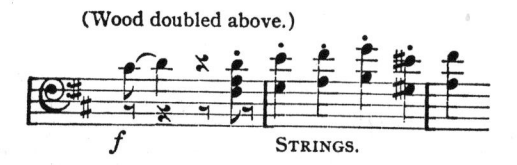

doubles to gay cadence.

The whole is clearly restrained from rushing pace of *Scherzo*; the point of gravity, since the Jupiter Symphony, has veered towards the *Finale*. And then there is ever a compensation in the

BEETHOVEN'S SECOND SYMPHONY

speed of beginning and end, of first movement and last. With all the quickness of *molto allegro*, there is a frequent breaking of the pace by recurring halts.

With all the speed, there is a poetic, almost dreamy touch in the second tune, whose motive is contained in four notes, beginning in bass, in close fugal woof of true pastoral madrigal, first in strings.

Soon the theme pipes higher in reeds, crossing the answer of strings in prettiest maze. After a more harmonious close, where the bass sings the motive in notes of double length, flutes and oboes ring the glee in higher pitch, against answers of lower strings and horns. Then all join in another friendly, gayer close in neighboring tone.

Our *Finale* seems all built on simplest themal lines. For, as strings strike a comfortable, rock-

BEETHOVEN'S SECOND SYMPHONY

ing gait, the tune of second subject starts with mere notes of chord in low wood:

begun, again, as canon of wind, while violins answer with almost flippant, chipper phrase that is hardly part of the theme, which goes winding on serenely, ever in alternating verses. Now it sounds in higher perch, now in minor, to wing to still bolder height, where comes curving cadence of quaint beauty. The idyl descends to

BEETHOVEN'S SECOND SYMPHONY

the first quarter, and ends, once more with active bustling of all the chorus, in phrases of general import, that gradually trip to the motion of first theme.

In the formal recurrence of noisy martial chorus is one of the strongest signs of the vigor of old tradition, that in later works merges into phases of graver meaning of truer symbol of strife.

The *Rondo* has no nominal claim of a period sacred to discussion. But the free course of later symphony blurred these formal lines of difference. The phase of themal disputation may come in song of *Andante*, even in dance of *Scherzo*. So here we cannot miss a certain serious intent, perhaps a little deliberate, to spin the stated themes to newer maze and meaning. The first theme is main text and, at the outset, the original motive; then the answer, changed in uncertain hue of tone. And the curve of bass, that seemed at first melodic, now sings in treble in inverted guise, playing the pretty dispute of bass and air, that seems ever a part of Beethoven's art. Returns the first motive and dives into all shades of tonal light. Finally on the very ending bit of motive the higher voices gambol in closest chase,

BEETHOVEN'S SECOND SYMPHONY

while the strings keep up the strumming motion. A gliding phrase of unison voices leads to a new subject of talk: the first two notes of theme, which the voices toss saucily back and

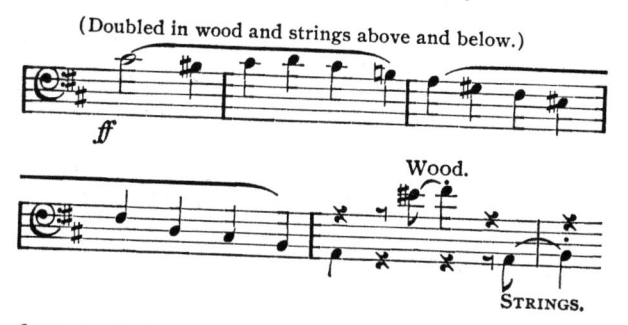

forth in lighter spring of dance. A hush and a belated note of the call bring us again to the round of full tunes. In its time the second theme appears in the tone of the first. That tuneful close has now a newer curve, still with the sweet and brave simplicity of old. All the themes have fuller setting than before. When we await the first in final close, here is a true jest, in a way of subtlest, both, and simplest fun. The comfortable swing of strings makes us look at least for the broad curve of second theme. Instead, the lower voices merely dance in softest tread. It is all like mere accompaniment with-

BEETHOVEN'S SECOND SYMPHONY

out the song, when we see the basses, in mincing step, descending the simple motive that announced the second theme:

The first quip of main subject soon adds to the spice of the joke. At the close, with cease of dance, the basses stride the same figure, with the trebles in reversed phrase, once more in solemn length of halved subject. Then into universal merry-making, where the clearest figure is the first bit of main theme, with repetition of the whispered jest, to end in simplest mood of mirth.

IV

BEETHOVEN'S FOURTH SYMPHONY

THE POET OF PATHOS AND HUMOR

BEETHOVEN'S Fourth Symphony, though often labelled of an "early period," shows some of his greatest traits. Most evident is a certain alternation of austere profundity and simplest hilarity. No one could be so severe as Beethoven, and, a moment after, so purely jolly.

It is an old and a new way to have a symphony begin *Adagio*. A man cannot always plunge right into the rush and strife of the first *Allegro*. Sometimes he must start the wheels slowly, have the figures of his stirring story grow gradually out of a certain mood of absorbed reflection. Haydn used to do it with a kind of conscious pose. But you have the true vein in the seventh, or in Schubert's C Major, and very specially in Schumann.

Here the poet begins his wandering thought in very simple phrases,—long tones descending in unison, answered by quick-breathed notes of

BEETHOVEN'S FOURTH SYMPHONY

violins. Right here is a bold touch in the minor ninth, sounded at the climax,—a chord that many think a later invention.

The quiet *Adagio* walk is wakened by the noisy, nervous snare of drum and the summons to the strings for a general gathering. Then forth breaks the main melody, first in violins:

BEETHOVEN'S FOURTH SYMPHONY

How this grows out of the introduction, so that we are sure it was not patched in afterwards, like a modern preface! Right out of those halting Adagio notes of the violins comes the *Allegro* theme, soon taken up by the whole band. And we must not be too wise and overlook the primitive childlike humor of it. Indeed, the true poet must never be afraid of simplicity. Not to quote Scripture, the truth must be much like the old verse: " Out of the mouth of babes . . ." There must be a guileless directness about all great utterance. So we have at the very start, *de profundis*,—out of the depths of revery, springing the most sparkling joyous song. It runs along through purling strain of digressive tune into a varied verse, and then, turning the corner to neighboring scene (what is wisely called the second theme), here are fagot, oboe, and flute frisking about, talking back and forth on a strain of curious charm, with a certain taste of demon mischief.

All the rest are drawn into the game, and the first refrain of melodies ends in a kind of big Titanic gambol. As soon as it has sung again, the meditative hue appears in the thin color, the logical sequence of phrases. But soon these are

BEETHOVEN'S FOURTH SYMPHONY

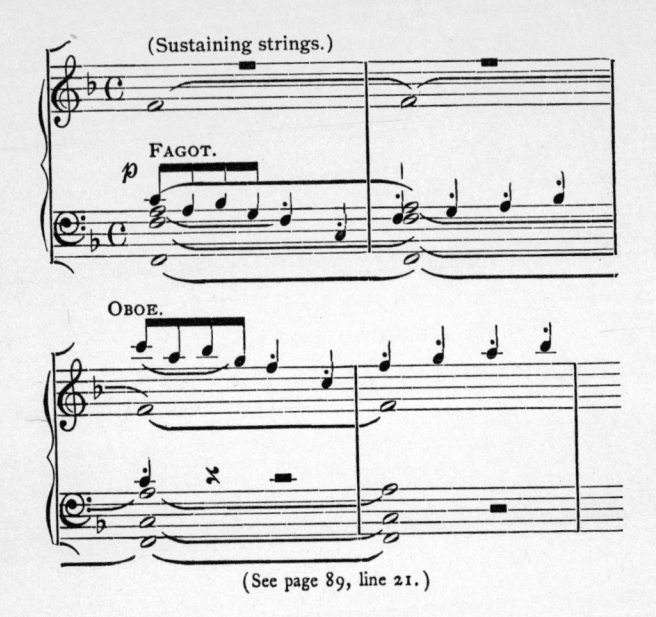

(See page 89, line 21.)

lulled and rocked by the magic of new rhythm. Suddenly the chief melody bursts forth; but together with its strain, taken up along the line, is a new answer: there is something more to be said on this question. And so you have the very element of discussion.

Ever a new group enter with the song, while the preceding or another sing the countertheme. Magnificently the noisy chorus tapers down to a still, sombre whisper, as if darkness had stolen

BEETHOVEN'S FOURTH SYMPHONY

(Strings, with main theme in fagots.)

(See page 90, line 6.)

over, nothing staying of the big dance save the pattering of feet in the steady rhythm. And even that yields at last to solitary strains from strings. Now little responses are heard; the night is lifting; the sombre hue vanishes. Gradually all waken and join with full throat in the main tune, as they sang it at first, save that they cannot restrain new, varying conceits here and there. Again comes the mischievous dialogue

BEETHOVEN'S FOURTH SYMPHONY

of woodwind, with a step of the dance, wherein Beethoven ever touches earth, and shows or renews his humanity. With a final joyous verse, mostly in the vein of the main melody, the movement ends.

The *Adagio* is pure German folk-song, culled by Beethoven, and endowed with all his art to express another side, a quiet lyric human sympathy. It is all mere evident song,—needs simply listening, while all the time there is an accompanying tap of slow figure, to hold a certain grave dignity.

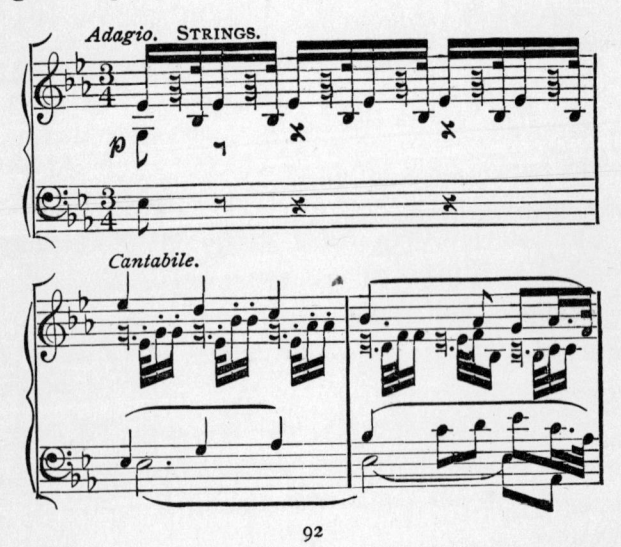

BEETHOVEN'S FOURTH SYMPHONY

It is another instance of how the mere successive sounds of the scale seem an inexhaustible fount for noblest melody.

The secondary themes have in themselves no special emphasis. They are all in the same strain of beautiful simplicity and dignity as the first; but they seem hardly more than digressive or discursive; they are like interludes between the main verses. The second melody comes in the same tone as the main one, and herein shows a purpose of the poet to avoid contrast and novelty; the main phrase is hardly more than answering cadence to another that is a rhythmic reinforcement of first motive of the theme.

The whole is mere after-strain of theme, always in loyal emphasis of its dominant rhythm, as of ocean waves. A tune of new pathos and beauty now sings in clarinets in neighboring tone. With all the distinction of its own tonal

BEETHOVEN'S FOURTH SYMPHONY

(Rapid arpeggic figure in lower strings.)
(See page 93, line 14.)

quarter, it seems again a mere version of main theme. But the melodic essence is in the text of variant, and not the rhythmic, as before.

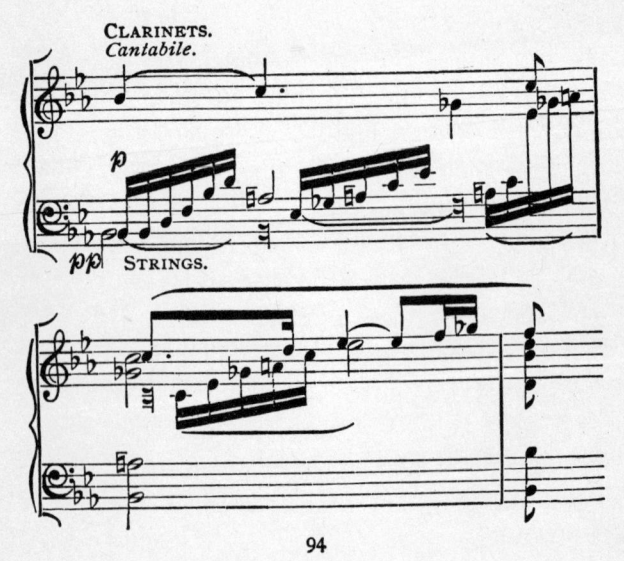

BEETHOVEN'S FOURTH SYMPHONY

To break frankly from an old rut, this dubbing of themes is often all misleading, a purely false view. Thus in our *Adagio* the truth, apart from trite lines of formal chart, is that, the first song over, an after-strain of true feeling sings, as it were, in the ebb between recurring tides of the big rhythmic pulse. Again and again, in higher pitch of sound and pathos, this appeal is soothed by descending strain in high wood, affirmed from still higher point, while strings add greatly to the rhythmic course of simple phrase of wood. In big rise of song the basses take up this very bustling course of the descending strain, that almost turns its soothing into terror, then sinks to solemn hush. The melody of clarinet thus comes in guise of plaintive, shy appeal, answered once more by solacing motive, leading to friendliest cadence, in hearty volume, too. A last brief, timid word that seems blended of plaint and soothing, turns trustfully to the full sound and big pulse of recurring theme. We must not forget that it is not always the tune that tells the story. Here the first rhythm's oceanic pulse has a faint sense of stolid Fate, against the human voice of the tune. The verse over, the wave-beat rises in tumultuous height of

BEETHOVEN'S FOURTH SYMPHONY

all the voices,—and sinks before the returning song. We have seen how, when the main melody has ended, big tides come swelling in between the phrases of after-strain, and then how a rhythmic vehemence is added to soothing answer. In the soft plaint of clarinets the motion is all but lost, but returns, welling gently like lapping waters, to the friendly answer. The full first pulse, even strengthened with redoubled course of strings, comes with the after-word that preceded the return of main melody.

Henceforward the theme in its regular song is softened by new grace of setting. But in the midst of this verse there is a dramatic play of opposite elements, In fullest volume of all the chorus a stern phrase, like evil dæmon of the gentle melody, descends, to big strumming basses. Suddenly out of the cadence, in new light, two voices in higher strings alone flit about in timid canon of vague, homeless phrase. They seek for refuge here and there, while the first pulse sounds ill-boding in dim depths. Then presently the home tone is found, where all the full song flows along to the end, decked in still friendlier figure. The trait of dual idea, of external fate and subjective plaintive hope, that

BEETHOVEN'S FOURTH SYMPHONY

finds full room in the Fifth, here spreads a graver hue o'er the less tragic song of early symphony.

Again the native vigor of the poet rings in the *Scherzo*. There he has cast loose the leading-strings of the graceful minuet. A certain roughness, an element of Titan, there always is about Beethoven's humor, not wanting right in these first bars, with the rude strength of the theme:

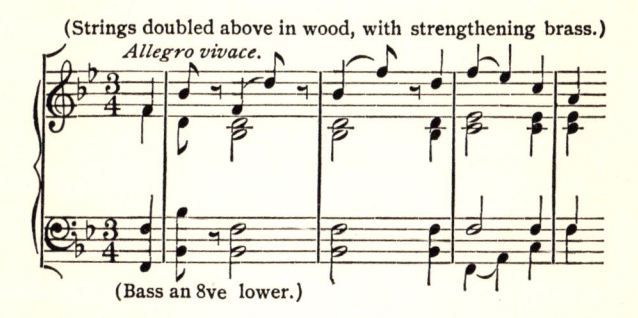

(Strings doubled above in wood, with strengthening brass.)

(Bass an 8ve lower.)

in great contrast with the misty flight of impish answer, in flickering shift of tonal light.

CLARINET AND FAGOT.

(Strings doubled below.)

BEETHOVEN'S FOURTH SYMPHONY

After repetition, the first motive flies off to distant scene of romantic color, and there has the pace and air of elfish answer, dancing about in mazing change of light and figure, darting high in the wood, gliding deep in strings as if in chase of its own echo,—all a mystic gleam of fairy-land,— then bursting into the clear, bright humor of mortals, as at first. The answer leads to tumultuous cadence on the first tone.

The Trio, since early days, has come to be a gentle retreat from boisterous fun,—at most, quietly playful,—often with a touch of special sentiment.

Here, the Scherzo began its rough revel in strange jolting against the natural pace,—in type of that broad, primal humor of Beethovens, that is ever balanced with a profound sympathy, as personal traits of his art. No doubt, to the world at large it may seem a word of shocking boldness: that nowhere in the whole treasure-house of art and poetry are these two elements of feeling uttered with greater vigor. The world is not accustomed, in strange lack of rounded view, to count the tonal poet among its prime influences, perhaps because he is the youngest of them all.

Yet to find a like note of deepest, firmest sym-

BEETHOVEN'S FOURTH SYMPHONY

pathy, we must pass over whole literatures of nations, of Latin or of Teuton, with doubt of old Greek tragedy, and sureness only in the words of highest moral teacher. It is quite true, though again it may shock our unaccustomed ears, that the depth of soothing in Beethoven's great Andantes is nowhere passed save in the prophets of holy writ and in the later words of the great Preacher on the Mount. That broad sense of brotherhood seems to have sprung first in the prophetic song of the religious race, and next in its crowning figure, the moral Savior of mankind. The later formulations not merely clouded the precious basic love of kind; they served as special means and cause of men's recoil to artificial privilege, of this world and the next. In the great burst for freedom and like human rights, Beethoven was the tonal prophet. The setting of Schiller's "Ode to Universal Joy," in his ninth symphony, was not the only evidence. In the Andante of almost every symphony Beethoven stands the clear sturdy poet of fraternity. The other cause for which men strove—the lesser, of equality—is uttered with Titanic force in other parts of later symphony.

But one truth needs strongest proclamation,

BEETHOVEN'S FOURTH SYMPHONY

that music bears the message of highest human need. In the great moral lines, Beethoven is the clearest prophet of the newer age. And once more we must not forget that one may feel the message without actual conscious sense of all its verbal import, although the knowledge will surely help the true reception.

The sense of justice and equality strikes in each least revolution. But the far deeper, underlying note of universal kinship sings a much rarer song. Here towers the stature of our master high o'er the mere Rousseaus, and rings his strain of keenest sense of kind, in deepest vein of all our Christian poetry.

It is here must lie the noblest trait of Beethoven and his work; and well it needs a noting in this very day. For, that greatest sense that man can have of other humankind, that final evolution from first stage of brute, as it is seldom felt, so it is most quickly lost. It could not come to Roman bard, against the conquering spirit of his race. Nor can it come to modern nation's poetry, where sways the brute pride of overpowering force. For, all opposed, a moral strife and victory is this, that joins both parties in the firmest bonds. The highest poets, whom

BEETHOVEN'S FOURTH SYMPHONY

otherwise the world acclaims, it is clear to all who read, have each touched on this great idea. Few they are in the force of message; and, of them all, since the first stirring words of golden rule, Beethoven is both clearest and most human. (Nor can the true music lover fail to mind, that praise of the master brings the greater praise of the art itself.)

So, in the subtler element of humor, there is no doubt again that Beethoven stands as one of the chief creative spirits. In Titanic boldness of thought and contrast, in big comic sense of rollicking fun, we can hardly prefer an Aristophanes or a Shakespeare. One gets nearer the mystic element in the wild fancies of a Jean Paul Richter; a Teuton sense of big truth, long suppressed through national neglect, is seen to emerge with irresistible vitality. The quality of this strange vein of all-embracing humor lies perhaps in bold surmounting of all human ills with the triumphant vigor of a resolute mirth. The woes and littleness of actual things are lost for them in the broad universal view. If we may rank poets as prophets, and mere seers, this humor is of the latter. The solace, of moral prophet, comes first; second, the cheer of humor.

BEETHOVEN'S FOURTH SYMPHONY

But there is more, still, in the vein of Beethoven Scherzo. The triumphant joy belongs more to last of word of *Allegro Finale*. There is, in *Scherzo*, an idea of pure amusement,—a common touch of oldest puppet-show. Here the stage is the great world of sparkling opposites, on which we look with perennial laughter. Spectators, here, we are, or seers. The cheer comes from the absorbed glance on this big cosmic comedy. Here lies the change from the mere joy of last *Allegro* phase, where we ourselves *act* in triumphant deed. The ethical phase here returns; the poet is prophet again. The change to earlier Menuet from the true Scherzo is almost to a vein of flippant fun. At least the strong, bold undertone is absent until the great symphonies of Mozart. It seems this a mighty step from mere effort to amuse and please, to a spontaneous, individual poet-vein. Most striking is the harvest of poetic thought that blossomed from the toil of formal workmanship.

In the *Trio*, as the rough jolting is gone, the tune seems to fly the smoother. With the lesser speed is more of intimate sentiment, as the boisterous fun recedes. Yet there is a sense of the pace that, in its height, approaches rest; the

BEETHOVEN'S FOURTH SYMPHONY

quickest flight does seem to bring all the delight of quiet ease. A very personal kind of confidence it is, too, with the utmost directness and naïveté.

Trio. Un poco meno Allegro.
p dolce.

(Oboe and Clarinet, doubled below in fagots.) VIOLINS.

And here it is seen particularly in the quaint childlike cadences.

And the cheerful flute sings a laughing strain of assent after each phrase of the melody. Later, the strings make a primitive kind of lumbering bass, to which the simple song of the theme is repeated, still with the same quaint cadences. Then the whole orchestra rise to a fervent climax as of pious hymn.

In the *Finale* is the chief difference in im-

BEETHOVEN'S FOURTH SYMPHONY

portance between this work and the more famous symphonies. Beethoven here still followed the older tradition, which was to leave the main stress with the first *Allegro*. Mozart's Jupiter was the first great exception, and Beethoven generally tended to shift the centre of gravity towards the end. The Finale is not so long nor so seriously conceived as the last movement of the third, the fifth, or the seventh.

It begins in a spirit of midsummer frolic, not without great breadth, on a theme broken between first and second violins:

BEETHOVEN'S FOURTH SYMPHONY

Then the strings run along in sequences on the first few notes until the leaders sing forth a real tune at last.

But soon they relapse into the whirling movement on the vigorous motive, until, resting on a neighboring scene, they listen to the song of the oboe with accompanying clarinet. It is carelessness itself, the second theme, a regular holiday tune.

BEETHOVEN'S FOURTH SYMPHONY

(Clarinet, with sustaining strings.)

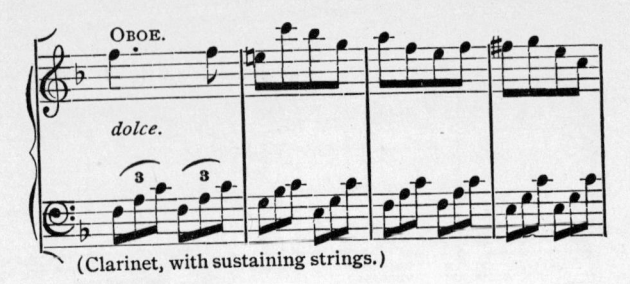

And then how fresh sounds the answer in simplest change of tonal scene!

(Clarinet with staccato strings in the harmony.)

On these strains the strings discourse a while, the tune singing in the bass with new melodic treble. The wood suggest a new idea to which all assent, and they ring out their nodding refrain to a climax of vehemence, where the original motive beats through the wild harmony. Twice this climax is relieved by a light cadence. The vehemence is lost, and the statement ends like an

BEETHOVEN'S FOURTH SYMPHONY

(With *tremolo* of violas.) (Added flute and horns.)
(See page 106, line 6.)

old round dance or song where opposite figures change places:

BEETHOVEN'S FOURTH SYMPHONY

After the discussion, the strings are chatting away quite aimlessly on a subject that seems not much weightier than the weather. Yet how relevant it proves to the main theme! But here are some curious things. As the garrulous strings keep running indefinitely on their old motive, suddenly there is a loud protesting single note, as if to say: this must really stop. Then the lower unison strings sing out the little answering air in boldest change of scene, actually without chords. All alone they sing the mere air alone, that, somehow, has its own implied harmony.

What is the mystery when single voice strikes change of tone, when single touch opens a new scene? It is the whole harmony of all the figures that marks the usual scene and color. One note may be of one or of the other,—as a single tree in landscape, though in the given region it may alone point the resting-place. It is in the relation of all the figures that lie the quality and charm of region.

In olden days, in grayest age of music's birth, there were but single tones; and so there was but one well-worn scene, or almost none at all. The word cannot be used without the sense of

BEETHOVEN'S FOURTH SYMPHONY

color. Here is the bold, charming touch of the stray voice groping back to friendly region, and then the others join in reassuring echo. Our voices may be of double symbol, of place and of inhabitant; yet the hidden feeling may become the clearer.

For a time there threatens a technical discussion by fugal rule. There is an echoing dispute, the simple and redoubled pace of new motive, that springs quite casually, though with melodic point, from phrase of bass while the original air is running in and out.

But the discussion is never very serious. It merely whets the desire for the rollicking dance in the whirling figure of the first phrase, which leads back to the main melodies. Once more come all the events of the first verse, not forgetting the little round, with exchange of figures. At last, quite needlessly, all join again in the main tune and dance to a fierce point. After the lull, as the basses stealthily hum the little run, like gentle drone of hurdy-gurdy, the high strings sing right at the same time the tuneful answer. A phrase of farewell has its timid say, answered by parting climax of the running theme. There is a pause. In pretty play of twice as slow a pace,

BEETHOVEN'S FOURTH SYMPHONY

the theme goes with deliberate step half-way and stops. The fagots sing four more notes to a halt, and so the low strings next. Then all the chorus with big festive noise and speed scamper down and—out.

V

BEETHOVEN'S EIGHTH SYMPHONY

AN EPIC OF HUMOR

THE Eighth Symphony has not the stress of the Fifth nor of the Seventh; its dimensions are less in every sense. Not that they measure the Symphony. It is frankly playful, teaches no lesson whatever. Almost, we might say, it came as apology for the sternness of the Fifth, the experiment of the Sixth, and even, as of future shadow, of the basic departure of the Ninth. It is most akin, in general cast, to the Seventh, but much simpler of pretence: one big *scherzo* of its own. It strikes no depth of profound sympathy. So it lacks a certain perspective or relief. As symphony, it is certainly not typical. The absence of true *andante* makes it exceptional. Its charm is therefore no less, rather greater, as undisturbed epic of merriment. There are no great contrasts of mood, few darker hues; the brightness has no help from contrasting shadows. Yet it has its broad

BEETHOVEN'S EIGHTH SYMPHONY

reaches, bold flights, big views. In a way it is a reversion to the old type of Haydn, the jolly symphony of the *salon* of good old times, where the composer had no business to do aught but amuse. A higher sort of court fool after all, in a way, was our "Papa" Haydn.

In complete abandon, careless of all responsibility and expectation bred of the master's earlier designs, this work was born; and in this defiant spontaneity lies assurance of its special charm. We may philosophize, if we feel we must. Just the right quantity of pathos cannot be determined by prescription to make a symphony. There may be a world all of humor,—a lifeview all of merriment. There has been such a philosophy. For the sage who went about laughing at everything, this work is a special symphony, a mirror of his world. If we must have a tragic symphony or pathetic, why not a comic? Humor has as much right to overemphasis as has pathos, perhaps a little more.

Clinging to our idea of the symphony as a kind of view of life of the poet, here the merry side has its own paramount place, a true comedy in the big sense of "Much Ado About Nothing," of "As You Like It." Secure, we listen, of no

BEETHOVEN'S EIGHTH SYMPHONY

deaths or funerals,—a jolly carnival though quite serious and sober in scope, not fearing to touch the ground note. But for once, instead of a sympathy big for all sorrows (like the Fifth), it cozens you gently and cheerily out of your sadness, wrings a laugh from the tears, brushes away the frowns with lightest touch.

A type of jolly serenity is the first theme:

(Full orchestra, with redoubled theme and harmony.)

Allegro vivace e con brio. Nothing ominous or profound. The tradition of Haydn's light abandon has lingered in the theme through all the stress of the Fifth, the sternness of Third, and the brilliant completeness of Seventh. The list of instruments is of old economy; trombones are not used at all. After the first theme is started in gay canter, it is carried on by galloping strings and a pompous figure dimly drawn

BEETHOVEN'S EIGHTH SYMPHONY

from main subject, where again the motion is more than the tune, and you can go indefinitely on the fillip in constant sequence of the slight motion; for, the smaller the phrase, the better for rearing structure.

The woodwind do no more than shout a regular acclaim as often as they are allowed. All this simmers down pretty solemnly, when out of the hushed and halted motion the second theme sings cheerily, though gently, almost timidly, with a touch, too, of jaunty humor in grateful change of tonal scene.

BEETHOVEN'S EIGHTH SYMPHONY

Our second melody emerges in charming shift of quarter; but in its second verse approaches the more familiar scene. Then, starting for the moment in anxious, hushed trembling, in gathering ascent of volume, it finally bursts in chorus on simplest cadent figure:

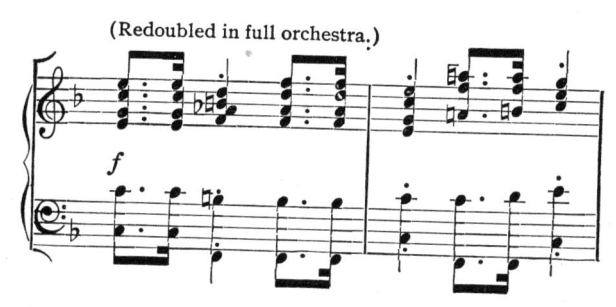

to which the answer is one of the most charming spots. It is gently sung

in solo voices of wood, each of which takes up the verse in turn, where quicker figures are entwined in the strings. Again bursts forth the noisy

BEETHOVEN'S EIGHTH SYMPHONY

chorus, just like Haydn's frightening places; and once again a responsive episode leads gradually to a big climax in the old way.

Now all is duly repeated according to rule. Then, as the bass keeps softly jogging the former noisy gait, stray bits of first theme are gently discussed in woodwind in a clear way that is somehow lost of late. In bursts the last noisy cadence. This alternating game, a little old-fashioned, reminding of Gluck, goes on for some time, but always with scenal change. Indeed this is almost the whole of it. As first we stray into dim shadows and suddenly dart into brilliant sunshine, once more wander into gray shadows and emerge into boldest light of all. Here the game is stopped. Instead, against trembling strings and crashes of wood, loud basses rumble the theme in rough minor. Merely the first theme rushes along, not waiting for the former answer, impetuously, as new text of its own, ever followed by united plaudits of wood.

The motive is transferred to high wood, group echoing group in eager cries. On a new height of the structure all the trebles hold the motive, echoed far down in bass. Once more there is a whirling mass of excited cries of this incipient

BEETHOVEN'S EIGHTH SYMPHONY

motive. At last, at the final climax, it is permitted to return to its original channel on full-blown theme. Only, it sings in resounding bass with trembling harmony above, though repeated in soft wood. But the basses are more important now; have much more to say. The lesser figure, which followed the theme with rocking motion, is more of melodic phrase, and is echoed by the bass.

As before, the gently skipping, cheery second tune comes singing along and leads to the same short burst of chorus. Charmingly as before follows the madrigal of timidly trustful voices of wood, entwined by tuneful figure of strings. Instead of ending, in a dim distant quarter the first melody sings or whispers a verse in slow clarinets. The answer is softly mocked by strings. Then all the strings in four groups play whispering a kind of canon, or game of chase with snatches of this very answer. They get noisier. At last all the chorus take courage and sing the main melody lustily with all the responsive play, inverting tune if needs be both ways at once, all in big frolic. Once more the plaintive madrigal of second melody is sweetly sung. But soon it is caught in the drollery and noise, and the

BEETHOVEN'S EIGHTH SYMPHONY

whole ends in shouting and shuffling on the first motive.

Allegretto. The great charm is this light dancing shuffle all in regular sprightly time, like chorus of dancers with the main figure behind the scenes, which suddenly appears with all usual grace. The most delightful prank in the world, as if a good confessor or confidant, instead of meeting you at the usual time, with long face

BEETHOVEN'S EIGHTH SYMPHONY

and responsive consoling grief, were gayly and roguishly to laugh you out of it all. For here is the second movement, the appointed time for pathos, sighs and tears maybe, and we are absolutely cheated out of our sad comfort and, what is more, made to dance a jolly turn instead with the gay deceiver himself. Can anything be more humiliating than to have to laugh at your own woes?

There is no resisting the mincing, dancing, rascally humor of the step. At the very start,— not too fast, a kind of deliberate, teasing, suppressed bit of humor, where wood are lightly shuffling and high strings are striking the tune, really a sort of duet as of mocked pedantry. It is marked all the more with a little echo way down in string basses.

On goes the sprightly strain with a slight change of tone and tune. A new prank comes, when, as the tune begins again, the whole chorus shout with most alarming volume, just for a moment, and then the tune goes singing right along with its old mock seriousness, as if nothing had happened or were ever to happen again. And here is another touch of drollery, as in dancing cadence high violins strike the light figure (which begins with

BEETHOVEN'S EIGHTH SYMPHONY

the theme), and instantly the clumsy low basses imitate, sometimes coming in in a belated, ineffective way and the more comic. More frightening bursts and other queer surprises,—unexpected lulls and stops. Then on again with the tune in all its innocent pertness of teasing, mincing step. But here a new jolly song rings out lustily, the tune in strings, shuffling step in the wood; in the low basses still the old skipping figure as if they had forgotten to leave off:

At the end the basses make an utterly unnecessary, terrible noise, running up and down the strings, and do it again soon afterwards, rudely interrupting a very harmless discussion of timid voices in strings and wood on snatches they had just heard, though it isn't quite free from a suspicion of mischief as the voices softly whisper in quaintly broken snatches taken up here, there,

BEETHOVEN'S EIGHTH SYMPHONY

and again, like dashing fire-flies. Now a broad, tuneful, sweetly serious sort of phrase

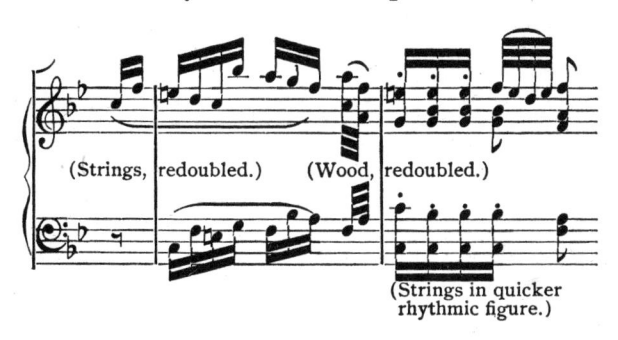

(Strings, redoubled.) (Wood, redoubled.)

(Strings in quicker rhythmic figure.)

comes sweeping along for a moment's rest from the fun, a true human word, a quick assurance of real sympathy, though there is still a mincing step in the answer. But it is repeated and the feeling is sustained a while, as the voices gradually return from the neighboring tone to the old, and the fun begins again, all the fresher for the break. Now the former course of tune and tricks all returns. But as the main melody repeats, after the basses have had their first refrain far down, a jolly variation of the air sings out, prancing gayly across the old outline, like daring rope-dancer, and coming out all right.

But here with all the fun, as the tune goes swinging on, a new feeling is blended. Some-

BEETHOVEN'S EIGHTH SYMPHONY

thing of intimate appeal creeps into the dance as the air beautifully extends and soon expands into lusty second tune, where still the comic basses are skipping away all alone in the old step, and again, as before, come breaking in with that frightful run in a most annoying way, with their very strange idea of a joke. Later the broad phrase of friendly assurance returns. Still the roguish whispers on skipping figure are more surprising than before, broken into by most tremendous shouts of every living throat about, all in quickest possible step, too, all ending in one more romp on the pure dance itself, though some are going two and even four steps to one, swelling once more from softest whisper to loudest din.

Menuetto. The minuet has an unwonted swing, though of course in three-step time, but it seems less like a dance than a sweep of one big motion for the three lesser ones, and the tune is a regular song with a good burst in the midst; you could sing words to it and forget to dance. After it is repeated with a special sense of freshness, it darts off to a neighboring tone; but instead of the full tune the first bit is passed down the line of strings by the

BEETHOVEN'S EIGHTH SYMPHONY

(See page 122, line 20.)

pleasantest sort of trick of retort, and then up again in a much jollier way still, getting noisily back to the first, the home tone.

Here the voices simmer down on playful phrase until the main tune returns, now down in fagots with low murmuring strings, with gently telling effect. Soon, of course, this mounts to another joyous height, where ends the first verse (the strict *scherzo*), with an odd sort of round

BEETHOVEN'S EIGHTH SYMPHONY

clog on the first notes of theme, where one group strike in on the heels of another.

In the *Trio* the fun has pretty much vanished. It is merely a true German folk-song in simplest lines and mood. Mostly the horns lead with the air just like an old song of love or hunt.

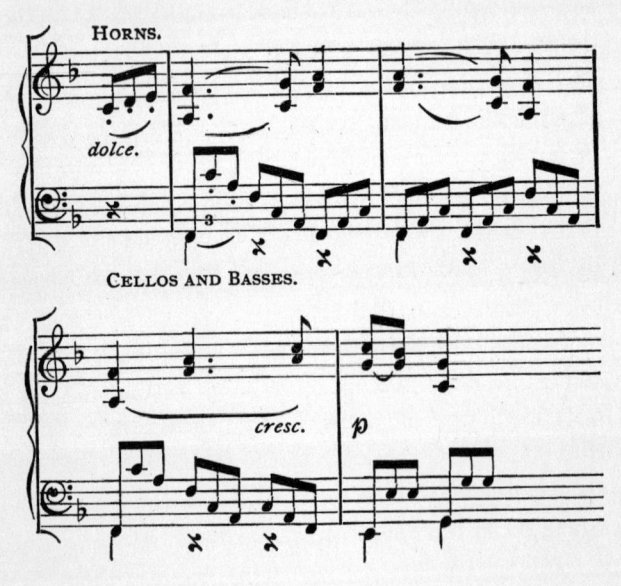

Oboes answer, followed in kind of canon by horns and cellos. In the Trio's second part (each is repeated) the motive of melody is simply played in dimmer minor, while the preceding

BEETHOVEN'S EIGHTH SYMPHONY

canon phrase still goes threading its consecutive course.

Soon a darker, shadier scene is reached, where the folk-song now sounds in full strings, the thread still running in the horns, and reaches a hearty conclusion. Suddenly it shifts to the old scene, singing the same heart-felt strain, now in horns. Carried farther, the song, in responsive and successive step, has a fervent though gentle burst, while the first motive ever sounds far down in basses with its slight trip against the smooth appeal of a newer cadent figure. Oft rehearsed is this burst, then dies down to a hallowed hush of horns and strings, whence the *scherzo* sings once more its merrier strain.

Finale. In the Finale is a bigger rhythmic swing (a little too big, perhaps, for traditional notation), one of those great reaches that Beethoven seemed to call from a stranger, higher sphere, conceived in a freer flight than we are tuned to in our scientific, "practical" age:

BEETHOVEN'S EIGHTH SYMPHONY

(Doubled below.)

The theme seems mere rhythmic idea; but the answer is more articulate song of gladness, on big soaring wing, though, to be sure, all in softer strings:

which play a while with strange hollow effect on the first motive. Then, in loudest unison of all, the whole song is rehearsed; or rather the rehearsing came first and this is the regular full verse.

In a new stride the basses have worked themselves into, they march ahead without heed of concluded verse, in a kind of special melodic consciousness.

BEETHOVEN'S EIGHTH SYMPHONY

ff

while strings are trembling on in the old way and bursts of wood point the pace. The high wood now have a feeling for the tune and sing it as it mounts reversed in the basses, while the strings tremble on in the first motion. The scene slightly darkens, and now the striding tune has lapsed into mere retorts *en masse* in full force. Suddenly, hushed in distant quarter, a real melody, that makes all the rest prelude to its song, sings rapturously in strings and, just before the close of phrase, the oboe chimes in a most sweetly concluding strain:

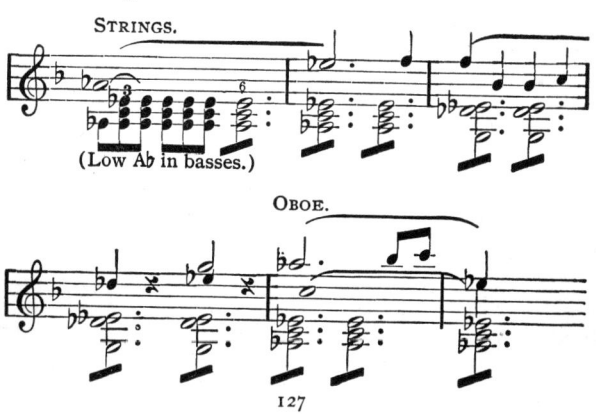

(Low A♭ in basses.)

BEETHOVEN'S EIGHTH SYMPHONY

The song wings on its freer course and then, with a fresh delight of returning to home tone, sings against broader swaying of strings, while lower wood now join, like the former oboe, in the tuneful concluding medley. On the latter motive, wood and strings start in timid, anxious ascent in strange cross-purpose of rhythm, then descend. The same journey is taken up by all in bold spirit, and on safe return the manful stride resumes to original tonal region.

Here, after a few timid tries at the motive, the main theme sings again as at first; but instead of echoing chorus, timidity reigns again, and against trembling strings a long, anxious, whispered discussion follows on answer of main theme:

BEETHOVEN'S EIGHTH SYMPHONY

voices entering without waiting for others to vanish. Three or four are attacking at once the same strain in different kind of suit and pitch; a few are singing bits reversed; the whole subject is gone over. Then some kind of order is restored and high cellos and low violins are given the floor. To be sure, they start together in opposite direction, but precisely agreeing in each rhythmic turn. Soon another pair are champions; the middle strings are sent off discoursing the same way. They cannot help getting tangled later with others. The strings seem to have a hopeless tendency to argue. For some time a strange call in two long notes has been heard again and again, here and there, above and below. It enters often crashing against the clash of quarrelling strings. Dimly we are forced back to the sounds of incipient second melody through all the strife of first, and finally it triumphs and brings order and a burst on united main theme in new scene.

Presently we have its original course home again. Of course it is enriched now with the gain of newer figures, mainly of striding bass; so the full refrain sounds far more triumphant, bigger with wonderful complexity of rhythms,

BEETHOVEN'S EIGHTH SYMPHONY

warring for the moment. The old course, as after original verse, continues, of melody, bass and retorts of massed groups. The second melody in full queenly beauty follows, though still in newer scene of sound, with rich accoutrement of melodic vassals, and again, as before, returns to sing on familiar ground. The anxious ascent and descent of wood and strings into discordant gait all recur with a full choral pursuit. We ought to be glad we are home again and rest for good; but we stray once more.

An entirely new pace is set, a new course of ideas. Out of the silence, in dim religious light, violins sound a chant, descending in notes of dirge:

It is answered by oboes and fagots, starting in opposite direction, but the old trembling

BEETHOVEN'S EIGHTH SYMPHONY

motion will not let go,—the one reminder of old frolic. Twice the chant is duly sung and answered, then in double pair of ascending woodwind against descending basses. They are met on high by a soft acclaim of the others; but the strings still tremble on. Now the motion is reversed. All this has been sung in dread hush of tones. Now it rings out as full religious pæan in four independent voices of strings against loud blasts of brass and clash of drum, while the woodwind shake a slower, though more solemn, vibrating call in big ecclesiastical magnificence. The chorus proceeds with solemn pomp. At last they break into quicker pace; the theme has a more playful ring; the trembling call quickens as of old. Then out flashes the old theme, but in strange, brilliant light.

Finally, in the gentle lull of the beginning it sings another verse. But a new spirit has somehow crept in; for anon all is stopped by full blast of chorus,—even the trembling motion ceases. Now, in overpowering mass the theme returns; but there is a strange tonal quality, an uneasy sense of omen. It is really a sort of mock fear. In the very height of triumphant joy, or rather on the eve of it, there is a note of

BEETHOVEN'S EIGHTH SYMPHONY

uncertainty, merely to increase the assurance when it comes, as it promptly does, in the old familiar scene where now lesser themes go chasing helter-skelter to give the chief a rest before the final verse.

But before him his queenly mate once more pours forth her lovely song in the very home tone, where she has not yet sung, where he himself had hitherto held sway. The beauty infects even rough basses, which are given leave to sing a sonorous verse against the higher harmonies of the others; and all the rest is great rejoicing as on home-coming, that seems, after all, to be the main purpose and the best of all journeys,—that leaves some truth in the old pedant who describes the movements of ancient sonata in all earnest: "The first to show what the composer can do, the second what he can feel, the last how glad he is to have finished." All things earthly and even above are, after all, an eternal round.

VI

BEETHOVEN'S SIXTH (PASTORAL) SYMPHONY

TONAL DEPICTION

"AWAKENING of Cheerful Feelings on arriving in the Country" is the title of the first movement.

"*Feelings*" here is the key-note that ought to pervade the whole symphony. If it did pervade, we should have a pastoral whole, as we have two real bucolics in tones. The first movement begins on simplest tune in the strings, that is like the song of a bird, if only in the leisurely pause before resuming, answered in four-voiced choir :

Allegro ma non troppo.

STRINGS. *p*
(Low C in basses.)

Later the tune steals into the wood, and soon rings out in full chorus with extended melody. At the end, as the accompanying clarinets and

BEETHOVEN'S SIXTH SYMPHONY

fagots pipe in triplet motion, the violins discourse freely on a strain of the tune, and glide with ideal ease into the second theme, really the first, so far as beauty lends dignity.

And here the wonderful art of the master appears. The most difficult feat comes without a seeming jot of toil. The perfect form does not appear at first, from its very perfection,—the soprano and bass are complementary tunes and at the end change places, without loss of a note, so that one does not know whether to find the melody above or below; it is all a double sort of melody. The highest art (what schoolmen call double-counterpoint) comes as naturally as the chirping of a bird. To write a second melody to a first is a feat of the older artisan; but to pour forth a double melody from the beginning, all unconscious of the feat, was highest of all, because done in a simple burst of feeling, not in pride of art.

Soon a third voice in high flutes strikes in the midst with the tune of the bass, and all the birds in the wood are singing bits of the double song, ending in half-unison, hymn-like cadence, dying down with a cheery call in strings and a carolling note in the woodwind. This leads

BEETHOVEN'S SIXTH SYMPHONY

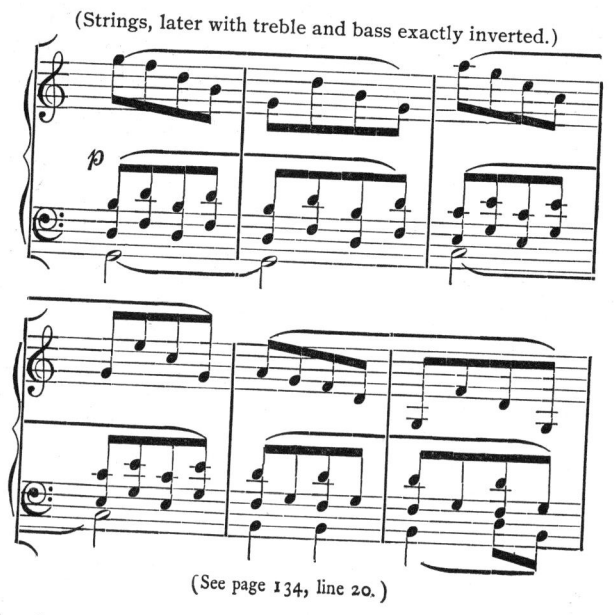

(Strings, later with treble and bass exactly inverted.)

(See page 134, line 20.)

back to a rehearsing of the tunes from the beginning.

The discussion proceeds, unhampered by labels, on the original strain. You cannot possibly talk freely in music if everything you say must have a verbal title and meaning. Fearless of repetition, the simple phrase runs along:

BEETHOVEN'S SIXTH SYMPHONY

modulating through bright changes of tonal light and shade to a kind of chorus where the theme is in the bass. Then the call is sung back and forth with perfect childlike or birdlike freedom. For the nonce, the first tune interrupts in fugal, reflective guise, but merely for the moment. The call sings on again through new modulations of tonal light. After a like appearance of the first tune we have the answer of the four-voiced choir. Its theme is carried first in low duet with strings, then in single song of violins, again in duet, and now in full hymnal chorus. Though brief, this is the climax, and, dying down, it leads straight to the rehearsal of themes as at first, with a trill instead of the pause. The big chorus and the whole second melody follow in full beauty. To be sure, the ending duet with cheerful phrase and carolling wind is much extended in length and volume, and there is added a rollicking dance tune, at the end of which the first theme sings softly as possible in strings, then in high flute, all alone, answered mockingly by a playful burst of the whole band.

Feelings, scenes, events have all been attempted in music. They have their place, certainly, in

BEETHOVEN'S SIXTH SYMPHONY

art. Has not each kind its special branch? For scenes there is painting; for events there are words, measured or unmeasured, prose or verse. So once more, from a different point, though not, of course, by a strict proof, we come to our old truth: that music is specially the utterance of feeling. Other propositions, various in grade, are all related: first and clearest, that feeling is the main burden of music; whether exclusive, is another question. A converse of the first, that by no means follows by mere deductive logic, is whether music is the clearest utterance of feeling. That it is not its only language is almost absurd even to mention. In one sense, feeling is the final theme of every art. A scene in colors or threads, an action or event in ballad or story, to arouse the least interest must spring from emotional motive, however unconscious, beyond the mere design of exact depiction or narration. So, to tell an event without interest, however faithfully; to copy precisely an object without a meaning, implies no art. All art must have its rise in feeling and must make its appeal to feeling. When, therefore, we speak of the utterance of feeling in art as against scenes or events, we mean merely the

BEETHOVEN'S SIXTH SYMPHONY

direct utterance without the medium of outside objects, of nature or of human experience. Here the strength of music seems to lie in freedom from interfering subjects, finally in the primary beauty of its alphabet. To be sure, we have seen that even here the depiction of feeling ought not to be conscious; its best utterance is a kind of involuntary betrayal, where the main interest is on the musical design itself; for indeed all work comes best from concentration, from an absolute absorption. For the poet to trouble about the emotional hue of the whole is like talking with one eye on the mirror; it is a hopeless diversion, a dissipation of effort. So, as we have seen, the best basis of titles in music is, as Schumann discovered, a kind of postscript: a final touch after the whole untrammelled course of the poem.

But this does not argue the impossibility deliberately to celebrate special subjects. Indeed, it is not for the hearer to inquire when the title was written, before or after; all must be tested by the work itself. But a natural guess may be ventured as to difficulty and danger of preconceived subject, an almost fatal cramping of its limitations. Any fetter of the fancy of the

BEETHOVEN'S SIXTH SYMPHONY

musician is a loss, and is never atoned for by the mere fidelity to a title. High art is the aim; the name, the label, is nothing. In the older arts, especially in verse, a name sprang from the necessity of conditions, because there must be an object. Prose and verse are themselves words; there a title is not derived outside of the art, it is part of the tissue of the work itself. Sculpture and painting stand midway. Names are not needed; but as they dealt always in outside objects, it was but natural to add the names that belonged to them. Most striking it is that more and more in modern plastic and chromatic art, of chisel and of brush, wholly fanciful subjects are vanishing, actual names are less and less employed.

In music, the necessary use of outside objects does not exist; with it the excuse, the reason for labels seems equally to be lost; they seem a mere vanity in every sense.

In Beethoven's day they were most pardonable; for the art was young, lusty, and unconscious of boundaries. Nay, the experiment, we may say, had to be made. If the greatest failed, the proof is the more complete. The very concentration of masters on their art left them witless of its philosophic theory. It was left for a

BEETHOVEN'S SIXTH SYMPHONY

Bach—highest poet of man's religious sense—to write a crowing cock in the Passion of Christ.

Therefore in the "Scene at the Brook" the words will be taken not in the narrowest, but in the broadest sense. "Scene" must mean the feelings aroused by a visit to the brook. As we shall see elsewhere,* the agreement of actual incident and its subjective impression may be so close that the musical utterance will answer, as does positive to negative of a picture. As composers do not split hairs, the use of actual story or song is most natural; their emotional meaning must, whenever possible, be implied.

The strings below are murmuring in steady course, the horns are droning in sense of quiet woodland, while the upper violins slowly sing themselves into articulate song:

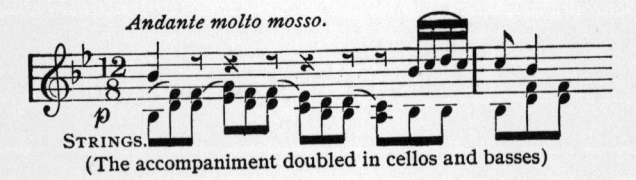

Andante molto mosso.

STRINGS.
(The accompaniment doubled in cellos and basses)

of which the close is clearer than the first notes. The lower background of vague strings soon

---

* See the "Lenore" Symphony, *infra*.

BEETHOVEN'S SIXTH SYMPHONY

grows to richer waving and swaying; a high trill, sweetly discordant, is added in the branches above, while the lower woodwind now sing the melody. Throughout is the special charm of the gentle clash of nature-sounds. The fool (and critic) might say in his heart: a vain displacing of art with brutal touch of nature. The truth is, the poet everywhere merely foresees a future touch of pure art which to the lay ear has ever the sense of clash, the herald of new experience. (Of course, it adds to the immediate poetic impression of the scene.) It is all easily demonstrable with the numbers of exact science, and were worth doing if the convictions of art were not always those of intuition rather than of logic.

The song soon breaks into a verse of more human clearness, first in the high strings:

(Murmuring cellos, violins and violas.)

now the cellos below and clarinets above take up the strain, while a like pair, violins and fagots, strike into the midst with a tune of the same fibre, aslant the skein of the first pair; and now

BEETHOVEN'S SIXTH SYMPHONY

even the high flutes add to the woof of song. Simply it ends and returns to the first murmuring tune of strings, spreading with new freedom of tonal moorings, and of melodic figure more cheerful of mood, ending in well-contented cadence of flute in a neighboring key:

(Full harmonies in strings, wood and horns.)

echoed by bassoons below. But the close is not real; a new scene gently appears with fagots starting afresh into song, while now higher strings alone are murmuring:

(Twice repeated, the cellos strengthening the melody.)

BEETHOVEN'S SIXTH SYMPHONY

the lower are soon strengthening the fagots; the singers trip into a jolly measure. The clarinets come crosswise into the dance; others add to the maze; but the end is in united chorus. The verse is repeated with richer interlacing of lesser phrases, but throughout all is a rural simplicity; the complexity is not of conscious thought, it is the sweet whirl of woodnotes. The best of all comes at the end of the verse, when the close playfully runs into another maze, richer, broader, stronger than before, on the more human, tender strain of the end of the first verse. As the vein, though not the tune, of the first theme returns, gentle clashes of single notes of strings (against the whole stream of song) grow bolder, bold even for to-day,—a century later. It is a clear case of the weakness of theoretic law when once the mind surmounts it, mastering the intent, in open transgression, yet true to the spirit of order. It is in a way a mystery, but it shows how the idea is all,—the outward, visible or audible effect nothing. The same note, written in ignorance of the law and therefore in false intent, would be false, because the idea were false. And Beethoven's idea seems false to the ear that is rigidly attuned to

BEETHOVEN'S SIXTH SYMPHONY

primitive consonances, refusing heed to constant change, to ever-expanding truth. (So, perhaps, nothing is true in the sense of rigid force of written dogma, and nothing is false in so far as it may find somewhere its right relation.) From a narrow artistic view, it remains true that the value does not lie here in a brutal intrusion of a hostile note in graphic depiction of nature; the beauty of pure art must be there and thus establish the truth.

Coming back to our song, the sense is almost an illusion of the sweet conflict of forest sounds of insects, birds, and waters. A new verse, through all of the old tissue, now sings out, echoed higher in the flutes. To be sure, like the second, it merely digresses from the constant strain of the original song which now proceeds with more readiness and variety of principal and lesser figures, succeeded again by the maze of the speaking strain of the second verse. This now spreads through stronger climax into a new tonal scene of the first. By a similar turn, still a new scene is found for the same verse, and by still further subtle changes the original key is reached, where the verse is sung complete as before (after the second), though with much fuller

BEETHOVEN'S SIXTH SYMPHONY

acclaim of all the voices. The contented cadence comes now in the original key; but it is again elusive and leads as before into the third verse with a dancing clause. Then comes again the friendly strain of the second and a final harking back again to the first.

A few trills in high woodwind, entering one after the other, may disturb the philosophic interpretation. They are labelled in the score: the flute's trill, the nightingale; the call of the oboe, the quail; of the clarinet, the cuckoo. They are answered by one more verse of the friendly strain. Musically they do not change our enjoyment. Beethoven's intent undoubtedly, it is more and more evident, is actually to depict the forest scene. However, it is wise for us, even in defiance of his conscious purpose, to get the best of the music. A composer, we dare say, is not a good authority on the value of his own music; the musical intent is his, and there he is authority; not so the verbal label. For he utters his authority only by his music, not by words. Never ask a composer what he means by a piece of music, nor a painter by his picture; for the composer's unconscious musical mood may be at war with the vanity of his desire to force an external meaning on his

BEETHOVEN'S SIXTH SYMPHONY

music. And here we may, nay we must, side with the true though latent musical purpose.

In the third movement, "Joyful Gathering of Peasants" is the first title. Who shall say it is the outward bustle, the mere view, the external action, rather than the enjoyment of it, the joviality itself,—all to a most expressive jolly jingle in quickstep of a real tuneful jig:

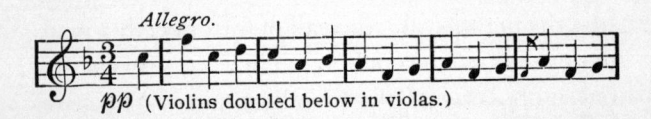

pp (Violins doubled below in violas.)

The answer has more of song than of dance. Later there are cross-figures; then all dance in unison, followed by a united burst almost of hymn, breaking off into a gay waltzing trip. Lightly as this constant skip recedes to softest, gentlest background, suddenly the ingenuous reed most naïvely blows a rustic air with all the bucolic freedom from measured limits:

VIOLINS. *dur.*

BEETHOVEN'S SIXTH SYMPHONY

Somehow it never strays far from the soft skip of dancing feet. Again and again comes the simple refrain, though never too often; and now the clarinet breaks in, in lower pitch, the comic bassoon even intrudes its three clumsy notes, and the horns still lower. Soon others are caught humming, even the lowest bass, when abruptly strikes a rudest jingle in rough time and harsher accord, in a primitive sort of tone common to all nations in barbaric stage:

In tempo d' allegro.

(Violins, with sustained strings.)

True, a later, more civilized tune sings above the receding jig and through a fine burst leads first to the beginning, then to a final verse of the first tune, whence again the united song breaks into the tripping rustic waltz, to be harshly disturbed by—"Rain and Storm."

Above the faint rumble of basses comes the light patter of a sprinkling verse in the second, and larger drops in the first violins; very soon the full storm is on, in furious tempest on the whole horizon of tone, with rough stride of de-

BEETHOVEN'S SIXTH SYMPHONY

scending violins, the winds driving big things, tumbling in heavy fall. Now thunder growls from afar; now strikes the crash; now again; now more peals in quick suit; then the former patter leads to a more furious storm than before.

Two things are true: first, we must never lose the possible sense of mere subjective impression, not of actually described event. The correspondence will become more and more close and exact as the outward titles increase in number. Under one general title the fancy and feeling may roam with great, though not with unfettered freedom. But here is a second truth: as the labels multiply comes the perplexing need of still more. We are driven to ask what is this and that and even every least note. Here is the tremendous increasing danger of titles. They are fearful tyrants and hold the imagination bound.

Even if the musician means to give but touches here and there of realism, yet the whole is transformed from free feeling to a graphic account. The question of objective and subjective, action or impression, is soon the splitting of hairs,—a matter of technical phrase. We cannot get away from the multiplicity of detail. Now

BEETHOVEN'S SIXTH SYMPHONY

this is mere negative. Think of the loss of all we have seen and gained in the free musical discussion of lyric melodies soaring to utmost ranges of structural height without the least fear of transcending imposed barriers, and then rearing the greatest possible art from the seed of the melodies and the soil of the poet's mood. And the real meaning, though we cannot define it in common words, is it not far nobler than theatrical touch of rain and thunder? Think of the value and meaning to the world, if only during a single year, of Beethoven's Fifth Symphony, which is all untitled.

The thunder and storm all crash together; heavy bolts descend through the blinding rain and wind. Lightning still flashes throughout. Now the tempest retreats; low thuds of pelting rain strike more gently; here and there a loud bolt recurs. As the last growls recede, the higher strings and clarinet sound a few notes of hymnal song, which seem the first touches of pure untrained feeling. But it glides immediately into the "Shepherd's Song,"—"Glad and Grateful Feelings After the Storm."

We have *feelings* again; the worst is over. The structure of song form is just like lyric

BEETHOVEN'S SIXTH SYMPHONY

poem, where first verse recurs in refrain. Clarinets and horn strike the pitch in simple rhythmic chord, violins begin the song itself:

of simplest ancient kind; rehearsing to make doubly sure, that all may presently join in full chorus, where clarinets, horns, and low strings take the air, the rest holding long tones in the chord or keeping mere time with skipping step. Almost as good and as joyous is the little after-strain:

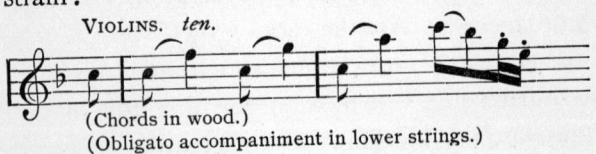

first in lower strings, answered by the higher. From out of this, as one subject of talk leads to the next, flows another separate verse of the song in neighboring pitch of tone, in mere mocking

BEETHOVEN'S SIXTH SYMPHONY

phrase, like things of the tree, ever higher in the branches, extending finally into an after-phrase almost finer than the main, and resting in the new home of tone, whence the quick return to the old leads back to the first verse with playful skip of lower figure. Hence quickly we turn in another direction to a third verse in another quarter of tonal scene. Broader swings the double air, broken ever by mischievous intrusion of chorus. Now we are carried into the freest phase, leaving the staid lines of rustic song playing about the end of the tunes, darting in strange colors of tone. Mostly the basses are humming in rough semblance of the main verse a tune of their own, while high strings are coursing furiously in rural bacchanale; but soon they all return to the simpler song, first of the original verse, though with whimsical changes, the strings still coursing lightly,—once more repeated with fullest chorus and followed by after-phrase and again by the second verse and its own postscript. And now a light carolling brings us to a formal round where our rustics try their skill, as one voice enters all alone, later a second in separate figure, the rest merely keeping time with hands and feet. The climax through another carolling strain leads to

BEETHOVEN'S SIXTH SYMPHONY

a feat of greater difficulty and complexity, where two separate groups are trying separate manœuvres, crowned by a tumult of loudest festivity.

Right at the close the old song sounds as devout hymn, all free of worldly dance, chanting its thanksgiving clearer than words:

It almost seems as if this were no longer our Shepherd's Song; as if, like the touch in the last movement, we had escaped from the title, we heard the poet's own finer thought of it all, his own purer note of thanksgiving.

VII

BEETHOVEN'S NINTH (CHORAL) SYMPHONY

THE FINAL NEED OF WORDS

THE Ninth Symphony brings us to a question at once most simple and most profound. What is more natural than the gradual striving for definite utterance of highest feeling, like the child breaking from the cooing rhythm of the cradling nurse? On the other hand, does this burst into words actually bring the definiteness striven for? Does it crown the insufficient utterance of the wordless song of the earlier symphony? To lapse for a moment from our exclusive view of the work itself, there is no doubt that the fact that Beethoven at the end of his last Symphony broke into words, must be a doughty argument for those who contend for the greater definiteness of verbal utterance in music. But we must not forget that while Beethoven may reach the greatest heights as a master, he was not infallible as theorist on the nature of his art. He found the latter only by experiments,

BEETHOVEN'S NINTH SYMPHONY

which were often failures, which we must test by our own intuition, which Beethoven himself would not have us accept in blind confidence in himself.

The last great work of big dimensions designed by Beethoven begins very freely, in vehement rhythmic strum:

that foreshadows rather than utters, soon breaking in loudest unison into a simple harmonic figure that is too frugal for melody:

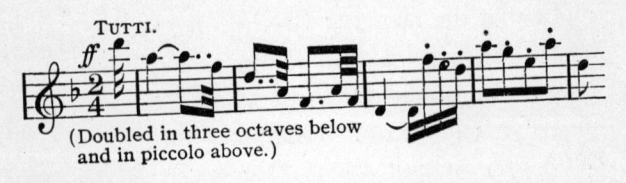

Indeed it is all introduction, very like recitatives heralding the aria. At times it approaches the tune:

BEETHOVEN'S NINTH SYMPHONY

WOODWIND.

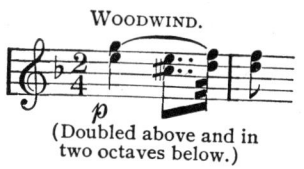

p

(Doubled above and in two octaves below.)

but soon we wonder whether the whole movement is not introduction. Often even all three movements seem prelude to the last. But presently a clearer phrase emerges:

(Flutes in 8ve of higher voice.)
WOODWIND.

p dolce.
(Doubled below.)

with antiphonal answer, and this but precedes a still fuller melody, though it is disguised by distribution among several voices:

(Tune in woodwind.)

Sempre. p
(Strings doubled in two 8ves below.)

BEETHOVEN'S NINTH SYMPHONY

There is an amount of noisy climax that does seem out of proportion to the modest tune; but it is all part of the solemnly festive humor that foretokens high rites. Out of this very burst of cadence steals a bit that we nearly lose, though it is of clearest ore. On the fillip of the previous clash:

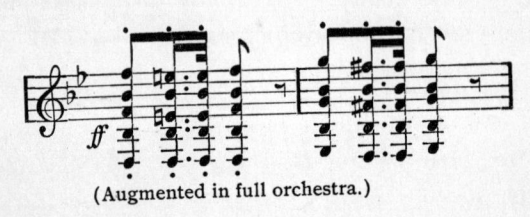

(Augmented in full orchestra.)

now rung softly far down in basses, a kind of motto hovers high in strings and wood merely for the length of a breath, in four sustained notes:

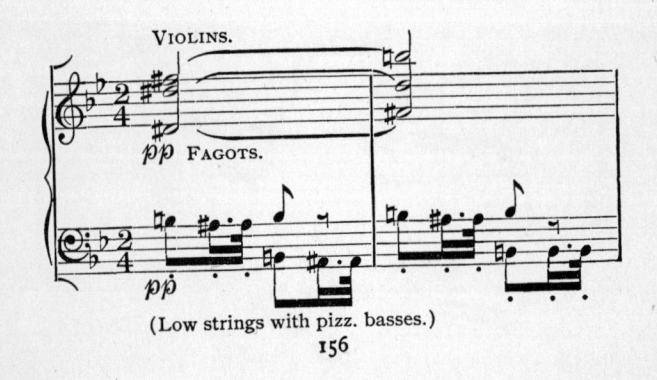

(Low strings with pizz. basses.)

BEETHOVEN'S NINTH SYMPHONY

But it is as integral as any fragment in this in-choate, chaotic, inconsequent prelude, and presently another melodic snatch sings in softest wood and strings, in outline like the reverse of the main melody:

Lower strings, tripping rhythm in drums.

BEETHOVEN'S NINTH SYMPHONY

Indeed, the whole is largely compact in mosaic of brilliant strains, all striving for dominance, none with clear sovereignty. After a still more furious climax, broken but heightened by momentary lulls, we enter again the stirring strum of the beginning,—a shadowy discussion of very shadowy subjects, where that earliest phrase in simplest harmony assumes more dignity:

Other thoughts, too, are crowding in for the lead, Here is one in cradling motion, which springs from an earlier motive:

BEETHOVEN'S NINTH SYMPHONY

The main frugal theme seems the very type of vague striving. So the whole has more and more of fragmental effect; the striving alone is definite; the vagueness alone is clear; each thought is rejected for the next.

Now, beautifully blended of the cradling phrase and the cadence of the big theme, springs a verse that sings its larger career first in resounding bass of fagots and strings, with the cradling phrase always somewhere about in other voices than the leaders. Now the tune is in high flutes and in violins; lower strings are rocking to the rhythm; now tune and phrase are confused in high strings and wood; finally, the melody remains on high and the lesser phrase sinks to a perfect bass in strings where, by a sort of verification, the whole is crowned to a glorious conclusion, swinging along in full discussion, which never loses the rhythm in the dispute. When it seems to have died away, we are in a sort of madrigal of responsive refrains on the cradling phrase, with more song and swing and sweetness and less dispute than before, whence we return to the main melody (not the first theme) in the strings. But, instead of the noisy tempest, the tune runs smoothly: first above, an-

BEETHOVEN'S NINTH SYMPHONY

swered below; then reversed; third, with new answer in the midst; and, finally, with redoubled answer dancing all above, drowning the song itself with very gayety. From out of the festive orgy the ominous strum of the beginning has suddenly driven the other figures.

It is wonderful, the magic of musical discussion. Is it the mere association of external similarity of phrases, hurled back and forth,—one view; or is it the marching in architectural array in magnificently prodigal profusion of ordered fragments, running by new dimension to massive structure?

Discussion shows the humble dignity of the separate lyric strain; it confirms the relevancy of the whole by the text and fibre of the motive, which is now merged into the infinite importance of the organic structure. The discussion from different melodic ends, fitting together, verifies and convinces far beyond the strongest force of man's logical proof. It is thus that poems and other forms of art stay longer than laws and institutions, which seem hedged in and buttressed by all the external means in the world. An unseen melody, a symphony that merely floats in the air, has the more powerful existence and perma-

BEETHOVEN'S NINTH SYMPHONY

nence because it is fortified by truth,—it is truth itself.

And now comes the original suite of strains, save there is an angrier dispute of the rude phrases of the beginning, clashing in contrary stride, marching in prouder step, with broader swing, with redoubled countermarching and cadence. Heralded as before, the main melody is again divided among its choir of voices, followed by the noisy tumult. Once more the gentle motto in four long notes, the bustling ascent, the swinging third melody that came before in the wake of the motto, the big climax. Instead of rest there is new discussion, still in the vague humor, striving for ever better, newer expression, not content with the theme at hand. The original subject enters softly for the first time, and is answered in more rational fashion, other voices chiming in in independent time. Then follows the climax, in earlier vein, of crossing phrases, which has something of mystic brooding. Through another lusty fanfare it leads to one of the best moments. That little blended tune of cradling phrase and cadence of first subject enter softly in major in the horns, while oboes and fagots sweetly interfere with the tune.

BEETHOVEN'S NINTH SYMPHONY

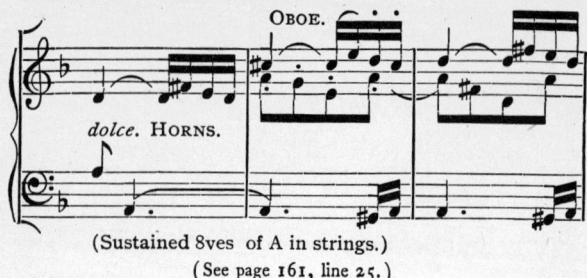

(Sustained 8ves of A in strings.)
(See page 161, line 25.)

The whole is colored by a more joyous hue, though once again enters the dispute of contrary stride. So the whole is a paradox in that the main theme and phase are lesser, in inverse proportion to official rank; and the best is in obscurest corners,—mere after-thoughts, not of the main design or text, yet betraying, through the pain of striving, a secret joyousness of humor. It is of course but a type of life, where the best often comes least awaited in humblest places.

So, near the very end comes another episode full of resonant charm, as the basses march gently to the active pace of the previous blended melody, and the horns and wood strike a call and trilling cadence, gradually infecting most of the band, ending finally in triumphant close of original theme.

Scherzo. The first canto has not ascended

BEETHOVEN'S NINTH SYMPHONY

(See page 162, line 15.)

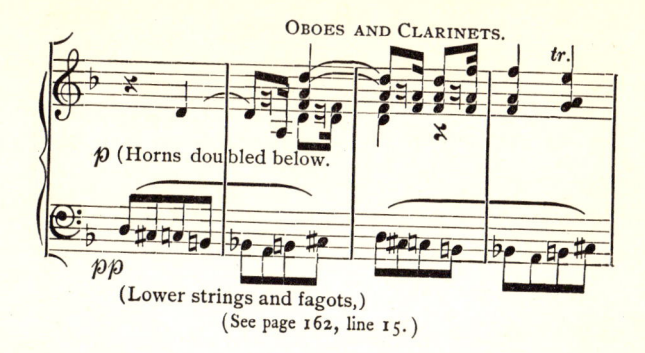

the heights of clear joy; the time for the calm lyric utterance has not come; the *Andante* must be deferred. Much clearer in tune than the *Allegro*, bright in tripping gait, the *Scherzo* is yet strongly intermixed with a mystic vein, a little like a dance of will-o'-the-wisps. It begins a dazzling filigree of five-voiced fugue on the theme:

which, most unusually, against its very nature is in the same tonal color (in the same key) with the preceding movement,—another sign of insufficiency, of an introductory function. It is this

BEETHOVEN'S NINTH SYMPHONY

reason, not technical of the schools, but poetic and therefore real. The departure to new tonal scene can only come when the whole structure—purpose, mood, and all—has been achieved, when the earlier striving has been stilled to utmost satisfaction. There is no other instance in a Beethoven symphony of identical tonal residence of the first two movements.

First tripping along in strings, with harmonies in the wood, the theme, no longer a fugue, plunges into full chorus in pure free dance with flowing answer. One continuous romp it seems—to the Trio. Still, one can distinguish, to the constant trip in the strings, the wood playing softly a slow hymn-like phrase:

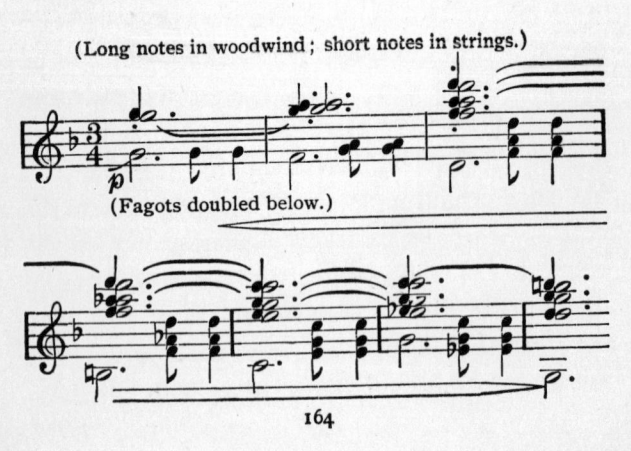

(Long notes in woodwind; short notes in strings.)

(Fagots doubled below.)

BEETHOVEN'S NINTH SYMPHONY

to which the whole chorus (all the brass but horns are omitted throughout) shout a tumultuous refrain:

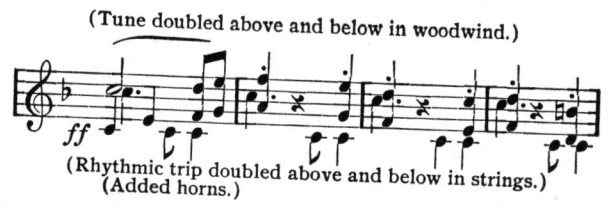

(Tune doubled above and below in woodwind.)

[musical notation: ff]

(Rhythmic trip doubled above and below in strings.)
(Added horns.)

The trip ever continues in the strings, soon prevails in playful repartee with the wood, and rushes through alternate gentle and noisy lines to a close. Whence first a complete repetition, then a discussion of the tripping motive, ever with mocking exchange between the choirs with playful pauses, climbing all the boughs of the tonal tree. Here is a new trick; the fugue has the voices dancing in, every three measures instead of four; so there is a double rhythm of dance, little and big, checking the great irresistible pace which must soon reappear when the voices restore the balance by entering, not on the fourth but on each successive measure. Finally, they let out their suppressed spirits and pace in pure repeated step, then burst once more into the former course of dance tunes with the same

BEETHOVEN'S NINTH SYMPHONY

triumphant close. Thence the whole discussion and refrain are rehearsed.

In complete transformation of scene and rhythm the *Trio* sounds a pious hymn in organ tones of the wood:

Playful, perhaps, is the first note of solemn lay that is soon to reign,—a touch of eternal fate, with all simplicity and even humor. Hymn-like, the second seems a mere varied verse of the first, where with dazing art the voices are reversed again and again, and the themes to boot:

BEETHOVEN'S NINTH SYMPHONY

so that the pervading sense of the thought remains without a single actual repeated strain, all in even monkish measure, though the quicker second pause still reminds us of the old fun. Now the horns below have the tune, and the high strings sing the former bass reversed, sounding even more fitting than at first; and so tunes and countertunes flow along far up and down without reck which is bass or air. An ascending play on the quick measure leads to the hymn in full canonicals, whence most of the Trio is repeated. In still greater array the hymn is borne to festive

BEETHOVEN'S NINTH SYMPHONY

close and the impish tune of the fugal scherzo returns. In big equipment the course of the gay dance is run through to heart's satisfaction, and even a line of the hymn is added with almost mocking effect. But we fear there is no proving of heresy on musical evidence.

Adagio molto e cantabile. The mood is purely lyric and the placid flow of tones has a noble simplicity:

From the second line there is a special sense, first of constant sequence, as in story; also there

BEETHOVEN'S NINTH SYMPHONY

is an informality of whispered echoes or refrains, breaking the stately flow of regular period. While the song begins in many voices, it breaks soon into passionate cadence of one prevailing soprano:

Finally the old fragmental, tentative air is soon felt as the pace of song halts, and presently changes from even four to triple rhythm into a verse beginning very like a lullaby:

BEETHOVEN'S NINTH SYMPHONY

The quality of the whole lies less in the melodies, but just in this discontent, moving with restless whim, scarce touching one beautiful, expressive strain before leaving it for another. After the second, the first returns much disguised in fitful figure of strings, though the clear tune is mostly seen in clarinets. As the lullaby re-enters in fuller numbers, it seems, as it were, joy cradled in extreme ecstasy, before abandon of outbreak. In the first there is more of calm, steady assurance of quiet content, though with strong-rising emotion and a stormy burst at the end. Indeed, they seem different phases almost of joyous suppression instead of utterance.

The next singing of the first verse is in dulcet fugue on the first four notes, between clarinet and horn, later between flute and fagot on a part of the theme, all in dim changing tonal light and halting figure of melody. But the twilight soon breaks into the clear first color and outline of the main tune in the wood, enriched by thread of strings coursing all about the song. But there is ever the conversing air, the quaint echoing refrain stopping the strict measure, the listlessness chafing against the bonds of rhythm, as when the melody is suddenly broken by trumpet blasts, which in turn are quickly hushed by timid whispered snatches, the fugue introducing the song as before. Again the trumpet blows, the scene and rhythm change for the moment, to return to the quiet flow of the placid song. Altogether, we do not find, as elsewhere, a clear quality. There are content and discontent, quiet delight and vague, almost mournful striving, and passionate outburst. We must be content with discontent. The sense, again, is clearly the very doubt of feeling, the uncertainty of its incomplete utterance; though the melody closes formally, it is still tentative.

Presto. In unrhythmic *fanfare*, in the escape from rhythm, we feel afresh the old disquiet; the phrase of recitative in formless figure shows a still stronger impulse towards new definiteness. The repeated fanfare leads to the stirring thrum that began the Symphony as a motto, —as a kind of password. Here it accents the tension for a new articulation. Again the recitative; now a strain of the dancing scherzo. Is it to return in search of the true word there; or is it a general view, a comparison of uttered ideas; or the mere sense, in this disjointed song, of comparison as the first basis of reasoning, of discus-

BEETHOVEN'S NINTH SYMPHONY

sion? Pure discussion, disputation, is unrhythmic. A new phrase, as of spoken words, marks further casting off of the bonds of measured melody; the quick changing of rhythm shows the striving for verbal definiteness in the restless harking back and forth to this idea and that. Away with the fetters of mere rhythm to *things*, exact ideas, free of the thrall of beauty's laws! Tear the charming scales from the eyes! So in review passes again the *Adagio* theme. Now a more thoughtful, promising solo phrase. At last a fleeting glimpse of a new song; back again to the thoughtful herald phrase: now at last the full course of the final song:

in basses alone without words; the refrain in stately array of full-voiced, fugue-like polyphony,

BEETHOVEN'S NINTH SYMPHONY

finally in fervent simple setting of hymning chorus, ending, however, with full abandon of phrases of the song, flowing to a free climax.

But this is a mere foretaste, a mere foreshadowing; for, once again the restless Presto breaks into the rhythmic course, ending with the first actual words sung on formless phrase of recitative,—words not of poet: "Not these tones, friends; rather let us strike a more pleasing and joyous strain." The words are not inspired; they are like a stage-direction, breaking into the text of the play; they are part of the scheme that renounces all previous attempts. Throwing off compunction and hesitation, the standards are flung aside; there is open desertion to the cause of verbal song. The resources of pure tones are abandoned for words: Schiller's "Ode to Joy," set to the new-found tune.

> "Joy, thou spark of Heaven descended,
>   Daughter of Elysian line,
> Drunk with ecstasy we enter,
>   Goddess fair, thy sacred shrine.
>
> "By thy magic charm is healed
>   Despot Fashion's cruel pain;
> All mankind are clasped as brothers
>   Under thy bewitching reign.

BEETHOVEN'S NINTH SYMPHONY

"Who hath won the highest venture,
    True friend's chosen friend to be;
Who hath gained a noble woman,
    Let him join our jubilee,—

"Nay, whoe'er upon this planet
    Count a single soul his own.
And who may not, let him, grieving,
    Steal away and weep alone.

"Heavenly Joy all earthly creatures
    Drink, of Nature's fountain source,
Good and evil all pursuing
    Joy o'er a rose-scented course.

"Wine and kisses Joy hath given,
    And a proven Friend in death.
And the worm hath share in pleasure;
    Cherub before God draws breath.

"Joyous as the suns are flying
    Through the heaven's vasty sphere,
Joyous as a hero conqu'ring,
    Brothers, run your high career!

"Be embraced, millions all;
    This kiss for the world is meant!
    Brothers, o'er the starry tent
Is a Father's kindly thrall.

BEETHOVEN'S NINTH SYMPHONY

> "Ye lie prostrate, myriads all.
>   Reck'st thou thy Creator, world?
>   Seek Him o'er the sky unfurl'd!
>   Brothers, o'er the sky unfurl'd
> Is a loving Father's thrall."

There is here no homogeneous art; neither fully developed song nor instrumental form,—neither *cantata* nor *sonata*. There is a straining of the one art to find expression beyond its bounds in the language of another. The intent seems very clearly to be a confession of weakness of mere instruments, and on highest authority. Think of the argument: on the side of verbal song the great Bach masterpieces, and Beethoven's final word of concession. And yet all this weighs nothing against the proof of the music itself. Not what it wishes to say, this Ninth Symphony, what it wants to express or to have expressed, not the conscious intent of the poet, is our question, but simply and only: What does it express by the force and beauty of pure art? The words, borrowed from another poet, announce *Joy* very clearly: they might as clearly announce any other idea or emotion. The words are no more convincing as to the sense of the music than a clumsy boy's label of

BEETHOVEN'S NINTH SYMPHONY

a drawing. The prelude of the song seems theatrical,—a preconceived idea, imagined in philosophy and forced upon musical utterance, lacking the wholeness of a work of art. It is, probably, spontaneously and sincerely tentative. But all attempts in art are not convincing merely because they are beautiful in separate parts. It is not impossible, nor infrequent, in the later career of the poet, for mystic philosophy to halt and choke pure fancy. We come back to the true basis of art, which is independent of announced purpose, works not with labels, is ever unconscious of its verbal meaning. It is quite possible for Beethoven to say: For once I wish to reinforce my inarticulate cries with spoken, indisputable words of verbal poet. It is an admission, if you will, of his own temporary lack of power, not of his art; it is really a reinforcement, a repetition in different terms, not one complete whole. Nor is it strange that the wonderful words of Schiller should occur to the modest composer as tempting crown to his symphony: the true composer never knows the full dignity and force of his work. Again, the composer's ideas of the nature of his art are of no value; the involuntary spirit of his work alone moves us.

BEETHOVEN'S NINTH SYMPHONY

There is no reason in the world why Beethoven should not wish to invoke Schiller's Ode in a setting. There is no reason in the world to hold his act as invoking the assistance of poetry to music in general. The fact that it is his last symphony has no weight at all, even if he knew it was to be his last. There is, therefore, no reason in denouncing Beethoven's intent, in reading into it a confession of weakness of the whole of music; although it cannot be said too often that the greatest master's ideas on the theory of his art are of small value, that he is very likely to go astray in vain experiments, as did Bach. The fact that the Ninth Symphony did not inspire a train of successors is of the highest import to our view. The only way the artist, after all, learns the nature and limitations of his art is by experiment,—merely to a small, preliminary extent by *a priori* theory. A Paradise Lost must have its Paradise Regained. Almost every success of a writer must be matched by a failure; even Shakespeare has his worthless moments, his unworthy designs; even Homer nods. The poet is to be measured by his best, not by a cool estimate of average. In Schubert we have masses of ore to a grain of gold. There is a Battle Symphony

BEETHOVEN'S NINTH SYMPHONY

of Beethoven that never reaches an audience, though the score be at hand. Haendel's wonderful melodies are not enough, even in the land of his special worship, to revive the ghosts of his ancient operas, though his oratorios hold the stage of sacred drama in the Anglo-Saxon world. There is absolutely nothing in the authority of the poet as to theory. It would be very convenient, indeed, if we had a text-book from Beethoven, like sacred articles of creed, telling us just what is good and right, what is to be liked, and what must not be enjoyed. Convenient it would be, but fatal to true art. The essence of enjoyment is ever the sense of discovery by personal discrimination. The sure knowledge that it is good takes away the true edge of delight and prompts contrariety. True enjoyment, like true creation, can never be gained by pure imitation. We must, therefore, find for ourselves as listeners the real value of every work, even of a Beethoven, taking nothing for granted from the halo of master or the tradition of past audiences. Indeed, the long run of public judgment, counted through the centuries, does do this, as we have shown,—has crowned this work of highest master and condemned that. But the

BEETHOVEN'S NINTH SYMPHONY

process is too long and costly. A long course of false enjoyment, of self-delusion, will lead to eventual revulsion; but it is not the only way nor the best. It is like choosing food by first sickening of poison, by the brute process of elimination or exclusion. What we need and want is the positive, instant choice of the best by intuition, whetted by constant and sober vigilance. Thus the keen sense of the leader is shared by each member of the flock; the truth lies much safer in the combined and tested judgment of many, where each is equal member of the court.

Now Schiller's glorious "Ode to Joy" runs on to the resistless pace of simple hymn, borne by quartette of solo voices and by added chorus. The music from this point takes the second place, the words of the poem are first; this must never be forgotten. The label is not the picture, nor the poem the song. The setting may be gloriously apt, overpoweringly rich; it may be more movingly beautiful, it may be infinitely more important in its poetic wealth and burden, in the strength of emotion which it carries and conveys; but it does not usurp the place of verse in expressing the artistic purpose. It may not

BEETHOVEN'S NINTH SYMPHONY

exceed this purpose; it may not start on an unhindered career to try its own independent burden. At best it is wedded to the verse in marriage of equal dignity as to beauty and power. As to meaning, it can no more than reinforce and enrich. The whole function of the meaning of independent music now loses its *raison d'être*, gives way to the definite tenor of the words. The meaning of music, as it can be given in pure instrumental forms, is dependent on the spontaneous, though inevitable flow of each part and of all the parts to a convincing whole, where the literal title is as small as the limitations are large. Little as it can be defined in prose words, it is overwhelming in its ethical import and its emotional power. The proof, as we have often said, lies in the verifying agreement of all parts in the whole.

All this, that clearly seems the noblest function of music, is least when refuge is taken to verse. So it is that from this point the symphonic quality, in the free instrumental development and discussion, disappears. As to form, we have merely separate verses of the hymn, set in varying shades of fulness, with no musical internal connection. The whole function of musical sequence, corre-

BEETHOVEN'S NINTH SYMPHONY

spondence, development, discussion, and final convincing climax has vanished.

There is no reason, however, in the special instance, why the enriching beauties of the setting should be ignored, more than in a song of Schubert; but our own work becomes secondary, much easier, of much lesser dignity, the mere perception of this and that detail. The keen scent for profound musical significance takes a holiday.

As the strings follow the singers in the first verse, an opposite melody appears high in oboes; to which a choir of woodwind soon rears a song of new beauty on the hymn in the bass:

(Woodwind redoubled.)
(Brass, reinforcing the hymn.)

cresc. *f*

By thy mag-ic charm is heal-ed

now the voices themselves weave a fuller harmony, the bass freely rolling through a melodious course

BEETHOVEN'S NINTH SYMPHONY

of lesser passing tones, to which the oboes and fagots give answering phrase:

SOLI ALTO, TENOR, BASS.

Who hath won the highest ven-ture,

(Rhythmic chords in horns.)

True friend's cho-sen friend to be;

(Oboe, doubled in lower fagots.)

as the climax is reached, the whole orchestra join, either in redoubled melody or in enlivened rhythm. Then the voices disguise the tune in varied manner, though the harmonic character is never lost, under the mask of outer change. The instruments either follow and echo the voices or spur them with trills and other rhythmic tricks.

BEETHOVEN'S NINTH SYMPHONY

SOLI TENOR AND BASS.
(With very light assistance of wood, horns and basses.)

Hea - ven-ly Joy all earth-ly crea-tures Drink, of Na - ture's fount-ain source,

(See page 182, line 7.)

Towards the end of this division the voices, of which the chorus and solo quartette have been singing alternate strains, leave to the woodwind the melodic text of the tune and sing a chorale to the line:

"Cherub before God draws breath,"

in phrase of utmost simplicity, ending in fervent climax.

Alla marcia allegro assai vivace. In spirit of march, in liveliest cheer, in tensest pace, heightened by a subtle sound of occasional clattering hoof, comes a new tripping pace of the old hymn, first in wordless tones of whispering band. In its refrain solo tenor joins the flight with a stirring verse:

BEETHOVEN'S NINTH SYMPHONY

singing the hymn or agreeing countertheme as he sweetly lists, adding, not doubling, a new swing of independent phrase, not bound to the slavish trip of wordless voices: now a resounding bass, now the tune, now a new melody; singing to the middle strain the line:

> "Brothers, run your high career!"

back to the first:

> "Joyous as a hero conqu'ring,"

BEETHOVEN'S NINTH SYMPHONY

to which the full chorus of men echo, ending the verse all together, not without special after-strain. Whence on double theme, quick and slower, both from the heart of the main tune:

too close-knit for fettering words, the instrumental wing of muse soars free to dazzling abandon of gayest fugal maze, where here the coursing motive, there the sonorous line of hymn, each in various crowning phrases, weave their festal woof, so that eye and ear despair of tracing the threads.

BEETHOVEN'S NINTH SYMPHONY

At the thickest, at least six independent melodies are singing at once their sweetly clashing madrigal. As the fray lapses for a breath, we discern for a moment dainty sequence of agreeing strides returning to the strife, ending in big stentorian unison calls to the mighty rhythm. Distant strains of the simple hymn approach and lead to chorus on the original verse:

"Joy, thou spark of Heaven descended."

But the lowest bass cannot be restrained and goes coursing in precipitous career to the fervent song of noble hymn. At once is poise of meaning and purpose, and exalted, headlong drive of resistless action "in drunken ecstasy,"—simply, with a refrain of parting line of first verse. The tumultuous march is over.

Andante maestoso. In majestic gait, too fervent for rhythmic utterance, the basses, sustained by the brass, shout solemn tones of new chorale of final call:

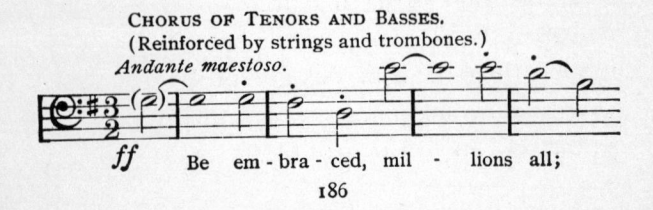

CHORUS OF TENORS AND BASSES.
(Reinforced by strings and trombones.)
Andante maestoso.

ff   Be   em - bra - ced, mil - lions all;

BEETHOVEN'S NINTH SYMPHONY

(Male chorus, reinforced by trombones.)

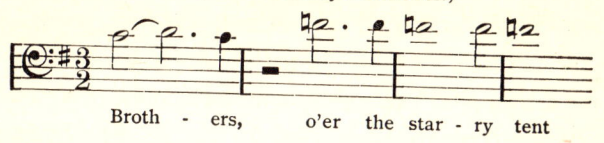

Broth - ers,   o'er the star - ry tent

answered by full chorus, universal, men and women, backed by all the band of woodwind and lower brass, while the quick motive and melodic reminder of the old air sound in statelier strum of strings, rearing a climax on the second line:

"This kiss for the world is meant!"

Again the solemn, simple strain of men and of brass sounds the next lines:

"Brothers, o'er the starry tent
Is a Father's kindly thrall."

On the same plan the chorus of singers and instruments affirm the great appeal; nothing but tripping strain reminds us of original air,—mere solemn fervent chant.

Suddenly we turn into still more pious mood, *adagio ma non troppo*, *ma divoto*, in all but slowest pace of prayerful song, where melodic quick beat has vanished, but the stern chanting tones

BEETHOVEN'S NINTH SYMPHONY

have more of devout beauty. As the woodwind and low strings lead and guide the hymn, the full chorus sound the solemn ending line of the Ode:

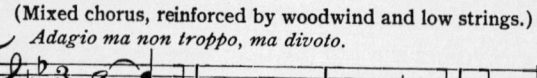

> "Ye lie pros-trate, myr - i - ads all."

In the third line:

> ". . . o'er the starry tent,"

trombones add their blast; in the last:

> "Is a loving Father's thrall,"

high strings and all the basses join in tensest whispering chorus. Just as all sense of tune has gone, the lay of original hymn dances into the midst, *allegro energico sempre ben marcato*, in clearest accent, though ever in liveliest, springing tread, and the singers, led by women, break without prelude into the original joyous verse:

> "Joy, thou spark of Heaven descended."

BEETHOVEN'S NINTH SYMPHONY

Acme of glee is added by nervous, quickest coursing, first of violins, then of basses of wood and strings; later by both groups.

The full instrumental freedom of the previous chorus might, after all, point to a combined form, where voices are but trumpet tones of legend, appearing here and there, the instruments being allowed a full formal career. The only weakness, then, is the limiting significance of words, which may, after all, be no more than Schumann's title, —*i.e.*, when they can be found exactly to fit the original mood, heightening and not weakening the pure musical meaning. They may then not dominate, but take their place in the ranks, though in simplest lines merely, carefully hedged from leadership and interference. Thus such a highest form would be, if not reached, yet suggested in the previous chorus.

But this is merely a half. Through the midst of joyous dance and high voices, and long tones of altos, sustained by clarinets and brass, sounds the solemn greeting:

"Be embraced, millions all;"

so that the whole, neither dance nor chant, is a completed pæan of universal profound joy, uniting

BEETHOVEN'S NINTH SYMPHONY

all of individual Ecstasy and Love, acme of the ideal state of art, when highest personal bliss joins in strongest humanity, crowned to perfect state of outer beauty and of inner detail, Greek ideal meeting Christian in simple spontaneous joy.

All through the two completing chants, the pagan bliss, the Christian kiss, are closely bound, interchanging voices and places. The basses now sing the blissful dance, tenor and alto hold the chant, interspersed horns and other voices ring out short invocations, while, all about, the rushing phrase, which first appeared at intervals, ever accompanies the hymnal melody, spurring and stirring the bacchanalian pace. One voice ends the phrase of greeting and another instantly catches it on lower or higher plane, or two chant it in duet, while the other two sing the dance of joy in canon; now double canon is sounding on both melodies, ranging the speechless armies, each in their lines. After final, united burst, low basses sing hushed, to dim strumming of lower wood, the after-strain:

"Ye lie prostrate, myriads all,"

all changed in rhythm, tune, design. Single-toned, to vaguest strums, each separate voice

BEETHOVEN'S NINTH SYMPHONY

sings the question in turn; all answer together in unison, joining in sweet accord on the last phrase:

"Brothers, o'er the starry tent,"

which ends the chorus in gentle harmony of calm faith.

Final Chorus. A new swing,—the chant is gone, the dross of monkish hymn is dropped, all is on buoyant wing, in highest poetic note, as solo tenor and bass sing the new strain:

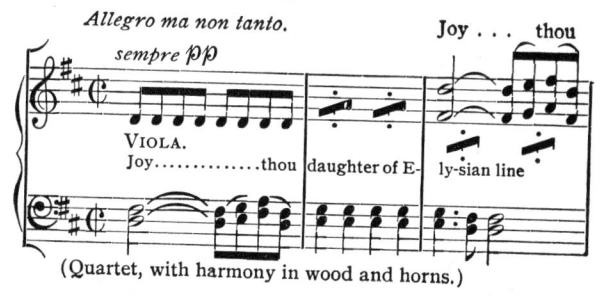

(Quartet, with harmony in wood and horns.)

to the first rolling verse, the verbal motto of the Symphony, while strings carry on the cheering trip which they have first played alone as prelude:

BEETHOVEN'S NINTH SYMPHONY

chiming softly against the singers in rhythmic and melodic clash of oboe, that sweetly grows in harmony. Treading on their heels, the higher solos try the same tune with their own friendly opposing flute. In the same pinching way, lower woodwind and flute continue the song, and now, without words between the verses, the prelude phrase is ever tripping along in contrary lines. The whole is a merry, exalted madrigal, where voices and instruments take equal part. Now they slide gently into the second phrase in purer, simpler song:

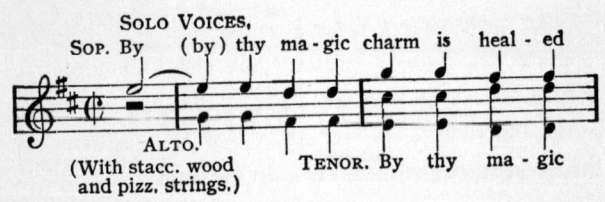

where bass takes up the air of soprano, which finds another tune above. Indeed, each of the four solo voices has entered in its separate turn on the tune, and each follows the chorus of the first, all singing away as in busy hive the sunny magic of healing Joy, while the song circles about in dizzy maze. Presently, when solo voices and instruments are thus started on the merry round,

BEETHOVEN'S NINTH SYMPHONY

the chorus steal in, whispering the tune in unison single phrase of the "magic charm," where all voices and band shout forth the line:

"Despot Fashion's cruel pain,"

in ascending figure, entering, in loud climax:

"All mankind are clasped,"

ending the verse in slow, gently winding cadence:

"Under thy bewitching reign."

Again the gentle ascent and strong burst of song; in closing, the solo voices light on a new pitch of tune and carol the ending line in freer course of trilling cadence.

Now the voices veer to the original tone; a newer, vaster gathering pace is struck, hurrying with increasing power into loudest chorus in fastest motion, a final cosmic appeal:

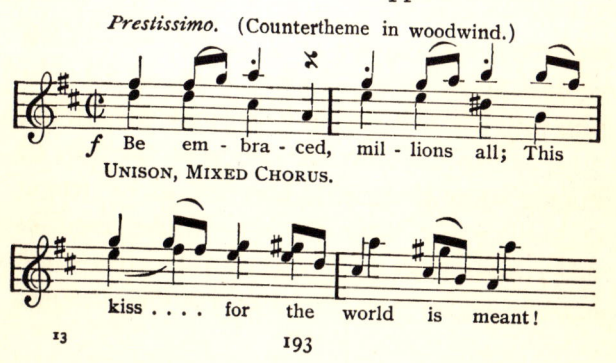

Prestissimo. (Countertheme in woodwind.)

f Be em-bra-ced, mil-lions all; This

UNISON, MIXED CHORUS.

kiss .... for the world is meant!

BEETHOVEN'S NINTH SYMPHONY

where the literal air, but not the mood or spirit, is new, with complete phrase in instruments; the answer is pure glee,—song of rejoicing, struck again and again by instruments:

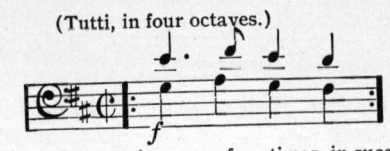

(Tutti, in four octaves.)

(Played four times, then sung four times, in succession.)

finally reaching the singers on the line:

"Is a loving Father's thrall."

The mighty climax is in slower notes of suppressed emotion:

"This kiss for the world is meant!"

To the dying peals, still in highest climax, the first verse, chant of the Goddess, returns, while in the wild maze of raging tones the motive of the original hymn gleams here and there, simply at first and redoubled in speed, all together in careless abandon of celebration.

VIII

SCHUMANN

FIRST SYMPHONY, IN B FLAT*

AT rough glance this first of Schumann's symphonies seems to begin in a way frequent with older masters: the premise of a motto, a basic theme of the whole. Such appears the beginning phrase, in horns and trumpets:

in slow, heavily measured stride, acclaimed by echoing chorus. Gradually the *tempo* quickens in the same figure, with ever growing sound, until from majestic march we have dashed into liveliest gayety. Now the theme is here in the same movement, though transformed in rate:

---

* Op. 38, composed in 1841.

SCHUMANN

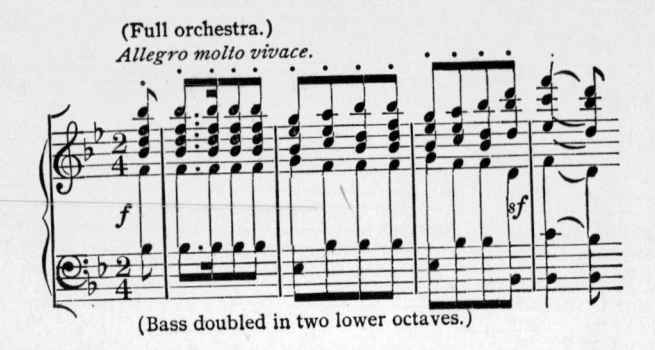

(Full orchestra.)
Allegro molto vivace.

(Bass doubled in two lower octaves.)

We might very well presume the basic quality of our original strain. But we must be chary in this kind of reading. It is best not to fasten a prejudice of meaning too early in a work. Let the poet develop it to our unbiassed ear. Perhaps the prelude is merely like one of those *Adagio* beginnings of Haydn, which in their restraint of emotion but whet our wish for the dance. The whole symphony has no deep, philosophic quality. It is simply unpremeditated joy,—written at the climax of the poet's happiness. We ourselves will enjoy it the more without too anxious searching for latent currents.

This *Allegro* theme begins with the most infectious spirit in the full band, answered saucily in a running phrase from violins:

SCHUMANN

(Violins, doubled in lower 8ves.)

STRINGS AND FAGOTS.

The jolly repartee continues until, in the second melody, there is an outward droop of mood. At least from the electric sprightliness of the main tune and its setting there is a sudden change to a naïve, personal vein.

On the wing of the little accompanying strain, moving ever higher and higher, we are borne back to the plane of the first melody.

Now, after the repeated sketching of characters, comes the telling of the story. See how spins the yarn of old ballad, literally from the

SCHUMANN

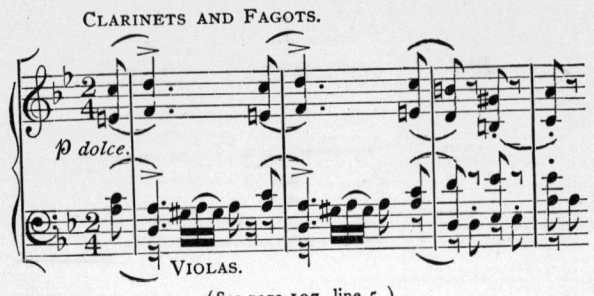

(See page 197, line 5.)

thread of the quick main melody. The low strings make a basic plot of ominous bustle, while aloft in the wood sings a clear idyl of delicate fancy, of a sentiment not free from a sombre hue:

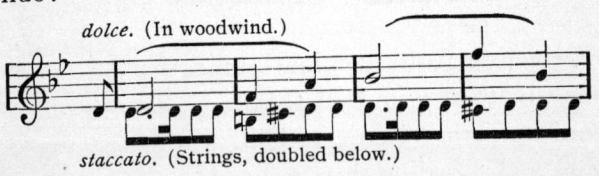

It is all most poetical. To be sure, there is a constant drift back to the gay dance of the first subject. But Schumann has the real story-telling instinct. Before you are aware, he has spun another thread into a sequence of narrative,—one that first appeared in closing the statement of subjects:

SCHUMANN

(Themes in woodwind, each doubled in 8ves.)

(Full accompaniment of strings in triplet figure.)

By natural flow in answering voices there is gradually massed an overpowering climax, where, as the woodwind hold the long chords, and the strings are running in doubly quickened figure, the brass sound the original big legend with greater solemnity than ever, ending in a long pause. Then back to the swing of the *Allegro*, with both melodies, now ending in a rollicking gale on the trip of the main subject, when suddenly—here is one of those puzzling touches of Schumann. New it is in melody, but integral part of the whole poem, like a figure that has long been in the background. It is that kind of secular hymn in which Schumann, towards the close, before the final burst, will give a special, poetic, conclusive confidence. Here it is first given in the strings, then it is published farther, with fuller voice in larger chorus. After its close the motto is sounded in fine conflict of brass and woodwind, followed by a spirited ending.

SCHUMANN

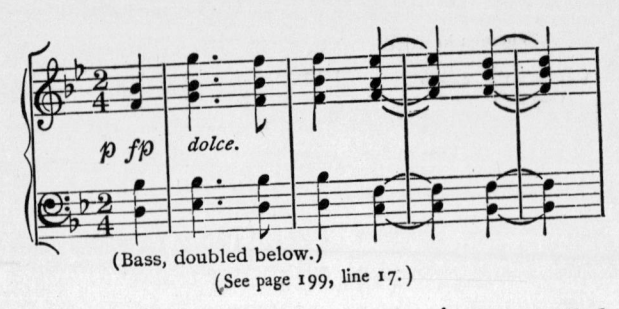

(Bass, doubled below.)
(See page 199, line 17.)

The *Larghetto* is one simple, sincere song, a stay of merriment; but there is no sadness, rather a settled, deep content:

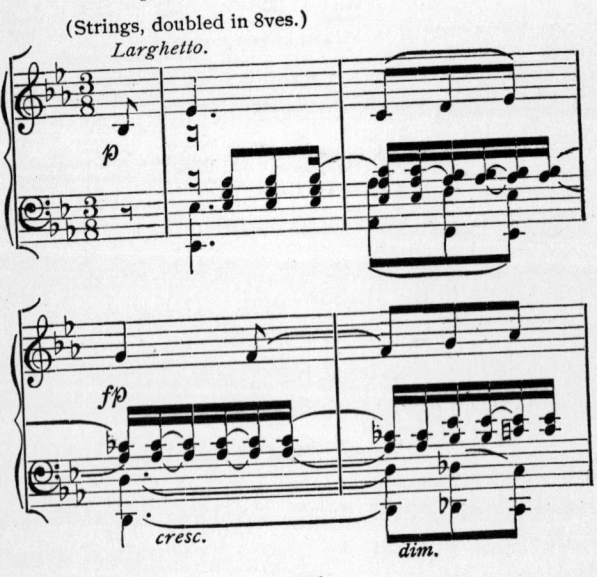

SCHUMANN

There is none of the strife of discussion, nor the thread of story; but there is the clear, steady outpouring of melody. Both subjects are sung clearly, almost beyond the need of quoting. The second is a mere episodal foil to the mood and flow of the first:

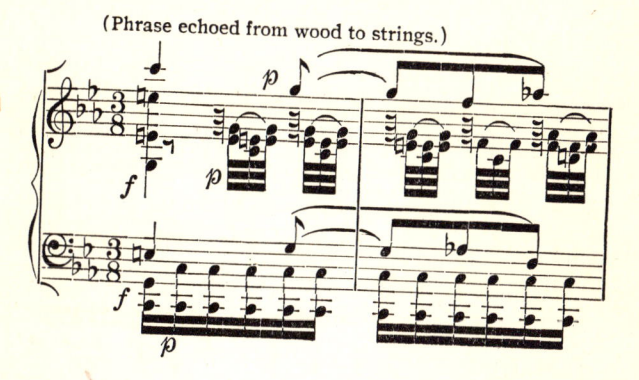

(Phrase echoed from wood to strings.)

But what would, in epic Allegro, be discussion, is here, in lyric Andante, a kind of tonal musing on a strain

gotten somehow from the close of the main theme, cast about in voices of wood and strings,

SCHUMANN

while cellos and violas are at the same time discussing another:

cresc.

The main melody, before sung in cellos, now sounds high in clear oboes and octave horns, with rich wreathing of entwined strings. Perhaps best of all are the last touches, like concluding words of sincere farewell.

In the *Scherzo* (*molto vivace*) is a return to pure individual exuberance, free from all burden of hidden connection or of deep meaning:

STRINGS.
Scherzo. Molto vivace.

There is no mistaking the clear succession of melodies. The minor key adds no sombre tinge, though it may give a certain boisterous air. By

SCHUMANN

contrast, the first *Trio* has the daintiest, most intimate naïveté in all music, though it is almost too quickly said to catch:

TRIO. *Molto piu vivace.*

(Alternations of string and woodwind.)

There is an air (or a trick) of leaving much unsaid, a sort of "you know" in tones, wherein lies the effect of this special confidence. Musically, it consists in omitting the transition from one chord to another, leaving it to the hearer,— also by the light suggestiveness of rhythm, hopping from a question on high to its answer far below. This responsiveness lends itself to much playful halting and coquetry.

The second *Trio* is rather the reflective stage; there are no new sensations or emotions.

The end is full of lightest poetry. The *Coda* is a last conclusive strain from the second melody

SCHUMANN

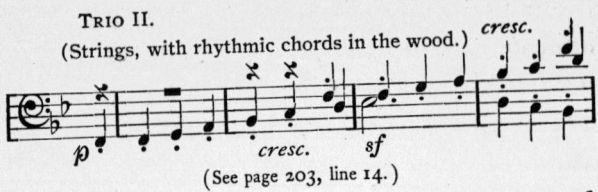

Trio II.
(Strings, with rhythmic chords in the wood.)

(See page 203, line 14.)

of the first Trio. Then, again, in discourse of wood and strings, the first melody of the latter breaks into articulate pleading, with a final confident, serene answer, where the chords of strings are quaintly followed, step by step, by echoing woodwind. The last note is a joint whisper.

Allegro animato e grazioso. The *Finale* seems to have the gayety of the ballroom. There may be darker figures here and there, but they only prove to be in masquerade, with an air almost of flippant frivolity.

The very beginning, to be sure, is a broader strain:

(Full orchestra.)

SCHUMANN

But it seems mere introduction, a more contained utterance of the joyous feeling, ending with a burst of childlike simplicity.

The main tune has the infectious gait of the dance:

The second melody has a legendary tinge that is belied by its lightness

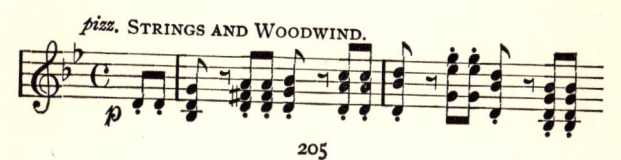

pizz. STRINGS AND WOODWIND.

SCHUMANN

and by the comic interruption of a rough unison phrase, which has a decided mock seriousness. Not until it has ended do we suspect that it is, after all, the same as our supposed introduction.

Presently it breaks in with full chorus, and now, though in soft wood, it spins a whole melody out of the brief phrase. When this is echoed in loudest acclaim and ends in triumphant, lengthy cadence, we are bewildered with the dignity of the brief strain that seemed mere prelude or *fanfare*. We are beginning to feel that it is the pivotal phrase of all. It seems here, indeed, to fill a special part, quite new in music, that Schumann himself discovered. It is like the last of the children's "scenes," where "the poet speaks."* For here we have, besides the objective melodies of official rank, another of more intimate utterance of the poet's own thought, hovering about the other two. It is exactly the free preface of the story-teller, his recurring asides and humorous sallies.

But the conclusion of the statement dispels flippancy and restores sincerity. At the outset

---

* Schumann, op. 15.

SCHUMANN

of the discussion we begin with the most serious end of our subjective strain:

in a sombre guise of minor, interrupted ever by the major chant high in the woodwind. And now comes the psychological phase, the brown color needed of a fine fugal rumination on a solid theme suggested from the earlier comic interruption:

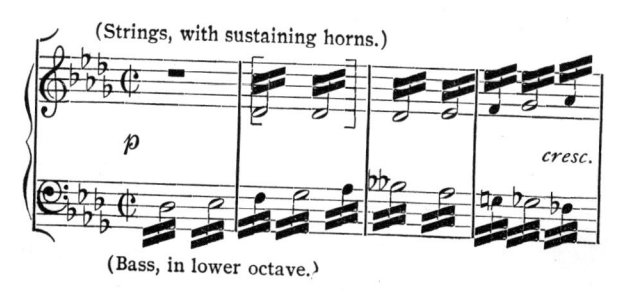

But here it is in sober earnest,—there is no pretence. It is very serious and all in the

SCHUMANN

thoughtful strings. Soon the theme extends, with the delicious duality and discussion which means progress to the thinking musician:

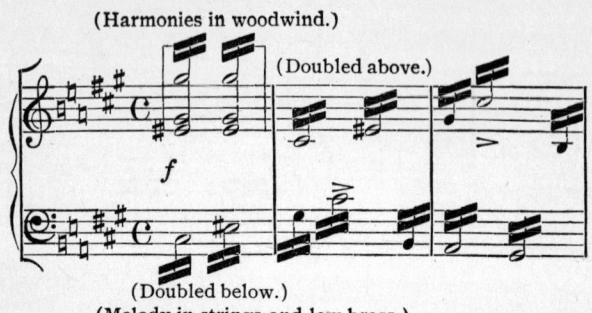

(Harmonies in woodwind.)

(Doubled above.)

f

(Doubled below.)
(Melody in strings and low brass.)

Now, as the strings subside into a mere humming background, the lighter woodwind take up the argument. But they are too friendly for serious dispute, and they soon fall into mere sweet responsive song ending in a lyric cadence in solo flute. After all, in the strings lies the quality of musing thought.

From the cadence we are back in the dancing main melody. And we have the full allowance of all the original tunes again. But, mark well. instead of ending, here comes once again the discussion,—not quite as before: less darkly musing; broader; bringing a big, deep con-

SCHUMANN

clusion from the full chorus. We seem even to hear the motto suggested in the brass. The "bone" of discussion, if not of contention, develops at the end into firm responsive strains between mixed groups of brass, wood, and strings,—equal factions of the whole band:

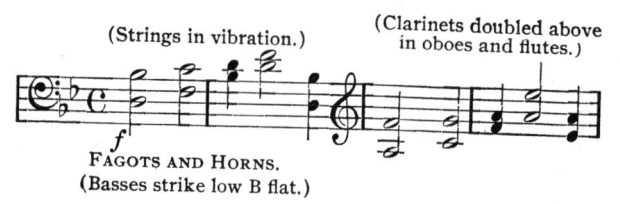

(Strings in vibration.)   *(Clarinets doubled above in oboes and flutes.)*

FAGOTS AND HORNS.
(Basses strike low B flat.)

We have hardly noticed that the reflection was all on the initial strain of the poet's thought. The nominal themes have, somehow, vanished to hazier distance. Then, by a last added word of rumination, the personal message is brought home more closely. Thus does the formal freedom of our master utter a certain reality of message. In the growing dominance of the poetic phrase, especially in the glad ending, we are borne back to the joyousness of the beginning of the symphony. There is, indeed, a clear kinship of these basic themes, of first word and last. In the freedom of the latest, with all its breadth, there is a new gain of intimate vein.

SCHUMANN

*FOURTH SYMPHONY, IN D MINOR**

INTRODUCTION; *Allegro, Romanze, Scherzo*, and *Finale* "in einem Satze,"—runs the title,—all in one. This means much more than mere absence of stop. It is a new kind of plan, and, in truth, makes a new sort of work. It must not be taken nor tested as typical symphony. But, by our habit, we will not prejudge, rather let the music make its own impression, in natural course.

After long note on unison tone, strings and fagots, in friendly agreement, glide down and up the dreamily poetic phrase:

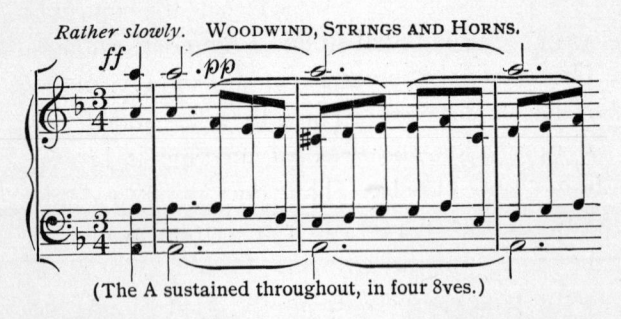

Rather slowly. WOODWIND, STRINGS AND HORNS.

(The A sustained throughout, in four 8ves.)

Clarinets then join the pleasant ramble, that has the magic of unending promise, dotted anon by assured rest in new tonal quarter, where the origi-

---

* Op. 120, composed in 1841, rewritten in 1851.

SCHUMANN

nal note, long sustained, points the cadence with sense of lesser melody. Still more voices are now gliding hand in hand, with much freer path, too. Though the placid pace is never broken, there is yet an almost exultant, swelling tone and movement,—and we have said nothing of the richness of contrary figures swaying in opposite ways, and meeting all in glorious harmony of large agreement. At the height of the ascent, all burst uncontrolled into big conclusive strain, that dies down to mere soft tread of basses. A new, quicker figure here enters timidly, singing

in ever rising curves, and spurring the older glide, until it bursts in full bloom of melody in spirited chorus:

Allegro.

SCHUMANN

But the heart of the *Allegro* is ever the former timid phrase; after the clear and definite cadence in home tone, it steals and twines with intimate charm its playful way in close, though gentle chase of voices,—like constant spray of brilliant fountain:

Soon, as the phrases are still rising from below, an answer sings from above with cadence of sweet assurance in neighboring tone:

The same pleasant close is rung in the first tone, and in another, yonder. Now, accompanying

SCHUMANN

the *Allegro* theme, a running duet comes tripping down in strings and wood, answered fitly in lower voices of each group. Another ascent, with something of strain, still on the quicker phrase, brings first a noisy descent, and then the merriest sort of close with abrupt stop, in which the melodious motive is ever eminent, clear though elusive. Thence the whole of this lively phrase is repeated.

The thoughtful phase must, of course, begin in playful chase of rising voices on the first quick motive; but it is all in far distant scene. For, a sudden bolt from the clear sky (one loud unison tone of descent) has shifted the whole plane of action, as if by magic. We are far away in the shade of some woods, without the least of familiar moorings. The chase of fairy strains has a more sombre sound. Now the first full phrase sings aloud, as at the beginning, in distant minor tone, followed by hushed, mysterious soughing of low strings and almost moaning of wood. Oft repeated, in ever new shifting tone, sings the strange plaint. Now a more peaceful sense steals in, and then in glad major the phrase rings out a last joyous verse, to start into being a new song, clear and bright of tune and mood, all

SCHUMANN

in simple, stirring chords as of war-song, in plainest rhythm (all changed from mystic rambling), that now holds its active course in lower voices, churning the current of rhythm in the pauses of the new song:

(All doubled in lower 8ves.)

The two are perfectly wedded, the running phrase ever in clear, insistent response, phrase for phrase, having the wonderful virtue of indefinite thread, as they wander and fly along through new lights of tone. At the last edge of the journey a third figure enters the scene, perhaps chief of all in beauty.

In quiet innocence or contained wealth of rhythm, it sings as it seems the consummation of all the story. It comes at the nick of the plot, as if all else had prepared for the full effect of its beauty. And it has the Schumann way of a tune speaking as if in words, and saying its message again and again, ever new and ever welcome. The strange part of it is that neither of these two

SCHUMANN

(See page 214, line 12.)

principal tunes has any official business with the design. They simply complete the others, are uttered of their own necessity, not for, but against formal reason. The final melody simply blossoms out of the discussion and crowns the whole.

The first *Allegro* theme intrudes its say as if jealous, but yields instantly to the quiet power of the new melody, returns again to the attack, and

SCHUMANN

now brings a bit of the martial song in its wake. Again follows the sombre verse in minor, with plaintive answer of wood and strings. Then sings the triumphant duet of first motive and joyous war-song, two songs woven in one, blended or wedded by force of their difference and contrast. To be sure, the sharp accents of the warrior tune hold higher sway over the phrases of theme, which merely fill the gaps, and it winds its full course unhindered, repeating or halting, as it lists.

And yet the companion seems ever in perfect place, almost part of the other. A true journey it is, of two; for, most clearly they appear before our eyes always in some new quarter (of tone), where they sing their gay story. At the top of the climb they both pause for a long breath. Then, as before, the latest melody steps on the scene, somehow solving all questions with the magic of its beauty, like fairy in old story.

But, of course, the formal hero is the first theme, that breaks for a moment into the latest, gentle melody, appears again with his martial companion, and finally sings the whole original refrain as at the beginning. Instead of the former airy chase of sprites (of the motive), there

SCHUMANN

is now a much more serious discussion. The whole first phrase sings and dins its say on rising scale of pitch, each tone clashing roughly against the last, with academic zeal. Suddenly it ceases,—as if the final triumph were not a matter of mere argument. Instead, a vague trembling of voices leads on simplest phrase, with broad swelling volume, suddenly to bright pace of war-song, followed ever by loyal phrase of theme. It is briefer than before, rises to higher scene before singing a full line. There is, indeed, a pent, electric state all about. Suddenly into the midst sings the fairy tune, like final essence or spirit of all the strife, and with a freer, bolder, and even more joyous wing of melody, stronger, too, of tone, and lastly, with actual martial force and spirit, so that we hardly know our gentle figure in the full equipment of *Pallas Athene*, taking sovereign possession, not merely entering gently as visiting spirit,—striding about with awing majesty. Though our first main theme returns, it is no longer as principal. There is no more to say. The rest is a mere general good-by, said noisily and frequently. The real last word has been spoken, and not by the "hero,"—by none of the principals,—by this

SCHUMANN

figure that entered with least importance, and by purest natural right took the lead of all.

The significant link of suspended chord carries us over from the *Allegro* to the *Romanze* without the usual formal gulf. All the air and fragrance of ancient (German) ballad breathes here. Words are not needed. The essence is there. That is the great truth about music, the directness of its power and beauty. In simple swing of minor strain lies a clear verse of ancient legend:

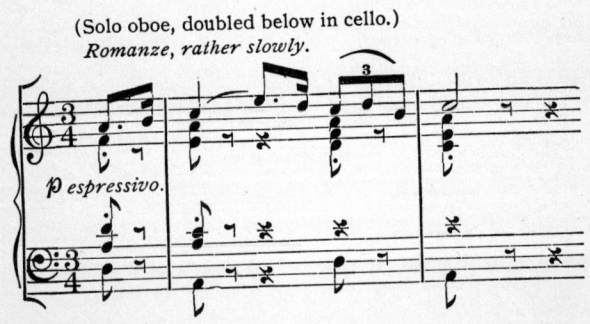

After a cadence flows the dreamy glide of friendly voices of the beginning, It seems now to find its true place and beauty. A special magic lies in the subjective touch of the original phrase of introduction, that comes after the line of ballad,— exactly as if the poet, after a verse of classic story, has another of his own modern thought

SCHUMANN

and say. With swelling chorus, really in big double movement, one group rising as the other descends, the broad conclusive strain comes sweeping down, and ends—most quaintly in a line of the ballad.

There comes a verse that makes us sigh for a mint of new words, to give sense of a more intimate poetry, a more delicate fragrance of special message than music seems ever to have borne. The former even glide is topped in high strings with accompanying gentle ripple of melodious flow:

It is all, one sees instantly, the subjective vein, not the legend, and it ends in a peculiar burst of confidence. This seems to prompt a melodic observation that, with perfect sequence of inner meaning, is outwardly all new:

SCHUMANN

STRINGS, HORNS AND FAGOTS.

and returns to the preceding vein of gliding phrase, again with the gentle ripple of high strings, and the appealing burst at the close. The latter phrase is repeated, and leads to a concluding verse of the ballad.

In lively, speedy humor the *Scherzo* dances noisily upon the scene. He comes in "like a lion," shaking his blustering locks. There is a whirling dance, of heavy trip but rushing pace, where every phrase is echoed below almost in comedy:

(Tutti, with reinforced harmonies.) (In 8ves.)

and the answer of main tune is a chain of halting, jolting thuds, singing in irregular beat,—like

SCHUMANN

a line of stone-hewers steadily striking out of time:

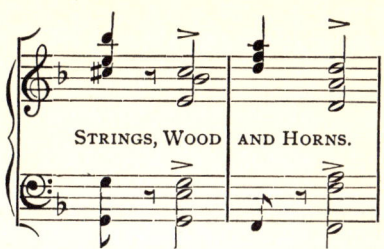

Strings, Wood and Horns.

This is all repeated, and the dance goes discoursing freely on main theme, soon simmering down more timidly, but with the constant play of mocking echo. It has fallen from the first fierce vehemence, but soon rushes to the original dance with stamping thud of main phrase and jolting strokes of answer. All this second phrase is repeated, too.

Schumann's Trios (of symphony) are his special spot for a quiet lyric, almost more than the Andantes. He confessed his own poet nature, as stormy "Florestan" and gentle "Eusebius." Nowhere is this clearer than in his Scherzos and Trios.

In many ways the Trio is like the indescribable first strain of *Allegro*, ever in outward line of waving strings; and this, we know, was but a

SCHUMANN

(See page 221, line 17.)

phrase of the introduction. Here, in the common kinship of themes, as well as in its unbroken flow, this work is unlike other symphonies; an air of quiet intimacy pervades,—a waiving of ceremony, that hardly fits with the big pomp of full-accoutred symphony, playing in loudest chorus to universal audience. In a way this poem is like certain plays that are meant for quiet reading rather than visible action.

The flowing curve of higher strings is like an earlier verse of *Allegro*. The melody itself descends most simply and rises again by single steps. But there is, between the voices, in each accent a special pinch of dainty harmony, that gives the whole the subtlest fragrance. Indeed, it seems too delicate for profaning words. The very rhythm is implied; the main strokes are merely understood; and so there is no final beat. But, after rehearsing, the light, downy phrase is

SCHUMANN

pregnant theme for free discoursing, and there is ever that gentle, magic turn of farthest harmony; and a broad conclusion is not wanting, leading back to discussion.

Of course, the noisy first dance of Scherzo returns, and it ought to end in tempest of romping frolic. But it doesn't. Without the least right in the world, the gentle Trio steals in again with all its special message and finally whispers the last word, not just haltingly nor timidly, but as if to single friend in softest tone. Thus "like a lamb" goes out our *Scherzo*. And without even a pause, the poet brings us in the same whisper, 'mid trembling strings, to a strain familiar as the theme of Allegro, but all in slow pace, long drawn out; the gay phrase almost loses its sparkle.

As the theme repeats, the basses moving dimly through changing depths, suddenly out from the brass starts a clear-marked chant, merely three tones. But they hark back, somewhere in the symphony; we know it is part of the fibre, though we cannot point precisely, until with utmost strain we urge reluctant memory to cadence of martial song in distant *Allegro*,—where it rang in gladdest, quickest song. Yet here it is, the same motto, in solemn tones of ancient brass.

SCHUMANN

And, while the quicker motive is almost lost in the increasing din, they sound forth in fuller legend, marking again the firm conclusion. Thence the whole phrase soon recovers its own gayer motion, and all the voices rise in swelling sound and speed to loud and long pause,— whence bursts the full flood of merriment.

Even here see the close knitting of common ties. Who ever heard before of the theme of first *Allegro* thus running most fitly in the fibre of the subject of the last? And more still, the answering phrase is the same as the late motto of brass and the early war-song:

Nay, the whole melody is, after all, nothing but our old triumphant duet of first theme and martial strain. Of difference there is really none. Only, now the answer is given a full say, spinning on its phrase really a new melody, with its own special answer. On it flows, seeming to start a fugal argument, when a new answer sings out in rollicking strings :

(musical notation: Strings. Melody doubled below in violas. Staccato basses.)

Here is the first real romp of the symphony, breaking at last through the gentle bonds of gauzy poetry, with soaring swing of the tune, scampering of lower strings, and, withal, a magnificent motion, as of galloping chargers. And they ride magnificently, too, ever into new scenes, up hill and down, 'neath sun and clouds, now in soft distance, now in loudest approach.

The gait suddenly changes. Smoother it is, and gentler in accent and movement; but steadily onward it flows. The speed all remains. A new song sounds above, in high wood and strings, as gay as the last, but with a more appealing note :

SCHUMANN

(Strings and wood, higher 8ve in flutes.)

p dolce.

Soon its dulcet phrase is sung in close, eager madrigal, though always clear of contention.

Indeed, the greatest charm comes just in these sweet rejoinders, all in succession down the carolling line. As the jolly refrain of themes nears the end, there are some skipping after-phrases: one borrowed from the ruling trip, which we might call the motto without peril of special meaning. Later there is, to be sure, some spirit of argument, as a fugal theme starts with running scale, and each voice treads rudely on the other's heels. But soon they fling into the old dancing gait, and return to the whole song of the themes.

The discussion is real, in spite of all the merriment. First there is a firm, almost harsh descent into a new tone, as if "play must cease; this is real earnest." The deep tone is answered twice by loud twang. It means clearly and plainly

SCHUMANN

nothing whatever but "Silence; room for the disputants!" There is something here of the academic flavor we caught in the Rhine symphony,—each party beginning in clear opposition, the audience applauding, not too often. The theme can be no other than the motto, the old phrase of war-song, now built to full, logical proportion:

Cellos and Fagots.

A discussion, to be real and worth its while, must lead somewhere. So, though we get into technicalities, and we have some narrow brushes, there is a true sequence that leads to satisfying harmony in all its senses. Soon the disputing voices themselves join in agreeing shouts of acclaim. Still, it is ever hardest for our Romanticist to give up the moment of meditation. Once again he returns to the maze, revolving all the related bits of thought in one, for final conclusion. Mysterious phrases sound about,—the first in horns and violas, below the theme of violins; a broader one in lower strings:

SCHUMANN

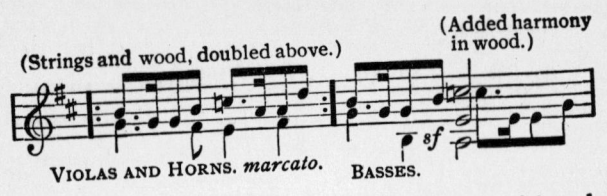

(Strings and wood, doubled above.) (Added harmony in wood.)

VIOLAS AND HORNS. *marcato.*   BASSES.

later, one of most solemn stride in united band. We can just discern in all a dim relation to the main fugal theme, in varying pace, each in slower imitation of the other,—getting finally down to real fundamentals, closed with pausing chord, whence, of a sudden, we are allowed to break into the old romp, halted playfully again and again by the pausing chord. The frolic runs here and there into changing lights and in wilder maze, and suddenly drops into the gentler scamper, with smoother motion and no less joyous humor. The short dispute on fugal theme of scale ends, as at first, in glad cadence and long pausing descent, with twang of chord. But, instead of the previous discussion, here is a new melody, though closest akin to the others. But it has the quality of Schumann of summing all the essence of the stirring poetry and thought into the honey of its melody. It is a kind of *summa summarum* of all the foregoing.

The rest, dispute though it seems, is mere pre-

SCHUMANN

STRINGS, WOOD AND HORNS.

(See page 228, line 16.)

tence, mere fun,—breaking out more openly in the next "quicker" phrase, where, as in Beethoven of old, bass and air change places, with equal completeness, then scamper in purest frolic to—a pause. Here, *Presto*, begins a mad fugue, literally a chase of voices one after the other in new coursing theme:

Sempre forte.

up to the final height, whence, after one more exchange of bass and treble, the end comes in melodious acclaim of all the voices.

IX

MENDELSSOHN AND RAFF
PROGRAMME MUSIC

IN various guises we see the symphony limited by labels. In Beethoven's "Pastoral" is a frank realism; actual nature-sounds are a part of the scheme. On the other hand, in Schumann's "Rhine" Symphony, the title is merely suggested. It is little more than an emblem of the spirit of Teuton Romanticism that pervades most of the German music of the century.

It is quite possible, where the greatest may fail in experiment, that a lesser may find the secret. Indeed, some forms seem best suited to a gentler flight of muse. Within a narrow scope it is true that the lesser form needs the lesser poet. Versatility is not a symptom of highest genius. Thus in the strange career of the symphony does it come about that in the limited field, where the feeling is narrowed to the sphere of some familiar idea, a Raff succeeded though a Beethoven failed.

There is no doubt that the true symphony is a very different poetry from the entitled, which makes much of its appeal by the mere trick of association. The former must stand or fall purely on the strength of its own content. Where pure music is the direct message, the other is diluted. The lesser is far the easier, leaning, as on a crutch, on the constant suggestion of the subject, as opera on its text. Yet there is no ground for its disparaging. There is no reason why music should not, in lower flight, hover about the special themes of folk-lore, with narrower, more defined scope of feeling.

The "Scotch" Symphony. That Mendelssohn should not have hit nearer the mark of his symphonies is a problem of its own. The elements of equipment seemed present in his art,—above all, a sense of exquisite tonal utterance of the poetry of outside objects,—that he shows in his overtures. A want of subjective power may have barred him from the pure symphonic utterance. Yet, in a way, he did not descend to Raff's use of the symphony, with the trick of more definite association. He strove for a more purely poetic unity, that he almost attained in the "Italian" Symphony. Thus one might say, there was as much distinction in his failure as in Raff's success.

It seems that for the sense of objective charm

MENDELSSOHN AND RAFF

that lies in place or story, the overture is a most happy expression, the symphony is not. Right here begins the difference of the two.

The form of the symphony, in four contrasted moods of intimate connection, grew from a spontaneous desire for self-expression. It must ever demand a basic purpose that binds the whole. A national cast is not enough, though reinforced with a title. That is just the wrong kind of unity that is merely external. But there may be all possible difference between this plan and the utterance of a poetic idea of a foreign land in several phases, such as was clearly conceived in the first two movements of the "Italian" Symphony. Though a similar vein may exist in the "Scotch," it is not palpable to the point of assurance.

All this does not prevent a glorious beauty. The well or ill choosing of a name cannot damn a work. We are concerned here with the question of the symphony, its typical idea. The truth is, music like this of Mendelssohn gives new enjoyment to the listener who casts off the puzzling mystery of the title. If, instead of symphony, it be frankly called "Impressions of Scotland," the mind would be far more open to

MENDELSSOHN AND RAFF

its enrapturing beauty. A title ought ever to be an under- rather than an overstatement of the aim. Its true function is a suggestion of the expressed intention, not a shadowy ideal which the poet vainly seeks. Indeed, the separate parts of the "Scotch" Symphony disclose a wonderful wealth of fine thought and of melodic beauty. It seems as though in their glorious workmanship they make up for a lack of organic poetic purpose. Fine touches abound of most delicate architecture. A clear, sincere process pervades. Yet, it seems, the profound idea is wanting that binds the whole in a convincing epic. With all its beauty, the work shows very well what is not a real symphony. The unity is external,—a national quality of tune. This unity might exist equally in four other Scotch tunes of varying pace and related tone.

But, to waive a subtle point of musical æsthetics, from a lower point of view the "Scotch" Symphony, if it be descriptive, is so in the deepest and broadest sense. It is born of the same thought as the Hebrides Overture, of the mind that reflects with new beauty outer impressions. After all, pictures need no illustrating. There is no subtle plan to search for.

MENDELSSOHN AND RAFF

Here they are, all charming melodies in the Scotch humor.

Beginning quietly thoughtful in the introduction, gradually gathering motion, rising to some bold height and descending again gently, here is a little overture of the national drama. In the solemn flow of the introductory melody

WOODWIND, HORNS AND VIOLAS.
Andante con moto.

there is a foreshadowing of the sprightly *Allegro* theme. It has the sombre merriment of the North. Treated with Mendelssohn's own grace and power of light touches, it rushes into a dramatic, stormy episode.

So the romantic and warlike elements are contrasted. But the statement of themes is so little of the work of Mendelssohn; it is the mere suggestion of what he is to sing of. You must listen to the tune in the bass; in thirds; or to the answer, singing at the same time in responsive

MENDELSSOHN AND RAFF

alternation. We are always in the strife and structure of many voices. Accompanied tune is not enough.

From the storm of this episode comes the lull of first theme in minor, beautifully answered

STRINGS. (Melody doubled below in clarinets.)
Allegro un poco agitato.

(See page 234, line 9.)

above, as it still flows along, making one continuous duet between viola and clarinet, working on to still newer melody in the major. Then the song is taken up in other instruments. With all the complexity of the climax there is perfect

MENDELSSOHN AND RAFF

clearness if the themes are heard. They are simple as any folk-song. Indeed, they are pure Scottish tunes, though made by a German. In Mendelssohn there is none of modern lack of

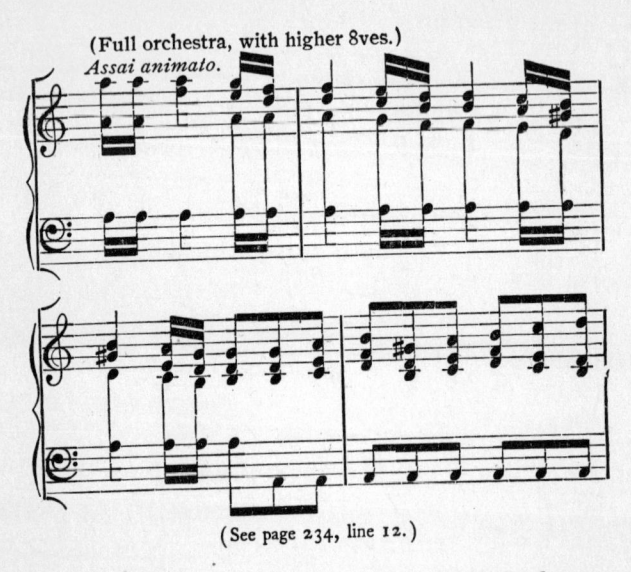

(See page 234, line 12.)

clear melody nor of turgid vehemence of treatment.

There is a kinship between German fancy and Scotch. Some Scotch stories are best told by Germans.* Both nations have a feeling for the

---

* See Hauff's "Märchen."

MENDELSSOHN AND RAFF

romance of rough scene and dread danger. There is a sign of it in the hollow fifths of the wood, which begin the story of the Allegro, after the tune-rôles have appeared. They are held while the little motive

goes on its stormy course, rising oft to higher tempest, quieting suddenly into the phase of pure song, but a song of many, grouped as by painter in fore- and background,—figures that seem independent in their harmony. We have the main tune in the cellos, little phrases in the first violins, and a flowing answer in the woodwind. Then they exchange parts. All this discussion is one glorious trio, crowned by a fervid burst of wild passion. It is Scotch in a profound and complete sense: in this savage vehemence, in the lyric quaintness, in the feeling of stern old ballad. This latter strikes us most in a long strain, low in the cellos. And thus we return to the original order of themes, with newer complexity of all the clans piping together, now with clash of furious storm, long continued, then gliding gently through the original *Andante* melody directly into

MENDELSSOHN AND RAFF

the *Vivace*, a real *Scherzo*. This is clearest of all, evidently a romping clog, with pipe and bag. It is the most Scottish, too:

(Clarinet, with strings lightly trembling in the harmony.)

How did the German poet ever catch this broad Celtic fun? There is a big to do and a maze of singing parts. But all is a jolly revel; the frowns are melted into a broad smile. One dainty verse is in brightest contrast. As the strings skip in lightest step:

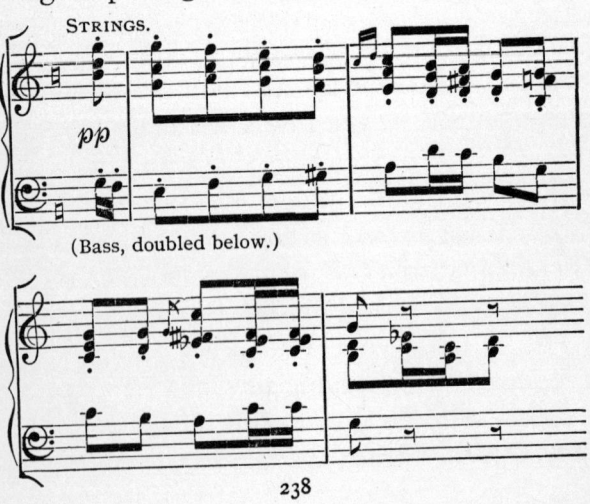

(Bass, doubled below.)

MENDELSSOHN AND RAFF

the wood are chirping a little answering rondel of their own. At times there is mere dance-rhythm without tune. But there is a full discussion of the humorous strains, with all their ins and outs. The perfect reflection of Celtic and English humor, now in its lightness, now in its very plainness, is itself a touch of genius. There are many narrow escapes from a broad, German, conclusive strain.

There is none, however, in the main melody of the *Adagio*. We can simply see that it is beautifully pathetic and large enough to include Celt and Teuton alike. But the second strain, in funeral march rhythm, has much of the grim terror of the North. The treatment is purely lyric, a song in varying verses.

The *Finale, allegro vivacissimo*, is a broad, joyous chant, tempered with a minor tinge. The first melody, in triumphant march, is a sort of new

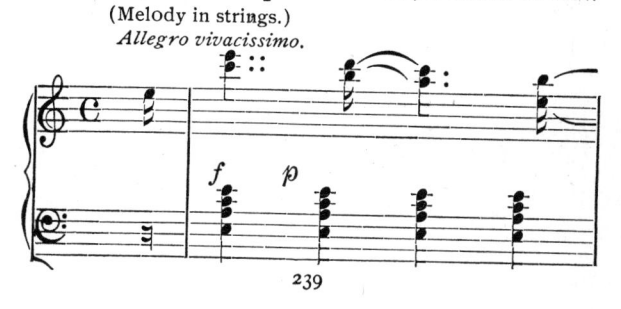

MENDELSSOHN AND RAFF

"The Campbells are Coming." Always firm in this feeling, it is never tempestuous. There is a strong contrasting theme, in full orchestra,

(Greatly reinforced in the whole orchestra.)

lacking the trip of the first. But ever comes the tread of nearing armies. Suddenly there is a bit of Celtic pathos that has outwardly no place in a patriotic piece:

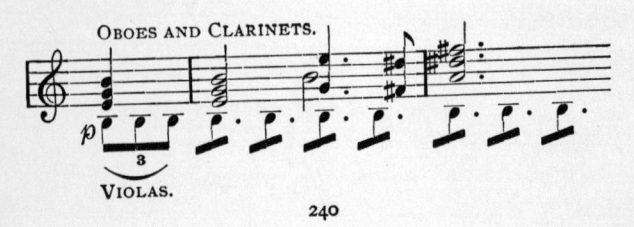

MENDELSSOHN AND RAFF

Breaking in as it does, it is just the mark of unconscious poet, and a type of the unconscious strength of music. In a wonderful way it strengthens the spirit of the national march. Though there is much of fugal depth, the simplicity of melodies, together with the power of Mendelssohn, rare nowadays, of refined thoroughness of detail, makes a clear picture of the whole. The conclusion breaks from the pervading key into benigner major, like the fugues of Bach, with the feeling of assured serenity. It has a clear trace of a subjective strain, of a wider poetic view.

RAFF'S SYMPHONY "IM WALDE"

We have shown how Raff's genius lies happily within the extremes of programme music; how he may be said to have solved its problems successfully as to symphonies, achieving here what Mendelssohn reached only in the overture. Indeed, without the symphonies of Raff, it might be held, for lack of supporting examples, that the true symphony cannot be burdened with a special title. More happily than Beethoven in his Sixth Symphony, Raff found the right relation of subject and utterance in the main by a predominance of the mood over mere description. The graphic aim was not pre-eminent, merely the suggestive. The two may approach each other so near as to be well-nigh indistinguishable. But the right attitude of the composer is clear, can never be actual delineation, but merely an utterance of the feelings aroused by the subject, whatever it be. As in negative and positive of a picture, there may be the closest correspondence of mood and of event, even in detail. And yet a true musical poem is never more than an utterance of feeling.

The division of the symphony is novel; there are three parts, of which the first, in Allegro, is entitled "Daytime, Thoughts and Impressions;" the second, "At Dusk," comprises first a "Revery," second, "Dance of the Dryads;" the third, all in one movement, is headed "At Night. Quiet Reign of Night in the Forest. Coming and Going of the Wild Hunt with Frau Holle (Hulda) and Wotan. Break of Day."

The poetic design fits perfectly with the

MENDELSSOHN AND RAFF

traditional order of symphonic movement and rhythm, and this harmony is a symbol of the fine touch with which Raff uttered his special sense of nature, of the great outer elements of life. His tonal schemes, with all their novel warmth of color and harmony and their objective realism, do not fail of a masterly grasp of the art in its highest reaches, of profound polyphony and of complete breadth of formal design. Indeed, there is no doubt that some of the melodic, harmonic, and chromatic manner that is all attributed to Wagner is quite distinctively Raff's own; that with him it is allied with a true mastery of the art, independent of dramatic illustration; that it is the sensational quality of Wagner's style, his constant reiteration of the same idea on the largest dramatic scale (lacking the economy of highest art), helped, too, by the attraction of visible story, that has stamped his name unduly upon much of modern musical discovery, of which he was not the only pioneer. This symphony of Raff was finished seven years before the first hearing of the Nibelungen Cycle.

Daytime is, after all, the prelude of the real life of the forest. The climax is night, of which the day is the mere dusk.

MENDELSSOHN AND RAFF

The first notes of the forest are a deep, sombre humming of low basses (in wood and strings), through which, at intervals, resounds the cry of the horn:

one of the chief elements of this bit of complex beauty. Presently appears the second, where the basses find a tune in their dim groping:

And then, third, the moving answer of higher strings, the motto of the forest:

In lighter pace the high woodwind join, the phrase of the basses grows to a fuller melody,

MENDELSSOHN AND RAFF

into which all the woodwind and horns enter in chorus. The low brass are first heard, on a sudden hush, in a new harmonic light, preceding another burst of the melody of the basses. In the silence of the rest, the strings sing softly and tenderly their former strain, in lower key, so that all the first seemed but a prelude to this, the heart of the movement, the sighing legend of the woods. The song is extended by a new verse sung in close rejoinder, the woodwind taking part. Presently the horns, sacred to the forest, take up the song, joined by the higher strings. The cadence has sudden brighter gleams of cheer as the last of the themal elements sounds in this epic of day in the forest. At the very close it steals in (among bassoons) so subtly as to be easily lost:

It stands a lighter symbol of the sparkling joy, the sunlight of the forest, clear of the dread and danger, and quaintly lifts the whole mood at the very end of the beautifully sad song, which is the principal theme of the woods. Though a mere phrase in a close, it flows along

MENDELSSOHN AND RAFF

in the constant cycle of its return, new voices ever joining,—growing to a whole song of praise into which the full band have at last been enticed. The motive has extended here and there, and now has almost the symmetry of full-blown melody. But the source, the tissue, is always the simple, sprightly, rollicking phrase. In its very last note, as it has simmered down to bassoons and lowest strings, is an interval of the fourth by pure chance, the first cry that we heard from the horns. Innocently the bassoon has awakened the sombrer horn to its old motto, which it now sounds again and again, while lowest basses are rumbling away through most solemn changes, at each step, of tonal hue, like huge kaleidoscope of deepest colors. The depth, the changing shades, the dim uncertainty of the forest are there.

For a moment lighter sprites interrupt with a tune that seems new, but is merely a friendlier verse of the old theme of the basses,—singing for cheer, while the dragons growl almost within sound.

And now we have the whole life of the forest, ever in blending of these moods, where dim dread is never quite absent. A lighter motion soon

MENDELSSOHN AND RAFF

begins and pervades until near the end. But it is the motion, not of birds and humming bees, rather of gnomes and fearsome elves. Much of their doing is of a strain of the song of the basses:

(Strings and wood with *pizz.* Basses and Violas.)

with a dancing kind of step or skip in the high wind. Presently comes a wailing cry from on high, which we hardly know as the beautiful legend of the strings, so distorted is the expression, so changed to a touch of anguish.

But now, with all the light dancing figures about, sounds a comforting bit of the rollicking strain, though it is not enough for the old joviality. All through flit shadowy figures of lightest motion, but uncertain of mood; a kind of secret hovering between the beauty and the terror. Nothing is quite clear; all the former melodies, of quiet beauty and cheer, are perverted; now two are singing together, distorted in form and feeling. Wilder grows the mad whirl, louder the chorus of all, when at the very top of the climax sounds the friendly song of the basses, now noisy with glad acclaim, where all are singing not in unison, but each with a different end of the tune,—later joining in a simpler, united hymn of a kind of deliverance.

Here we are in the same chorus which the basses had first enticed on their original melody, and now follows the same career of lesser strains, of the principal legend, of the rollicking phrase with its climax. Again comes the changing hue of low bass sounds, with the horn call above. There is still a lesser phase of uncertain humor; but the distorted melodies are absent. There is a sense of coming cheer, and soon the song of the basses bursts forth with utmost brightness in final climax of the rollicking phrase. At the very end is once again the solemn call of the horn through the changing choir of lowest sounds.

At Dusk. Revery. In the cool air of evening, in uncertain light, the strings grope through searching tones, the clarinet trills a strain seeking a clear utterance. Presently the strings (aided

MENDELSSOHN AND RAFF

by bassoons) fall into a melody of great beauty and pathos:

STRINGS AND BASSOON.

which is really the burden of the whole, in pure lyric vein. Between the verses the clarinet sends forth its vaguer rhapsodies, much as a bird, stirred to carolling by song, vainly tries to echo the melody. Other voices, flute and oboe, join in answering snatches. And now the horns send out the golden notes of the tune, while the flute, instead of listening, continues its carolling in sweet accord.

In the midst is a madrigal of forest voices, started by the first strain of the main melody. But in the graceful interweaving (with new color of tonal hue) there is missing the human note which comes with new force in the final verses of the melody.

The Dance of the Dryads, still in the twilight,

MENDELSSOHN AND RAFF

tells its own story, unless we refuse to take the title with literal fidelity. The dryads cannot be a very distant kin to the fairies, who seem more at home in the northern forest. They are creatures of the same kind of humor; indeed, their humor is the best of them. But these dryads or elves have a way of varying their guise in the midst of the dance. The fairies of the first tune are more impish:

in the slower second they are almost human. At the end the poet has the lyric mood of the

MENDELSSOHN AND RAFF

revery blended with the humor of the fairies, whose dance hovers about the song of the *Largo* in the strings.

The Wild Hunt of the raging host — *das*

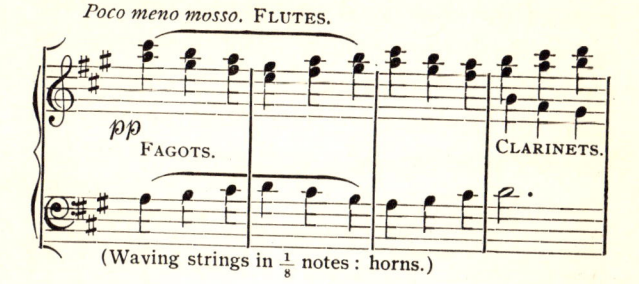

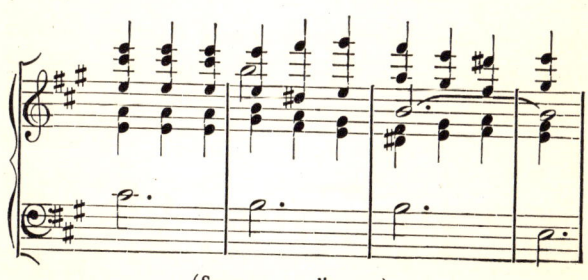

Poco meno mosso. FLUTES.

pp FAGOTS. CLARINETS.

(Waving strings in $\frac{1}{8}$ notes : horns.)

(See page 250, line 10.)

Wütende Heer—of *Wotan* and *Frau Holle* belongs to the ruder world of German folk-tales rather than to storied legend. In oldest saying *Frau Holle* lived in high mountains, in lakes or in the sky, and was good to mortals, as her name *Hulda* shows.

MENDELSSOHN AND RAFF

Indeed, she probably had a mistier past as *Erda*, or Mother Earth herself. She was even later ever a motherly sort of goddess. She certainly made the snow when she shook the feathers of her bed. Says Grimm, she is cross "only when she sees discord in the household." The home, spinning, marriage were her special interest; but, like Diana, she had a hand in the chase as well. In the strange tale of the raging host we see *Frau Holle* in a later time, when Christian cult was degrading heathen creed before killing it. The good dame never became savage and ugly—she was once white and fair—until the Christians came and displaced her with Mary. It was the natural way that the very kindest of the gods—strongest in the people's heart—must be specially attacked. So gradually *Wotan* and *Hulda* sank to a sort of devil and his grandmother. They had a quaint kind of place, too, in the Christian world. The gods die hard; they do not vanish in a day. For a time they are doomed, like a conquered race, to a nether sphere of evil spirits; and they were, in a way, not without their use. To *Wotan* were sent the spirits of men who had died of violence, and *Frau Holle* was given charge of the babes that died unbaptized. And thus the mighty

MENDELSSOHN AND RAFF

march of worthy gods and heroes became the wild hunt of the wasting host of lost souls and devils.

A whole of the three divisions is of Night, the real element of the forest; or perhaps the forest is her home. Day, after all, the clear sun, never really reaches it. The darker the night the deeper the forest,—which is equally true reversed; and so the darkest depth of the forest must be at midnight.

In the "*Stilles Weben*" of the title is a clue that seems obstinately to refuse utterance other than in its native figure. It means a fulness of life and motion with the least of sound. And so Raff takes a theme from his magic bag of tunes, that fits this humming woof of night in the forest, tingling with the pulsing throb that is busiest when most still:

CELLOS AND BASSES.

Raff's fugal themes are rare, almost unique in being melodies. And so the course of these gently murmuring voices on one tuneful motive is a most poetical utterance of the busy sway of night in the woods, as true whether we read as child or naturalist. Above the strings presently sings the horn (the new voice stealing in ever before it is expected), and, too, the bassoon in softest humming.

Then a new throb is felt in steady ascent, while horns are sounding a distant rhythmic call. Now the approach of the wild hunt of the gods is clear with the new pace of galloping steeds:

STRINGS, CLARINETS AND WOOD.

rising higher and louder as it nears. Suddenly the band is upon us, the thud of the hoofs ringing all about. And now a more measured hunting chorus breaks out in the strings with supporting brass, only to return, later, to ruder clangor alternating with the hunting chorus song.

Now comes the maddest whirl of clash and din, where the one thing clear is the unceasing thud of clattering hoofs, though, at times, strains of the (second) hunting chorus are heard. But

MENDELSSOHN AND RAFF

presently even that is distorted out of all guise.

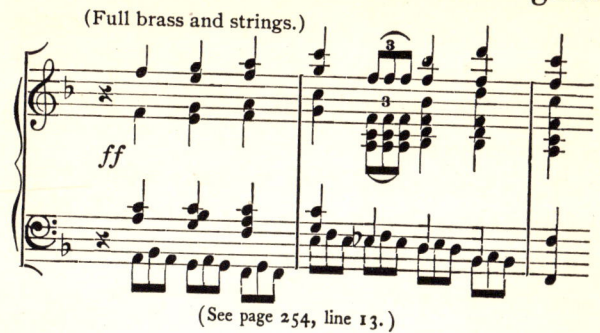

(Full brass and strings.)

ff

(See page 254, line 13.)

The answering cries of the horns ring ever

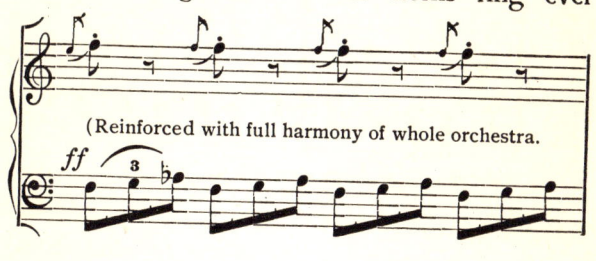

(Reinforced with full harmony of whole orchestra.

ff

(See page 254, line 15.)

higher; but all is disorder, with no sign of

common (tonal) plan. A vague sort of march time seems patched from shadowy snatches of the hunting songs. Suddenly out of the worst of the din a clear strain pours forth, joyous and festive, without the terror, the brute noise, sweetened and lightened, without loss of pace or freedom:

And still one melody sings out of the night, most human of all, but is presently lost in the renewed turmoil of wildest hunt. At one time when the sounds, uncertain still, have hushed for the

MENDELSSOHN AND RAFF

moment, the first motto of the night can be heard dimly struggling through the incongruous elements. Through the cycle of all the strains the wild course continues, but reversed, so that when

(Woodwind with *tremolo* strings.)
(See page 256, line 9.)

the last hoof has died away, the *Waldesweben* is heard in its original stillness. At the end, in climax of the whole symphony, the united chorus returns, with break of day, to the legend of the first movement.

THE "LENORE" SYMPHONY

THE complete title-page is:

FIRST PART . . . . . THE JOY OF LOVE.
Allegro ; Andante quasi Larghetto.

MENDELSSOHN AND RAFF

SECOND PART . . . . . . SEPARATION.
March; Agitato.

THIRD PART . . . . REUNION IN DEATH.
Introduction and Ballad (after Bürger's "Lenore").
Allegro.

One of the greatest flowers of the species "programme music,"—so ingeniously misunderstood,—the "Lenore" Symphony needs, for intelligent enjoyment, a knowledge of the romantic legend of Bürger's poem and of the divisions of the composer's plan.

But "programme music" is like dangerous medicine. There ought always to be an accompanying warning, much like Beethoven's in the Pastoral Symphony—"rather an expression of feeling than a painting." So, to the "Lenore" listener we would say: Don't find the literal touches of the ghostly ride of the bride and spectral groom. Don't find the

"Tramp! tramp! along the land they rode,
Splash! splash! along the sea,"

nor seek the "coffin'd guest," bidden to swell the nuptial song,—when "the shrouded corpse arose,"

MENDELSSOHN AND RAFF

> "And hurry! hurry! all the train
> The thundering steed pursues,"—

nor where the felon

> "Swings 'mid whistling rain,—
> The wasted form descends—
> The wild career attends."

Nothing is clearer than the composer's intention: to express the feelings kindled in the story in the free manner proper to the tonal art, unhampered by the detail of narrative. The simplest way to enjoy the symphony is to read Bürger's poem or Scott's version; then to resign oneself untrammelled to the musical treatment.

Three of the four movements are mere prelude to the story of the poem, but they are far the most important part of the symphony. The lovers' early happiness shines in the opening theme:

(Bass an 8ve lower.)

MENDELSSOHN AND RAFF

bubbling with joy, breaking into the placid pure delight of the answering melody:

The shadow of a sigh in the strings

MENDELSSOHN AND RAFF

is hushed by a laugh in the wood:

Thus passes the opening *Allegro*, while the

MENDELSSOHN AND RAFF

Andante seems but a more complete deepening of a perfect bliss:

Indeed, there is nowhere out of the range of songs, in pure tones, so loftily poetic an utterance of love's happiness.

It is Raff's freedom from an over-sensuous taint, of "emotional" fury (where feeling is falsely measured by the mere violence of passion), that has for the time obscured his music; it is the same trait that will bring it the more lasting place.

In the flow of melodies, with their general whim of interference and interruption, the first is full of a quiet, almost fearful ecstasy that slowly plays into the strong assurance, in the second, of absolute content.

Separation comes first restrained by a patriotic,

MENDELSSOHN AND RAFF

warlike mood. Nothing betokens sadness, unless it be the grave cast of the whole march.

(Strings, with clarinets and flutes.)

Cantabile con espressione.

(See page 262, line 16.)

But suddenly, out of the close ranks, the spirit breaks into tumultuous rebellion, from which, after a sombre calm, it rejoins the war-march.

While hitherto all is of the clearest, the *Finale* is, by the nature of its text, restless, undefined,

MENDELSSOHN AND RAFF

uncertain. There is no distinct melody or

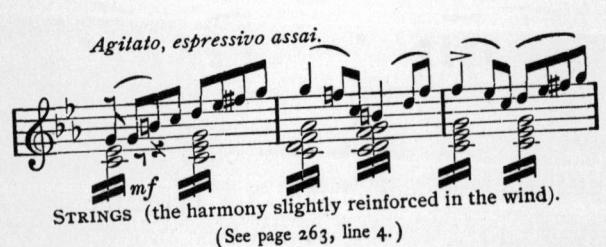

In march time.
Pizzicati STRINGS AND CLARINET.

(See page 263, line 2.)

Agitato, espressivo assai.

STRINGS (the harmony slightly reinforced in the wind).
(See page 263, line 4.)

thought, save reminiscences of former ones, and these are all distorted into a hopeless wail. The

MENDELSSOHN AND RAFF

wild pace of the basses knows no rest until, at last,

> " Her soul is from her body reft ;
> Her spirit be forgiven."

The soothing chorale ends the poem.

It is, perhaps, just to say that other interpretations have been current and even dominant. Many insist on finding in the third movement an approach of the army; in the *Agitato* a duet of the lovers (in the violins and cellos), Lenore pleading, Wilhelm resisting and finally joining the soldiers.

It must be admitted that the temptation is of the strongest, in the last movement, to find the actual incidents of the ride, funereal and nuptial in one. Nor is it well to cling blindly even to the best theory. At times it seems most clear to hear the whole story from the moment when to Lenore, despairing of her lover's return from the war,

> " —— slowly on the winding stair
> A heavy footstep sounded ;"

how he bids her ride with him

> " O'er stock and stile, a hundred miles—
> Before the matin bells ;

MENDELSSOHN AND RAFF

then the events of the furious ride, as the spectral guests join the nuptial throng, until

> "Sudden at an open grave
>   He checked the wondrous course.

> "The falling gauntlet quits the rein,
>   Down drops the casque of steel,
> The cuirass leaves his shrinking side,
>   The spur his gory heel.

> "The eyes desert the naked skull,
>   The mould'ring flesh the bone;
> Lenore's lily arms entwine
>   A ghastly skeleton.

> "The furious barb snorts fire and foam
>   And, with a fearful bound,
> Dissolves at once in empty air
>   And leaves her on the ground."

The strongest reason for the descriptive interpretation lies in the whole cast of the *Finale*; the reckless, ruthless discord of shrieking wood and clanging brass. In lieu of a musical reason it does seem natural to turn to a dramatic one.

The truth is that in a special subject like "Lenore," with its rapid chase of startling events, the line must be narrow between objective description and subjective utterance. Raff may have crossed it in momentary violence to artistic possibilities. When feeling is thus at the mercy of legend, emotional expression must bear strong resemblance to actual description; it will be a kind of negative of the picture.

But where there are two possible interpretations, the true lover of music will choose the one which lies within the natural sphere of the art.

RAFF'S "WINTER" SYMPHONY

ALLEGRO. "*The First Snow.*" Convincing, and it seems classic pieces of programme music are Raff's symphonies. It may be set down as generally admitted that they are not descriptive. They help in their own way to settle the nice boundaries of entitled music. What Raff himself intended (or thought he intended) is hardly relevant; it is certainly not conclusive. For if we agree that the power of music comes from its utterance of the unconscious intent, the deliberate purpose of the composer is just what we do not care to know. When we consider that all our perceptions are subjective, surely art, in its permanent expression of them, ought to have that attitude,—above all, that particular art whose medium is invisible.

MENDELSSOHN AND RAFF

The first division of our symphony is fragrant with the breath of early winter, with its blended tremor and delight. If we cannot see in every phrase a definite symbol, or even a relevance to the subject, we can always be content with the abounding beauty itself. We cannot quite believe that an interlinear interpretation is, somehow, really essential to the true enjoyment. The feeling of winter is there throughout, however indefinable in words.

Against hollow octaves of oboes sounds the frigid, unhoused theme of the fagots:

MENDELSSOHN AND RAFF

answered by a shrinking murmur of strings. This duet introduces the prettily dreary song of the main melody, first in the flutes, with graceful trip of accompanying strings:

Though lightly tinged with sadness, it has a strongly human, almost domestic quality, which is rudely shocked by the interrupting strains of the first phrase, figures of hostile nature without, ever answered by the fearful cry of strings, succeeded again by the placid song. Other graphic touches of the unfriendly season are ever breaking into fragments of the melody, chiefly a running phrase in the clarinet, with picking strings and chirping flutes. During one of the strains of the main subject there sound, deep in the basses, rough, hammering blows, rasping against the other harmony, growing louder and fiercer:

Presently, with unlessened noise, they somehow merge into lines of agreement, and then, with full chorus of each lusty voice, rings out from the very din of the blows a glorious, fervid song that draws all man and nature into its ranks.

If we had to say something wise about meaning (which in music is as bad as the moral of stories), we should guess, say, this. First come rough blasts of the storm, driving man and beast in terror to their lairs. Then, presently, man is

MENDELSSOHN AND RAFF

seized by the very spirit of the winter; dauntless he revels in the snow; fear itself is turned to fun and frolic. But the stirring song, like day, must end. The frosty first theme comes moaning again, and the strings hum in sad harmony. We must never tie ourselves to any story which links our labels of successive phrases. Otherwise we

(See page 270, line 11.)

quickly lose the guiding hand of the poet, blinded by our own sense of a preconceived path.

A gloomier hue is cast, of darkening shadows. Night is added to winter. And now the first melody becomes a pious chant in proper fugue, and loses the human note. But the mood grows lighter and brighter. There is more energy in the surrounding figures. Soon the song sounds in all its first fulness of human feeling and of earthly color. Again it ends with the chill strains of the woodwind. Then among symbolic sounds of winter is a new figure in the wood, with humming strings. This is presently doubled in pace, whence it grows cheerily playful, throwing off the cold reserve:

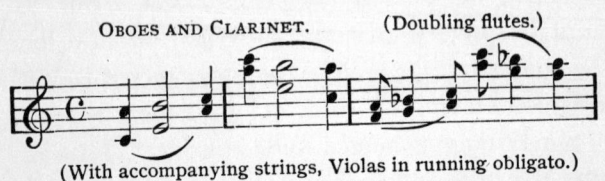

OBOES AND CLARINET. (Doubling flutes.)

(With accompanying strings, Violas in running obligato.)

And the earlier running phrase joins in the gambol, growing more boisterous, when suddenly a theme of mysterious meaning sounds in the basses. As it steals nearer, we greet it as the herald of the joyous song. More and more the spirit infects the ranks; all are summoned, and then out bursts again from full throats and hearts the great chanting praise of winter. And now, though all the blasts blow fierce and cold, they but add to the joy of the glad tune. The true climax of all this first act (of the season's drama) is surely where the first melody turns its sad minor to glad major, and, the fierce winds in

MENDELSSOHN AND RAFF

captive background, crowns all the strife with triumphant joy.

Allegretto. The second movement is the most mysterious, if we must seek for something more definite than the mere "Allegretto," which the poet has written. The want of a title does seem purposed; and so it is almost impertinent to insist on finding it in spite of the poet's intent. But it must be yielded that the provision of title for the whole and for each of the other scenes leaves a natural craving for some enlightenment here.

Surely there is here a lyric episode. That is, after the strife and energy must come a phase of quiet thought. The dramatic element has now subsided. Nothing happens, or very little. Nothing is done. The lyric is definite enough; but it is itself,—not translatable. A quaint song is here for winter evenings, perhaps a ballad, a household glee; for the voices move all together in four even parts, with marked time, clear tune, and sharp cadence. This is evidently the beginning. We might imagine some old *Minnesong* set to the notes. The tune is rehearsed with dainty interplay of two groups of woodwind. The melody is varied with much delicacy, so that when, later, the simple tune reappears, it seems new.

MENDELSSOHN AND RAFF

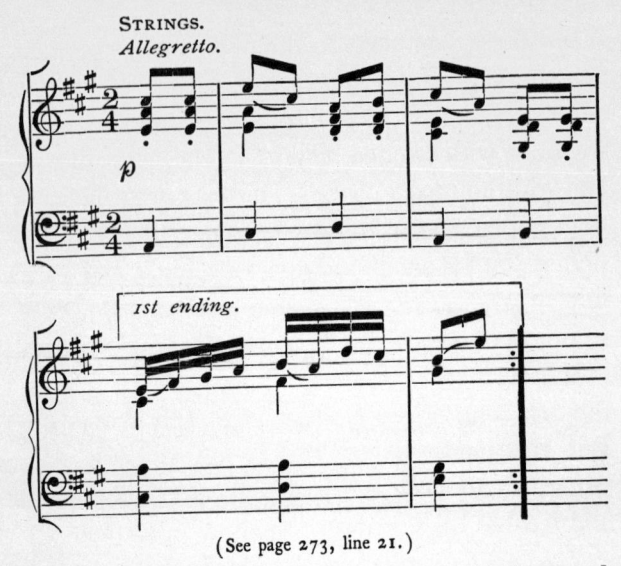

(See page 273, line 21.)

There is in the middle a swelling glide of strings and a whistling of flutes that is very like the howling of the wind without,—even if we must defy the critics. An ominous theme sounds once in the bass:

MENDELSSOHN AND RAFF

Then the ballad sings in the minor, with changed surroundings,—no longer a simple glee, but a single voice with trembling strings, while others break in with excited refrain. The wind moans and whistles most clearly. The song descends into unearthly scenes of tone and of tale; that warning phrase sounds again and again on high, and in a lull of the storm (in major hue of the latest strain, freed of its tragic dross) a hymn is blown in the clear tones of the trumpets. Very earthly the first song now sounds, as it timidly reappears. But the pious air of the hymn prevails. A ballad we are sure it is, with cheerful beginning and terrible haps, ending somehow in heaven.

Larghetto. "*Am Camin.*" "At the fireside" saves us much thinking. But we must have guessed it. How like members of the family the voices steal into the deeply enchanting melody, each appearing somehow after joining unobserved in the circle! Each entrance of new voice has this quiet way of taking us by surprise. Raff's melodies have a strongly human quality, fragrant of folk or legend poetry, and this is one of the most glorious of them all. The whole symphony was worth writing alone for this tune. The rest of the movement is clear in the intent of the music and of

MENDELSSOHN AND RAFF

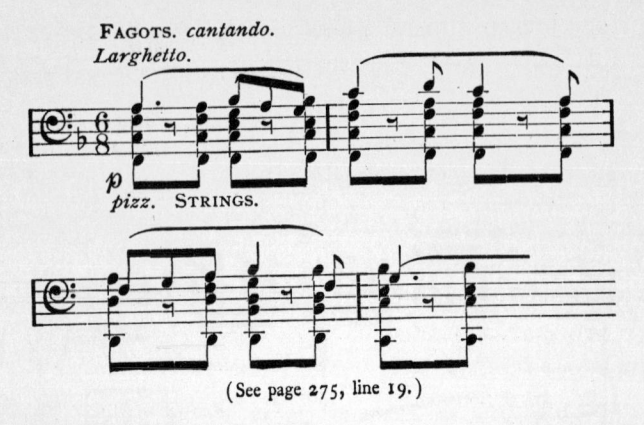

(See page 275, line 19.)

the meaning. What might strictly stand for a second theme is a light, mirthful phrase in the wood answered more thoughtfully in the strings.

But the whole middle phrase has surely a placid, chatty feeling: *häuslich* they would call it in German,—a sort of domestic idyl, without strongly romantic heights. When the first song of the hearth re-enters, the setting is in a way reversed. Before, the fagot played to the strain of the strings. Now, woodwind and horns give a bright color of background, whence the cellos emerge in solo song, followed again in the surprising way of the beginning by violas, second and first violins. Through a stormy burst we wander again into the lighter mood of sprightly

MENDELSSOHN AND RAFF

laughter and friendly chat, which turns by natural path of thought into the last verse of the serious tune.

Allegro. "*Carnival.*" There are many frolics in the classics of music. Indeed, most of its

(See page 276, line 3.)

poetry might be called a simple utterance of pure exuberance of spirit. And it is curious how in such phases of the masters the greatest art is somehow called into service to express the very simplest

MENDELSSOHN AND RAFF

feeling. Indeed, highest art seems closest akin to primeval emotion.

Of that kind is the *Carnival* of Raff. But it has a way of its own that specially fits the name: something of the unending spinning of the top, the ceaseless buzz of Mayfair, that adds to the subjective feeling the graphic touch of the scene. At first, figures are romping about, more and more frequent, to a figure capable of a most wonderful momentum:

Presently the wood adds a frivolous air that fits the other at almost any point; and so we are dancing away without fear or care of clash. The dance does seem to sink for a while into song, but not for long. When the second tune comes in:

stacc. STRINGS AND CLARINET.

the general din and vague bustle seek the more regular lines of a round dance,—that is, each is

MENDELSSOHN AND RAFF

dancing the figure his neighbor had a moment ago, and there is a general maze of successive steps. (It makes us wonder why a dance could not be devised to such counterpoint, the steps answering to the interdependent voices, on the principle of "three blind mice.") Finally the dizzy medley ends in a common burst of general chorus. But a few are caught stealthily dancing away to the first strain, and the rest are gradually infected just as before. Now it must stop, with reluctant skip; and there comes a song that with all possible grace and lightness has a certain speaking way:

In the return of principal theme things are somehow reversed, as in Alice's Wonderland. At first the heavier figures began, the low voices rousing the higher. Now the lighter trebles lead off and are joined each by a bigger neighbor.

MENDELSSOHN AND RAFF

Finally the frivolous air is sung below the dance figure by clumsy basses of strings. There is the same maze as before, and the round dance of the second tune. But now the episode is new. Here we break away from all the general impersonal din and mob. This is the best of it all, without a doubt,—a moment of personal confidence, sincere, yet tinged with the lightness of the scene and of the dance's rhythm which holds our talk in its sway:

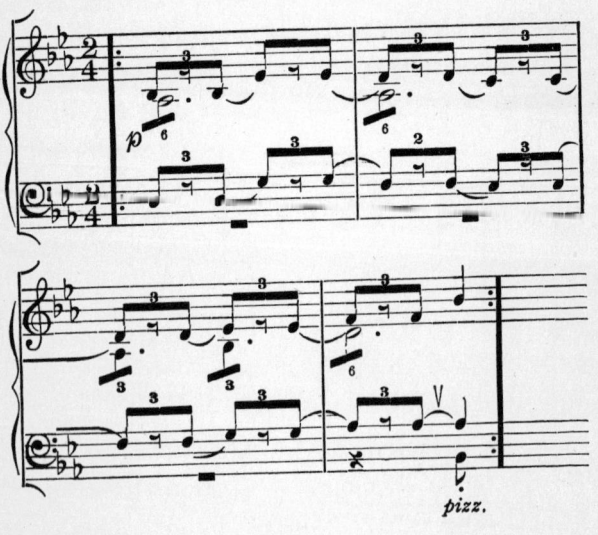

And mocking voices are spying and laughing

MENDELSSOHN AND RAFF

about. It is a *tête-à-tête* snatched from the festival's whirl. Somehow we are loth when it ends, and we are hurried back to the general dance which begins once again. And now the mad frolic rages in real earnest. The former maze was real child's play. Four separate groups at least we can see dancing the figure, each at a different point, all in perfect agreement of motion. For some reason the brass are sounding a big signal blast in the midst. And now, in purest fun, they dance the step just twice as slow, the big basses leading off. At last, with much more diminished speed, all sing the strain together, ending, of course, with maddest clog of all.

X

BRAHMS' FIRST SYMPHONY

THE first symphony has its own interest, like the maiden speech, and in highest degree when it is written in our time. It is like the philosophy of a new teacher. The man's spirit, his personal tone, is specially stamped therein. And in the first there is the added charm of novelty.

To be sure, with many, with most masters it is but tentative,—is, after all, a mere academic essay. No one thinks of Haydn or Mozart's first symphony. Beethoven's had little of his musical individuality. It did not emerge from the shadow of his elders.

It is interesting to count, and to find merely two, Schumann and Brahms, who in the first symphonic work gave an important message. It is somewhat a matter of age. Brahms had waited longest. It is not strange, therefore, that his first word is far the boldest of all. One can imagine none of the earlier masters hearing it without wonder, not even Schumann, who knew Brahms in the piano sonata.

BRAHMS' FIRST SYMPHONY

To be sure, this radical trait does not, itself, insure greatness. The past century has been marked with no other quality more than this of novelty, until it has proven its own refutation. Originality has a bigger meaning than strangeness. The conscious striving for *bizarre* effect is a fatal symptom of poetic weakness. The true poet must begin in full sympathy with the best that has gone before him. True individuality must be an unconscious trait of expression. It is not by rejecting, but by crowning the preceding art that a new poet earns high place.

At once an austerity and a mature, fully developed originality appear with the first note. The muse of Brahms seems truly Pegasean, seems to have grown out of the regular course. You do not see the paling lines of older masters' influence. From the beginning he seems to have his God-given manner, like a later Zeus-born hero of song. The whole process, the fragrance of melody, the lesser figures, the very orchestration are his own to a degree almost beyond belief.

There is, in truth, a sense of harking back, with other poets of the age, to elemental things, through myths and legends. In Brahms this primal fragrance of motives is ever fresh in the

BRAHMS' FIRST SYMPHONY

pure crystal of spontaneous form, that is like organic growth. His scheme of colors is, above all, clear,—not sensuous, for its own sake.

As we read of the young Beethoven coming to Vienna "all for the grand,"[*] so Brahms was filled with true heroic temper, not lacking in most expressive melody.

It is good to have lived in the time of such a man, a great gift of the gods to know him when he comes, a sad fate to fail to see the mark of a great spirit. The truth, after all, is, the people are not the test; on the contrary, the certain test is just the other way. The true audience for living genius must always be those who see far ahead. It may be said, as a rule, that never have the people instantly hailed a true genius; when they have praised an early utterance, the poet has never proven a classic.

Amidst the maze of lesser evidence is one very simple sign of great tonal poetry: an *Andante* melody. Smaller men may roar themselves into a bacchanale of sound and fury, but they cannot think the quiet, measured melody of

---

[*] Grove's "Dictionary of Music," Vol. I. p. 166; Thayer, *Leben*, Vol. I. p. 237.

BRAHMS' FIRST SYMPHONY

sober pace. Here alone is a sure proof for Brahms in all his symphonies, not least in the first. Not since Schumann have there appeared such melodies to hold the ear and comfort the soul; nor do we find them in the works of any others living in the time of Brahms.

Reading this prologue of *Sostenuto*, we are struck with the solemnity of message. No bubbling spirits break forth, as in Schumann's first symphony, which, in the new light, seems a little like Haydn. Gathering masses move slowly down (in the wind) in doubled thirds, against a rising phrase of strings:

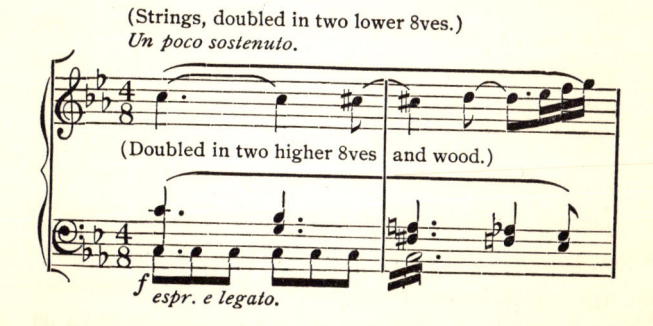

Slowly the double pulse rouses the rhythmic motion, ending in trilling cadence. Now hollow picking of strings

BRAHMS' FIRST SYMPHONY

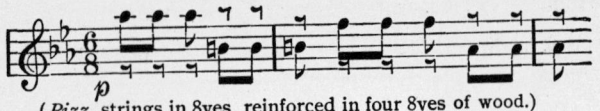

(*Pizz.* strings in 8ves reinforced in four 8ves of wood.)

and piping of wind—of strange token—are answered with the first fervent strain of human appeal

(Strings, doubled in fagots and higher flutes.)

that is a most marked trait of Brahms as a later Eusebius,—his own note of rare tenderness that ever comes after vague striving. Like Beethoven it is, only in the fervent strength and sincerity of feeling. A big conclusive sweep of descending tones leads to the first budding sign of main theme, still in *sostenuto* pace. Gradually it hurries and confuses its arpeggic gait, then turns back for one more splendid march of the first heavy figures. A new answer here glides in, in softest chase of wood and cellos, the very essence of

BRAHMS' FIRST SYMPHONY

delicate poesy, most fragrant as it steals its gentle path upward and down, in rounding phrase

daintily clear as spoken words,—to the sudden force and motion of *Allegro* theme:

(Basic theme, in strings and fagots.)

Yet—such is the maze of interrelating motives—this new strain is hardly more than countertheme

BRAHMS' FIRST SYMPHONY

to another, a brief, quicker form of our first phrase of slow moving harmonies. For, with new vigor of motion, these surging chords, closing with electric run, are the real theme of *Allegro*, as of *Sostenuto*, and even of later phase. The new motive is now, to be sure, the more eminent; but the older phrase is pressing on in a steady flow of answering canon. The newer has the apparent dominance; but the other is really basic. Thus the sense of pressing onward, groping and struggling through heavy masses, first dimly, in the *Sostenuto*, then with joyous hope, is the clear fundamental idea.

Of the especial *Allegro* theme, we must see first that the quality is less of fullest melody, in older sense, than of spring of motion and promise of coming achievement. Yet in its bold wing on high it has presently rounded a tune. And now the answer is of phrases of the prologue, of picking strings and intimate response:

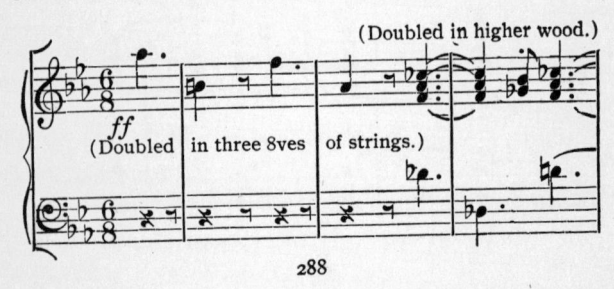

BRAHMS' FIRST SYMPHONY

Only they are both transformed in brilliant strength and masterful stride. The note of sympathy yields to the very opposite, of heavily clanging chord and clashing rhythm, yet rising hopefully to bright climax and returning theme.

Here is the splendor of deeds and motion of former promise. Through bold light, the mobile theme darts to new tone, still of minor. Brahms dwells in the sober realm of contained, almost fearful joy. But the melody itself wings in freest career, losing all but semblance of its rhythmic gait,—now in three voices, one on high, two singing below in opposing motion, until they meet in united fall of crashing chords. Even then the motion cannot stop,—the momentum is too great. So in the mere shadowy phrase of close, the big chords tumble along in constant mutual chase, rising to altogether new scene:

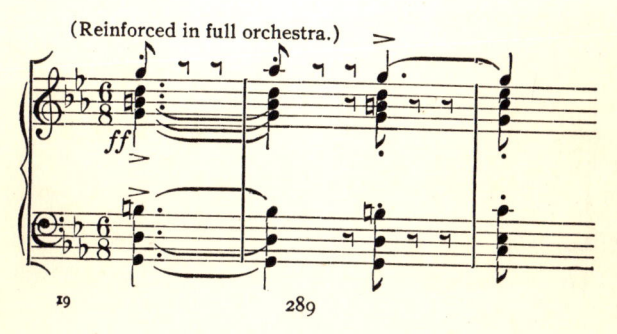

BRAHMS' FIRST SYMPHONY

The chase is pursued in lighter steps of lesser phrases. But, before we go farther, we must note two things,—the fulness of thought of our invocation, holding indeed all the germs of *Allegro* song; second, the mastering movement of it all. The sense of Titan stride is the pervading element.

In the run of light figure the chase is more flitting, as of pairs of butterflies, answered, in moments, by curving cadence, where the first theme sounds from below. The chase seems by nature endless, in the change of flickering shades of tone.

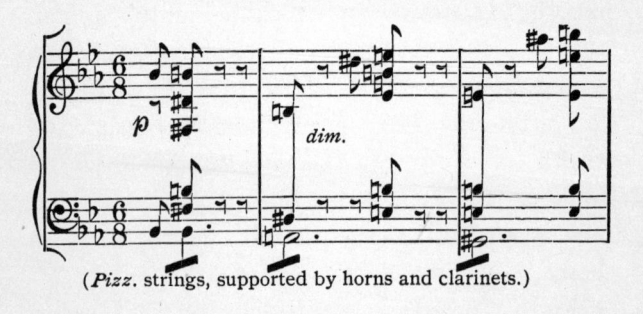

(*Pizz*. strings, supported by horns and clarinets.)

For a moment comes the temptation to see in technical devices how the tone seems to shift by less than the smallest step of modern music. By boldly holding the bass, while other voices

BRAHMS' FIRST SYMPHONY

move through least of steps, a strange intermediate tone somehow shimmers through, with magic sense of new discovered tonal prism, as of an insect world.

The symphony is full of Olympian moments of a certain quiet beatitude, that carry us to the isles of the blest,—a vein out of the nervous humor of the times. So the swing of a placid cadence is reached; the horn begins a friendly call, echoed by the wood. The whole movement is on so great a scale that the structure refuses to betray its lines, though ever giving convincing evidence of its big perfection. It is like the dazzling view of cathedral, where you cannot pierce the maze by clear sight of balancing figures, and yet you feel the overpowering completeness. Here is just such a bewildering wealth of lesser melodies. But there is no doubt at all of the ruling idea of *Allegro*, which now reappears in the double figure of main theme.

And so, here it is again, starting from basses and spurring to friendliest conclusion of wood and strings. A new expressive answer of oboe ends in cooing duet on the simple call. The voices have stolen into the dim shade of new

BRAHMS' FIRST SYMPHONY

Sempre molto piano e dolce.

region, where the call is sounded softly by horns:

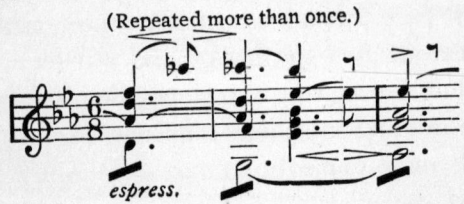

as of answering night-doves in the forest. Still darker grows the scene,—then a sudden energy starts the strings:

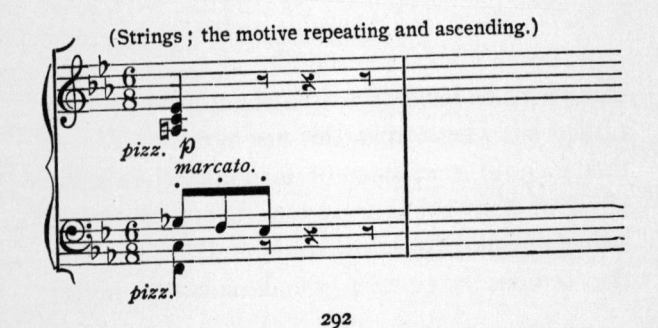

BRAHMS' FIRST SYMPHONY

and though it grows to full, vigorous strain of its own, we feel the main theme coursing in the bass. Presently, in inversion, we are merely in the climax of the rehearsed sounding of themes.

The next phase has the galloping motive in full chorus, in various voices, like unruly horses that run amuck. But it is a mere brief vent of spirits before the figure goes gently browsing in slowest pace through strangest pastures, resting a moment in new tonal spot, and wandering on. Suddenly the nervous throb starts in the strings, and, ascending in strange sequence, bursts into a loud hymnal phrase

that seems to have grown, in thought, out of an earlier bit, where, after the first verse of *Allegro* theme ended in cadence of tumbling chords, the chase of harmonies keeps on. It is here a more articulate and extended strain. Together with the nervous motion, it sounds again in higher

BRAHMS' FIRST SYMPHONY

scene; then the shorter phrase of hymnal chords, as in brilliant chase, soars along in canon of briefest theme, through glinting light.

As this has come to resounding close, with gentle echo, we see the mystic enigma of the close knitting of all this thought, without the plain themal lines of older symphony. For here, in softest passing of hazy chords against higher phrase, is again the gentlest, steady journey of fleecy clouds that hold the eye in trance of rapt absorption:

(Strings, brass and wood, doubled in higher 8ve.)

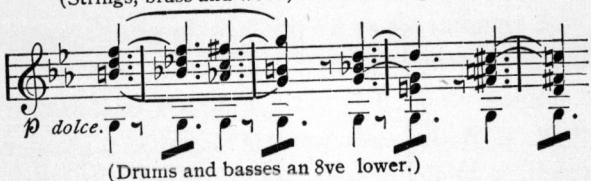

(Drums and basses an 8ve lower.)

and this very bit of musical thought that seems exactly in its place is the first line of original *Sostenuto*. But the mystic trait of these harmonies is the wonder of this first word of latest symphonist, as they speak a primordial truth from grayest ages,—before man had lost a higher sense of deep wondering in the nervous bustle of small concerns. This vein we see throughout Brahms, confirmed in different way in each symphony.

BRAHMS' FIRST SYMPHONY

It might be all unwitting to the poet (and this is really all beside the mark), save that here and there, in lesser works, he has noted a line of verbal verse as index of his thought.* There seems no doubt that our master uttered a profound sense of elemental beauty, in the hue of ancient legend.

Just how music will give this sense without the titling word, though it can be clearly shown, is not here our special field. By a close glance at the elements, of rhythm, harmony, even the *timbre* of instrument, the subtle association could be surely established.

A certain trait of all this new breath of poetry is an elemental ease of movement, a leisurely lounging along, beyond the touch of hustling time, as if the ages were before us,—a greater reach, a bigger view than the muse has taken through all this century of tense Romanticism.

The drive through stress of shifting masses, that comes as the first vision of the symphony, pervades the whole, independent of first phrase. There is no doubt the discussion is largely on slower motive of main theme, augmented at a rate Beethoven would never have dreamt of. The

---

* See Brahms' Ballads and the *Andante* of Sonata in C.

BRAHMS' FIRST SYMPHONY

hymnal strain grows, as do the best melodies in Schumann's symphonies, after and out of the principal themes. When the whole cycle has sung, the elemental groping through moving masses returns, tinged with a sense of prismatic wandering. We must not fail to see that the nervous motion is associated in the *Sostenuto* with the main theme. Indeed, all this thought can be seen in the germ in the first prologue.

The dim journey of browsing meditation has reached the lowest point of descent, and now turns slowly upward.

We might well say that the detail of small phrases and their connection ought to be ignored; that the true intent is the total impression, from an unstudied view; that in the close search much is lost of the whole conception. In most masters we have the landmarks of larger themal melodies. With Brahms, in their frequent absence, the smaller motives seem to get a certain symbolic value. Then, the vague sense of former origin may be all we need. Yet the actual and exact discovery is a most pleasant confirmation of our own perception and of the poet's art.

As the thoughtful wandering mounts towards the light, the quicker phrase, without the nervous

BRAHMS' FIRST SYMPHONY

strum, plays above. At the height, instead of the hymnal strain of yore, comes a broad conclusion, descending in irresistible sequence, in clashing duet of the brief motive and of the quick phrase that first preceded the main theme:

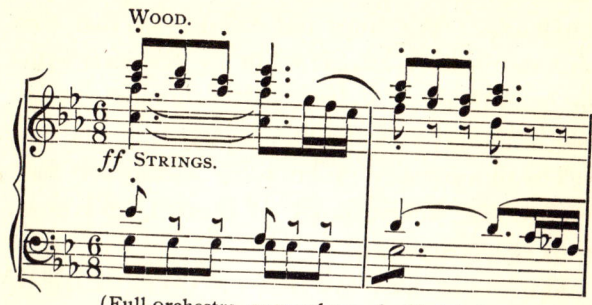

(Full orchestra, every phrase doubled in 8ves.)

Continued in sequence.

that was indeed its origin. This soon glides into the slow chromatic chase, the oldest and the all-pervading figure. Thence by natural though overpowering climax the cycle of themes is reached.

BRAHMS' FIRST SYMPHONY

In one way we must keep our view off the small themes, or we shall lose the big sense. The consummate art, in its correspondence of phrases, is here tempting against its own best reception.

The *reprise* is like the original statement, but for the second strain of first theme, with climax of tumbling chords. So the germ and, of course, all trace of the hymnal song are wanting. The whole expressive phrase out of which springs the cooing duet of dove-calls is there in full length. Still, we are held more and more by the predominance of the one idea, to which the others are foil, and with the clear prophetic sway of the *Sostenuto*.

The big ending of the first refrain of themes is lengthened and strengthened to the liveliest accent of the old, driving iambic gait:

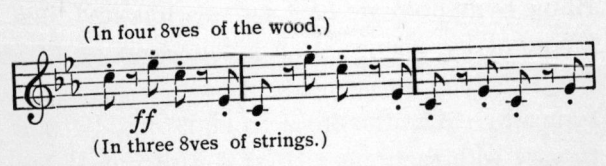

(In four 8ves of the wood.)

(In three 8ves of strings.)

Towards the last line, the slow-shifting cloud masses (of first beginning) return on the lively step of the theme, and end in broad cadence of serene assurance, gliding into one more phase of the *Sostenuto*, in solemn and transfigured mood.

BRAHMS' FIRST SYMPHONY

The first link with earlier thought is in the *Andante*, that is certainly German folk-song in fibre; yet there can be no denying the abounding color of a new personality. The vein of true Andante had not been struck for a long

Andante sostenuto.

STRINGS AND FAGOTS.
HORNS.

time, not since Schumann; and there, while gaining a certain intimate charm, it may lose something of broad, world-wide sympathy. In the Rhine Symphony we have rather a folk-idyl than a note of big plaint. It is a dangerous ground, this, searching for elements of such a quality as sympathy. On the other hand, it may be said to vary with each poet, so that with one it has lost all sound message, is a mere weak, personal lament. We have distinguished the fanciful, eerie strain of Schubert and of Mendelssohn from the human of Beethoven. Any kind of feeling may be eminent: legendary, say, idyllic,

BRAHMS' FIRST SYMPHONY

or intimate. Rough though these labels be, there is a certain kind of tune and of poetic mood where a broad sympathy mainly pervades. This is most clear in the first of our latest master's symphonies. The feeling seems to crop out at special points, as at the beginning, or in the answer. It will

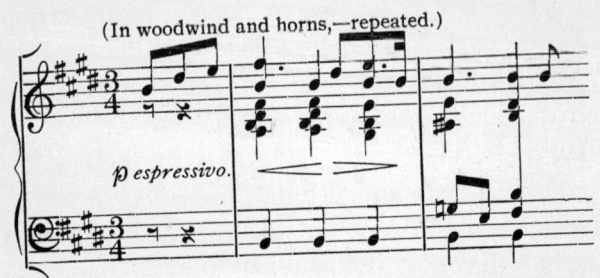

yield before the spark of Promethean boldness, to return with new assurance in the cadence:

above all, in its firm second assertion.

BRAHMS' FIRST SYMPHONY

And then the best often comes in the after-phrase, as here of cadence, and in the great wide-hearted sweep of concluding strain.

All this seems the full enjoyment of a simple tune, until we stand in a certain novel amazement, when, perhaps on second hearing, we catch down in the bass of conclusion the whole theme over again. It is here that the art and genius of Brahms take on something of the marvellous,—that prompts the use of strange words in superlative. There is in such a discovery a sense of delighted wonder, as when, with the aid of lens, we find the hidden beauties of a snowdrop. With such a master one can never reach a state of high disdain; for the lofty critic can never be sure he has not missed some secret treasure in the vanity of his easy survey. There is never room for the satiety of listener; one can never feel that one knows Brahms " by heart." There is ever a danger of an entirely new view and tonal purpose that has altogether escaped. There is a bit of the delight of a child's game of hide-and-seek : one may ever be on the invisible heels of the quarry.

Again, we cannot resist a wonder at the strange harmonies in mere cadence, in this first

BRAHMS' FIRST SYMPHONY

symphonic word, and finally in the new way—privilege of highest genius—of saying simplest thought.

We might speak now of the art of the following strain (really a part of the original answer):

with its thread of melody above the canon. But the spirit and feeling must never be lost in this smaller view. And so, canon and closer imitative woof are all lesser in the fervent afterverse, all still in tone and vein of the first. But

BRAHMS' FIRST SYMPHONY

it prepares gently and perfectly for the flowing second subject:

that pours a free carolling song from the oboe. To be sure, in its midst another voice from the wood, in ideal mirror of nature, is roused to the same strain,—not waiting for the leader to end, though it does have a new sense of answer in the varying tune. With the same abandon a third breaks forth in lowest bass. Before we are aware, all this carolling is joined to the human strain of first cadence. With wondrous beauty, as the third voice begins, deep in bass, the second breaks with sudden upward curve, all with spontaneous fervor, though unlooked for, into the noble melody of the beginning. And yet the new carolling song keeps on, and the whole is richest blending of both strains.

BRAHMS' FIRST SYMPHONY

There is something in the complete contrast of these two melodies that gives their union a sense of special delight of big truth. For this new running bird-call is the most careless of bucolics, recking nothing of note of pathos, not even of melodious outline, finding its charm somehow in this very tuneless freedom, in the rare clash of its elusive course against the dainty harmonies in strings, and other forest notes. So when the second ingenuous bird-throat strikes the lay, the whole is enchanting idyl of nature's polyphony. It is all completed by the resonant voice far in the bass, in deeper vein, while at the same time the main theme is sweetly insinuated in freer phrase of clarinet, in crowning cadence of the whole. Ever the main subject stands against the former abandon, for a world-wide sympathy. The wonder is, how perfectly they join in the fervent close, how the lighter phrase becomes aglow by contact with the main theme.

The two are constantly playing each against the other; and so the feeling of one heightens the other. The fervent main subject, or its phrases, will come as foil to the impersonal elusive fancy of the other. To be sure, the first is main theme, and so it soon holds sole sway,

BRAHMS' FIRST SYMPHONY

heralded by most expressive duet (between strings and wood) of two of its appealing phrases. As now the main theme sings, to a gentle triplet tread of bass, a new melodious air is woven about, in high strings, that has just blossomed from the heralding duet:

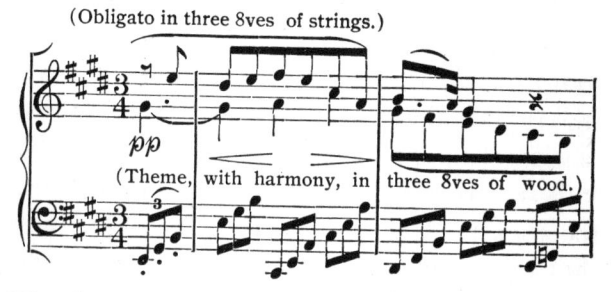

The full course of the song is more moving even than at first. The homeward journey gives the harmonies a new fervor. The phrases have a more varied guise, and thus, in their union, a richer choral flow. At the end, the big conclusion, with theme in bass, sings its hearty farewell again and again; the after-phrase, on canon theme, closes with repeated strain.

The humor of Brahms is curious, like all higher forms of humor, which is a matter mankind differ about as much as possible. All men

BRAHMS' FIRST SYMPHONY

laugh; but all men will not laugh for the same cause. So, when it comes to humor, who has the right to speak save of his own special sense? Who may deny another's gift because it is not of the same strain as his own? When two strange nations laugh each at the other's lack of humor, the true jest is for a third.

Brahms' humor does seem new in kind. In other moods he has been charged with striving in the path of Beethoven, for no better reason than a like heroic mould. In their Scherzos the masters have nothing in common. For one point, with Brahms the pace is less than of the first Allegro, instead of the greater of Beethoven. And so the humor is more delicate:

It does make its insidious appeal here, in

BRAHMS' FIRST SYMPHONY

quaint, rollicking phrase of clarinets, extending against all law just one measure, with the dulcet countertheme of horn. The answer is conclusive in every way, not failing in the stolen measure. Now the lightest sort of phrase dances down in double notes from high wood on buoyant wing of arpeggic strings, ending in playful cadence:

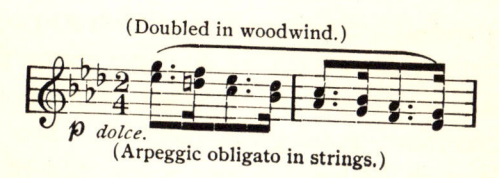

So now the slower, staid song of clarinet returns, the humor is far clearer,—a quaint mock dignity, of short stride, fearfully balanced between hurry and halting. The novelty, the delicacy and boldness withal cannot be denied, and, too, in a first symphony. The vein of reposeful humor, reflective,—that corresponds to the dry wit of words,—is Brahms' own. Humor with him did not mean high excitement, big rushing movement. It lay rather in the strange taste of a tune, the slow jogging gait, the subtle touch of elfish phrase.

In the second melody, though it begins gently:

BRAHMS' FIRST SYMPHONY

CLARINETS.

p espress.

(With $\frac{1}{16}$ rhythmic harmony in strings.)

we have presently a moment of pure, exuberant, joyous motion, playing hide-and-seek with the

(Doubled in 8ves and wood.)

f

(Accented in strings.)

repressive strain. There is, to be sure, a difference between joy and humor.

What would formerly have been called *Trio* is a new scene in the midst of the Scherzo,— new in color and region of tone, and new in the manner of motion,—a slow swing of two paces, of which each has three lesser steps, well designed for big gathering mass on simplest motive. Contrast is a basic element of humor. It is in the quick conjuring of tonal opposites that Brahms is behind no other poet.

BRAHMS' FIRST SYMPHONY

This Trio, in its natural, swinging trip, after the quaint gait of Scherzo, is again a pure buoyant

utterance of high delight. The relapse to the weird tread of the first melody completes the humorous cycle. Yet we must beware of our own terms and symbols. They are, after all, mere images that we have conjured to give shape to the sense that we feel. So there is a touch of exquisite refreshment in the last run of main melody, when the tune extends to charm-

BRAHMS' FIRST SYMPHONY

ing after-phrase with freer rhythmic utterance, leaving the staid rut of clownish clog. But there is a new touch of friendly meaning; again "the poet speaks," breaking through the guise of his puppet figures. With a like transformed song of all the strains, the movement ends.

Adagio begins a dim passing of chords like clouds across the tonal horizon, all in the spirit of the first thought of the symphony. But now the harmonies of the woodwind are topped by a clear melodic idea in high strings:

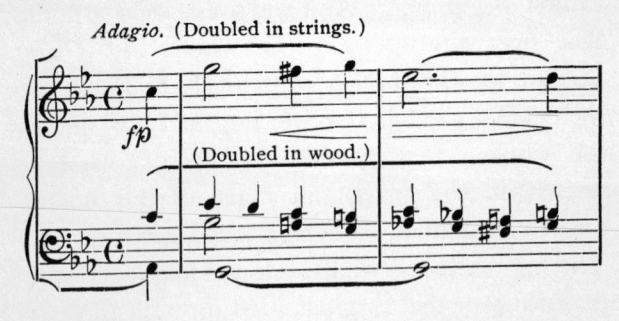

Adagio. (Doubled in strings.)

(Doubled in wood.)

that marks a new token. No reminiscent phrase is here that harks back to earlier prophecy; the outcome is at hand, the bright result and reward of the groping and striving. As yet it is shadowy

BRAHMS' FIRST SYMPHONY

and infrequent. Scarce is the stately pace defined, when in breaks an opposite, fragmental, halting gait, of shortest motive:

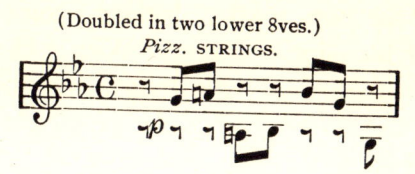

that soon hurries nervously to big height of sound, whence returns the first placid song.

But, although the main idea of the *Finale* is new and crowning, yet we must not fail to see the common woof of lesser figures here and in earliest beginning. And we must yield a point that may almost seem the whole. It is not needful for the listener consciously to know all the detail, to catch the true ring and purport of the whole. It may even be possible to lose oneself in the mass and maze of this undergrowth,—to miss the whole wood for the trees. The big result is—we have found long ago—the personal tone that is transmitted through all these subtle feats of highest art. The true answer, again to sum in former words, is the balance of clear view and tense enjoyment. Though there may be too close a gaze at the visible notes, yet

BRAHMS' FIRST SYMPHONY

this danger, in truth, exists, at most, for the single student. In the great world of listeners the lack of balance is all the other way; the fault is a basic ignorance of the dignity of the art, the spirit of the old Philistine to whom it was all tweedledum and tweedledee, or, almost worse, a certain modern hedonism that awaits the mere physical stimulus of tones, cares nothing for a spiritual message.

To feel this common background in first movement and in last is the important need. It is best pointed and confirmed in the concrete phrase. In the very first line was a waving motive of three neighboring notes:

In the second expressive strain is a slight change of outline:

The third is much like the second:

BRAHMS' FIRST SYMPHONY

Such phrases abound in the background of the *Adagio* that begins the *Finale*, and bring with them the groping mood that does at last strike sweetness and light. Nor does it spoil this sense of the poet's meaning that the very theme of the Finale itself, symbol of the new joy and truth, has grown out of the old.

If we compare here the basic motive of Brahms' Second Symphony, we see the master's tendency to find a motto, in smallest atom of tonal figure, for the work of greatest depth and reach and breadth.* Nor can we miss the close likeness in the two *sostenuto* preludes of first and last movements. The second halting passage is foil to the groping chords, as a like phrase was in the beginning.

After rehearsing of both strains, a new pulse of nervous hope stirs first in low strings, while the old symbol of dim search is singing faintly above in the wood. Then the expectant mood possesses all the voices, rising on the line of the halting second phrase.

Finally come mere pelting accents (still of an ancient motive)

---

* Vol I. Chap. XIII.

BRAHMS' FIRST SYMPHONY

against basses marching steadily up the chromatic line. There is an overpowering mass of heaped and strained expectation. As the answer

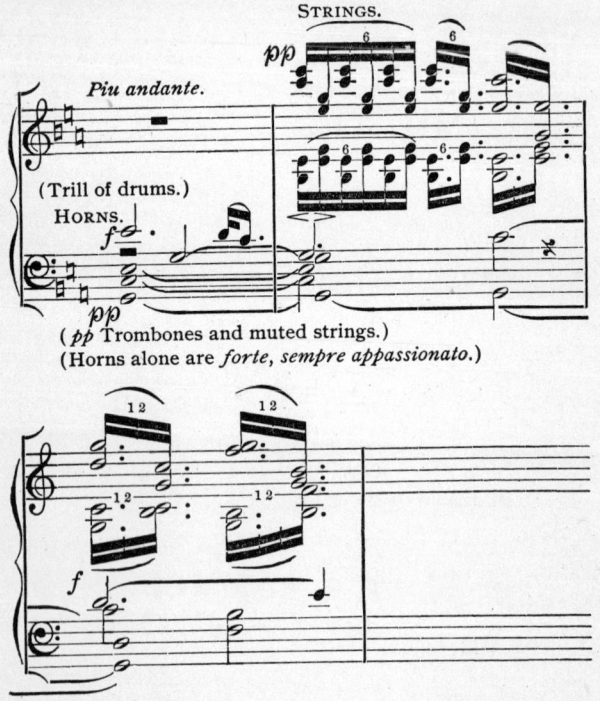

(*pp* Trombones and muted strings.)
(Horns alone are *forte, sempre appassionato.*)

sings 'mid softest hum of light wood and lowest

BRAHMS' FIRST SYMPHONY

brass and strings, in clear and passionate notes of the horn, here is one of the most overwhelming moments of sublime beauty in all poetry.

We do not care that even here we can trace the theme in small origin; for the mass of intricate striving and groping is all of the past. A transfigured melody here sings in all clearness and with freest reach. And all other sounds have ceased save the restrained hum and harmony of trembling strings and sustaining basses.

There is a ring, here, like no other song in music. Something there seems to be of the tones of Pythian oracle, of celestial message, in the clearness, 'mid the sacred hush. Nor is the song of one voice alone. Slowly a madrigal of responsive voices is reared. In the midst is a single strain of pure hymn, in low brass and wood, in strict choral steps,—a passing touch, in

BRAHMS' FIRST SYMPHONY

still higher empyrean, as of pure religious truth. Even the hum of strings has ceased. There is somehow a more human ring as the clarion message bursts out again, more joyously, with new echo in companion horn. The pace, though faster than the first *Adagio*, is still a serenely slow Andante swing. As it moves, now with almost feverish glow, we feel dimly that it is itself mere herald for the new song that breaks forth in firm array of martial tones and step:

Allegro non troppo, ma con brio.

poco.f
STRINGS AND HORNS.

It is, to come to a quick point, the symbol of clear achievement, undisturbed by the very pangs of joy,—a true song of the happy hunting-ground.

In its own way, the herald figure yields nothing in beauty to its proud successor; so that the high point of the symphony seems to lie just in this entrancing moment of breaking light, like the first red ray of dawn. Indeed, it is possible

BRAHMS' FIRST SYMPHONY

to lay too much stress on the formal eminence of one theme over another.

The marching song is the final distilled flower of the idea that began the Adagio, when higher phrase of strings topped the dim moving chords in the wood. It is the realization of all the lesser motives into a tune of firm serenity. Another answer is this to the charge of imitation. The tune cannot be another's; for we have seen it grow from smallest seed.

The tune swings along in leisurely sequence, and, after full-rounded close, is taken up with added choir of wood. Lastly the brass joins in loudest chorus. Now a new stir and strum of rhythm appear. The repose of steady march is lost; a new answer to the first strain of the tune sounds in quick notes of ancient motive. A new, broad, arpeggic stride is in the violins, above tumbling violas, crossed by another in the basses; then a nervous hurrying of voices in quick coursing phrase,—all in tempest of tonal torrents, ending at last on high, where, with the old solemn clearness, the prophetic figure sings in highest flute, echoed by magic note of the horn, the sacred song in intertwined strains.

In such a moment it seems that the world has,

BRAHMS' FIRST SYMPHONY

as yet, no approaching idea of the greatness of Brahms, as he looms up more heroic than ever in all dimensions of his art, in every mood of poetry. For, after this brilliant glimpse of glinting beauty, of ecstatic joy, here is our second melody (of the Allegro), in serene reserve and sustained humor of contented pace. Wonderful is this sudden descent from Gothic passion and sweetness to Olympian calm. It is alone a mark of the widest reach of human conception:

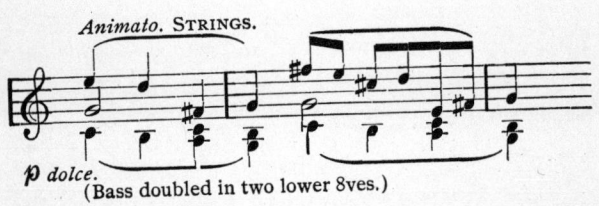

Animato. STRINGS.

p dolce.
(Bass doubled in two lower 8ves.)

This second melody (of Allegro) but stresses the true quality, and in its line of newest melody confirms the intrinsic novelty of the first. There is not the usual contrast of themes; for both melodies, instead, stand opposed in quiet, assured, triumphant stride to the toil and throes that precede the magic song of the Pythian strain.

More than the first has this second Allegro tune the comfortable charm of endless delight. The golden vein seems to lead us in boundless,

BRAHMS' FIRST SYMPHONY

pleasant quest. But the gentle motion does end with a new nervous stir and jolting pace. Yet, though the quiet is gone, the joy is not. Rather is there a faster pulsing of rising delight that must have a more tumultuous utterance. For a while we relapse into serene glide on a responding phrase of our tune:

Soon, as this is taken up in doubled time and ragged beat of strings, we are whirled into the midst of half-unison pæan, in fullest chorus:

(Redoubled in higher and lower 8ves.)

BRAHMS' FIRST SYMPHONY

If we have caught the clinging habit of tracing themes in their mystic course, we see that, from the beginning, of movement and even of symphony, there was contrast between the even flow and eccentric pace. The former was, we have seen, first a dim groping, then an approach of light, last a confident serenity. In the intervals, the ragged rhythm uttered the uncertain mood, the increasing stress that ends in triumph.

Against a line of it a new motive now appears, in petty conflict of its rolling figure:

Quickly it envelops all the previous song and crowns it with a new touch of glee. It may be quite needless to search for a dark origin; but there is no doubt of the identity of one of our ancient motives, that is here recalled in changed spirit of gladness. After a moment of subdued mood, there is a sudden burst in loud chorus, in duet of the rolling motion on high, and a masterful stride of march that has grown out of the eccentric song. The climax is the joyous flood-tide of the symphony, as the rolling phrase

BRAHMS' FIRST SYMPHONY

and the stride, now in even pace of triumph, play about in confusion of delight, first one, then the other above, the march carrying the main song, but the merry motive adding the final sparkle.

Now, after a half-pause, re-enters the stately tune of main march with a more festive brilliancy, a prouder ring. The earlier song of Allegro melodies returns with little change, save that new scenes are touched in homeward path. All the joyous episode of stress returns and leads to the magic of the prophetic call, and then to the serene humor of the Olympian melody. So follows, too, once more the big climax, with the ancient motive entwined about the second melody.

Here the old refrain ceases. Instead of a final verse of main march is here a mystic spot with solemn echo of earliest phrase in high wood against dim figures below, while the strings are running their former quickened, nervous strain. But the tonal light gives the strange hue of sombre mood, with grim sense of barbaric lore, that slowly presses towards the light, in symbolic style of responsive voices of the canon, which at the full flood plunges with utmost joy and speed to the final *fanfare*. First there is mere

BRAHMS' FIRST SYMPHONY

noisy whir of strings against blast of wind. Slowly the exuberance finds a melodic utterance in the old pace of serene triumph. Just one phrase is chanted to and fro, as by delighted children,

in ever higher tone.

At the top is the mere beat of glad foot, until of a sudden is poured forth from loudest brass and strings the hymnal line that sounded gently once before in earlier *Adagio*, that gives once more the seal of religious truth to the plot of mortal stress and triumph.

In the last line of mad revel the voices start a half-articulate glee, where the vague theme strongly recalls one of the elemental motives.

In structure, as in poetic sense, it is clear that the first pervading struggle through slow-moving masses, the basic figure of the first Allegro, returns in the last for final solace and overpowering triumph.

XI

BRAHMS' THIRD SYMPHONY

THE intense ethical or moral element of Beethoven, the human, the fraternal, is less in Brahms. But his is not the animal materialism of much modern art; it is too sanely balanced, it has too high a stand and standard. There is in Brahms the consummate patience, both of big design and of least detail, that assures a sound poetic message. This is, indeed, the one test of high art. In humor it is a recoil from the tension of Romanticism. As we have said, the high perfection insures a high tone; but the calmness, as of Mozart, leaves the message less tensely clear than of Beethoven and of Schumann. A broader, freer, clearer outlook is Brahms', oceanic in a way, if not quite cosmic. Strange how the view onward is made clearer by a big harking back to earliest ages,—a correction of too straight and strict religious sense by the more primitive significance and feeling of pagan cult. A bad time is this for dogma. It is too definite and is doomed. One might say

BRAHMS' THIRD SYMPHONY

that nothing that can be defined or formulated in human speech can possibly be permanent. Truth is too big for that jargon of small things. Dogma must go, and, with it, the cult and creed of narrow religion or philosophy. Christianity in its small sense has too long overshadowed the world. Music is the first to proclaim the new message, though elsewhere the legendary element is also prominent.

The harking back to the sense of old lore is important, not for itself as for this recoil from narrow view, to teach the world that all truth does not date from the last two thousand years, that great poetic divination was felt elsewhere than in Oriental lands,—in ancient times, when truth was uttered, if not in individual verse, in legend and belief. This is in common between the two opposing champions of latest music. The one chose, in a literal way, to turn to old legends with full drama of personal god; the other sought the freer, less limiting way of pure art, whose breath, without label of words, somehow stirs man's spirit much as does the air of woods and meadows, calling him from the narrow thrall of dank cloister. There is also a mixture of frugal simplicity with high complexity, that

BRAHMS' THIRD SYMPHONY

profoundly kindles our sense of ancient truth. To be sure, a special legendary subject cannot be read into any symphony; it lies in the neo-ancient quality of melodies and color of harmony and instruments. Brahms did not mar his message by perverted tales of ancient lore, redolent of animalism and fatalism that must die for lack of buoyant truth. He appeals to the pure musical intuition, and has no outward indices save where, as in the Ballads, an actual verse from Ossian points the mood.

We can never neglect the very beginning in Brahms. In many greatest works it is often purest introduction, preface, not integral; in Haydn it is often irrelevant, nay, literally impertinent; at best, like grace at table. In Brahms, push it aside as we will, it reappears ever with haunting meaning, seems ever like overshadowing motto. Here it is two chords, loud and long; one in the clear bright light of day, the second dark and sombre; we are between clouds and sunshine. In this April light we proceed. In a way, Brahms seems to have the symphonic point of view more than any one,—that is, the element of big design. The perfect placidity of his poise helps here; he is the sanest, perhaps, of all secular

BRAHMS' THIRD SYMPHONY

masters (where Bach is absent); at least, he has least frenzy of poet. Beethoven would begin with that wonderful reversible way of his: melody of bass and treble which can be inverted with equal effect. Think of the mastery for that unconscious art! Somewhat similarly we catch in Brahms a special profundity of design which

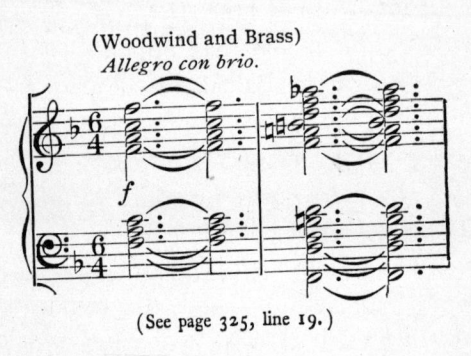

(See page 325, line 19.)

does not lie on the surface, so that you can never study him in a hurry.

Here in the symphony one can easily neglect the fact that the motto of the first three bars is instantly the bass of the next in contrafagottos and strings, the ominous motive at the foundation of all. The main theme, which here begins, sweeps down the simple lines of tonic chord, too free for modern melody. Strange

BRAHMS' THIRD SYMPHONY

how there is here a blending of the new and very old! As always, the greatest truth is most simple. The simplicity is all in the general spirit; for, looking at the parts, here is at the very beginning a double rhythm, the main one of basses fighting the swing of the tune:

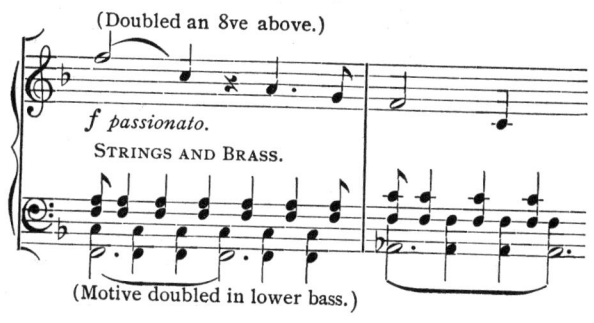

But, through the melodious woof, on goes the actual fugue of the motive of the first three bars. For immediately, in the midst of the tune, the motto answers its last entrance in the bass with another, redoubled in time, in neighboring key of low wood, straightway followed in the original tone on high. Subtly pervasive is this underlying legend, but so subtle that, while feeling, it is almost impossible to see it with conscious eyes. To be sure, it now ceases during the lesser tunes and second theme, but this pro-

BRAHMS' THIRD SYMPHONY

found view-point is the rare symphonic quality, wider, bigger, saner than much of romantic rhapsody.

Equally with the jolting rhythm is the rude jar of sudden harmonic change; beginning in clearest white light of major tone, it plunges the next step into dark, cloudy minor, and so it climbs the Parnassian height through quick varying tonal hue. There is a sense of ploughing through heavy waves of resistance with jolting motion, listing now here, now there, up in the bright sun, down in dark depths; but it does come to a gentle haven, though ever with a certain heaviness of gait, never a smooth grace, until the next tune, which hums for the nonce like lullaby:

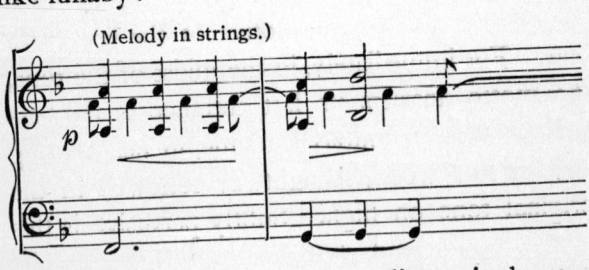

(Melody in strings.)

Quickly, however, rushing to a climax, it changes the tonal light, and sings again from a new quarter. There is no return to boisterous theme,

BRAHMS' THIRD SYMPHONY

—a line or so of sighing strings with soothing wood, and then, still in remote tonal scene, here is the real second theme, a song most sweetly quaint and appealing, almost plaintive:

with a swing (of $\frac{9}{4}$) that is not dainty nor awkward, but seems in one moment the one, in the next the other; is certainly naïve,—novel yet natural; on the whole, gives the spontaneous song a tinge of slow dance. The rare charm of the song is blended of limping basses of strings and of a high note of flute piping in at oddest moments.

The verse is repeated with some change of parts in the voices and with the same gay overflowing of cadence. Now the inverted first strain of the verse is sung through succeeding hues of tonal light, straying far away and suddenly

BRAHMS' THIRD SYMPHONY

coming home again into the original tone, where above the lower melody is a pretty bit of phrase, descending to meet the rising tune:

Here is a sudden ominous halt of placid pace. In sombre tones the motto intrudes its dread message, followed by a phase of light flitting figures above and below that are most mysterious:

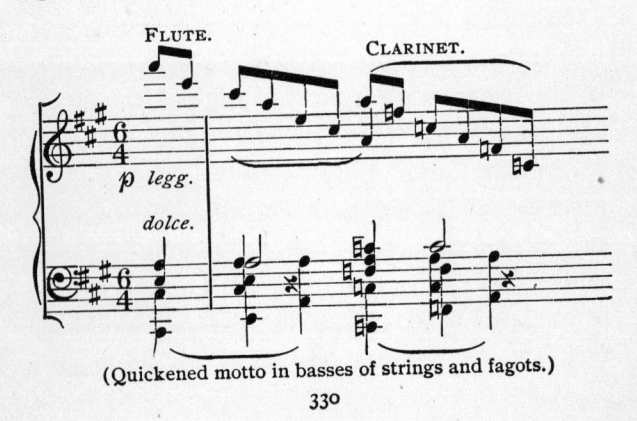

(Quickened motto in basses of strings and fagots.)

BRAHMS' THIRD SYMPHONY

All of Brahms is much more detailed, minute, than any other master. Broad lines there are and pervading; but they pervade as arabesque figures entwined in obscure plan. Are they more in artisan or workman than in poet phase? However, the fact that they are not reducible to language is no reason against or for their greatness. But it is strange how, after Mozart, symphonies rushed to a more defined stage of intense content and romantic message, and then reacted completely. The reaction of Brahms is not merely from Schumann or Schubert; it is the reaction even from Beethoven. Thus, to show the minute process: in this difficult phase of the symphony, before repetition of themes, the sense of arpeggio figure, of harp-like descending chords, haunts us with a dim sense of relevance which is most difficult to realize. To be sure, in one sense an arpeggio chord is always relevant (like an adjournment), especially in mere pointing of the harmony. But it must be more than this in a melodic voice. Our first search gropes to the second theme, whose cadence breaks into falling tones of a chord. But this cannot be the source. We feel with the sudden change of hue (and the ominous motto) a total break from

BRAHMS' THIRD SYMPHONY

the chain of melody; we must go further back for the trace.

Arpeggio, the harp-like ripple of chord, is itself a sign or touch of the primeval. It is one of the unconscious traits of Brahms in all his music. Throughout lesser figures we see it—too humble for mention. If we go to the theme itself, the main subject, what is it but an arpeggio? Remembering now Brahms' way of doubling and redoubling the pace of his ideas, augmenting and diminishing, every arpeggio gains a new meaning, a special relation to the subject to which it is akin, so that our phase with motto (redoubled) below and arpeggio above is all part of the fibre of the central idea. The phrase here seems to get an added fitness as a guise in quicker notes, still of the shortened motto, that is moving below and about. Even when all resemblance of outline is gone, the quick change of harmony at each big step breathes the same air of ominous harmonic suspense of the first two bars.

We understand now better the meaning of the interruption of second theme,—as a return to the motto, of which, we remark, the full phrase has four notes:

BRAHMS' THIRD SYMPHONY

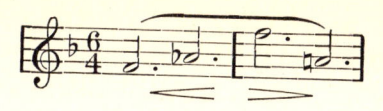

so that the first sounds of the symphony are not the whole, but a motto of the motto, a spirit of the essence.

It is the melodious texture, the perfection of big design and small, that make the art of Brahms sublime. Such absolute honesty of fulfilment can come only from great thought. The world cannot withstand the insistent evidence of this workmanship. One feels as if the sacred verse, "He that is faithful in a very little . . . ," were meant specially for art. It is the perfection and correlation of the smallest details that make the greatest art. Of course, it is not done as toil —that must not be forgotten; the spontaneous thought alone brings on exultant flow the perfect utterance. But the patient toil has gone before in student years, and by slow labor has tested the right spirit, the spirit that learns all thoroughly before it teaches.

The quicker figure is pulsing down in high wood, while from below slower notes stride upward. There is a long discussion, misty, until we see quicker forms of the motto rising like

BRAHMS' THIRD SYMPHONY

spirits of the legend all about, while against them are gentle cascades of harp-like tones in the wood, interlacing the whole. Still, as the shadowy discussion continues through cadences that are ever nearing the first tone,* while the motto is rising here and there in vapory figures, the quicker descending phrase has become more definite. The gentle cascades which come trickling down in the wood, above the phantoms of the motto, are seen to be of the closing phrase of second theme. So, in a way, are united the ominous hue of motto with gentler grace of second melody. The whole statement ends in triumphant coursing of final phrase in overwhelming climax, not only of first theme, but of the whole integral texture of the vital thought of the movement.

After the repeat, the shorter motto first still strides noisily about, descending as well as ascend-

---

* *Tone* is here used in its true, complete sense, embracing with a note or sound its whole tonality. It is, too, historically, the original conception, when there were no chords of simultaneous sounds to reinforce tonasity. It is a conception harder to realize as we are removed from the old epoch of single-toned music; but it makes for the true meaning of "Gregorian tones" and Church modes.

BRAHMS' THIRD SYMPHONY

ing through rough changes of tone, until, in a remote minor, a changed form of the second theme appears.

(Upper figure in four 8ves of woodwind, the next lower in two 8ves of strings.)

(Repeated with new ending.)

(Lowest figure doubled in basses of strings.)
(See page 334, line 15.)

We must be prepared in our latest master for a disguise of themes more occult by far even than the subtleties of Mozart's "Jupiter" Symphony. Inverted, augmented, or diminished in pace, changed in harmony, the same virtual idea somehow resides, brought out the more by variation and wrought out to higher meaning and conclusion by the life of the discussion.

So we plunge through a clash of guises of the motto into a new phase of second theme,—no longer sweet-humored,—in sombre, almost gloomy minor of low basses, the old quaint step gone—instead, a pace of anxious, eager striving,

BRAHMS' THIRD SYMPHONY

with here and now a gleam of delusive, ephemeral sweetness of major. Now eager strings take up the agitated song. All trace of the old quality is gone; but outwardly it is the same figure, and it ends, as before, with chain of cadences seeking a familiar tonal home. But the solace of sweet close is not there. Instead, by timid, halting steps we meet—a surprise: to smooth humming motion of strings the horns sound the motto in a new form of beauty:

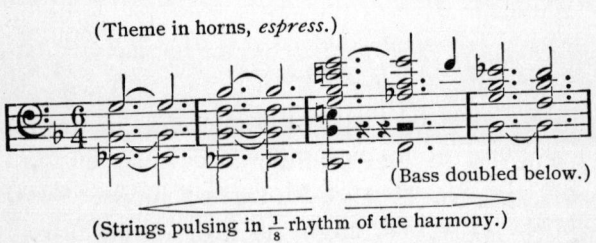

(Theme in horns, *espress.*)

(Bass doubled below.)

(Strings pulsing in $\frac{1}{8}$ rhythm of the harmony.)

with new swing, with moving tenderness. It is as if the melodies had exchanged humors. The sweetly quaint second, in sad distress, is consoled by a new soothing strength of the erst ominous motto, and is followed with the same cheer of oboes.

Through untroubled cadence we come to a mysterious strain of first theme, soon darkening in hue of minor, in various figures gliding down

BRAHMS' THIRD SYMPHONY

in shadowy chase, suddenly broken by the motto, as at first, heralding the main theme in full force and stirring freshness, and yet ever entwined with the dim sombre motive sounding below or hovering above, which it throws off in the clearer cadence. Then, as before, to more human, appealing, lesser melody, to distant tonal scene; again the sigh of wood echoed by low strings; now the full former grace and quaint charm of second theme with strange halting dance. Once more the chain of cadent phrases, through prism of colors, and finally home again to sweetly concluding strain in reversed melody. In breaks the motto, as before, and the dual phrases of themal fragments, so dim of origin, the quicker theme ascending, the arpeggios trickling down to meet the theme and crossing each other. For a time the latter gain the mastery; but the true climax is again reached with motto figures rising from the depth of strings while the harp phrase extends to more definite theme, which seems to have a dim relation to all others, and a clear one to none, though, mainly, it is of the text of the motto. In final verse comes the main theme in bright array, motto and all. Losing the gloomy sense of change, of human vicissitude,

BRAHMS' THIRD SYMPHONY

it is transfigured to one of steadily coursing joy.

The stress on a former brief figure of the subject

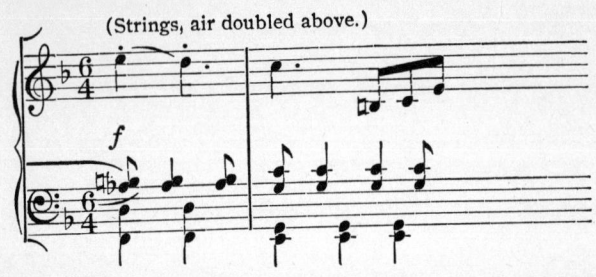

is now all brilliant with victory. The ending phrase, also from the first verse of main melody:

comes in fervent climax, with a new conclusive breadth and relevance, subtly sealing all former doubts. There is, too, a new turn at the end of

BRAHMS' THIRD SYMPHONY

intimate strain, in cradling swing,—a human touch before the last lay of fateful legend.

The *Andante* is in the simple classic vein hallowed by rare masters, that fearlessly begins in full tonic chord: stable, absolute, not wavering nor yearning; not at all romantic; settled, assured in placid repose; childlike and ingenuous. Beauty is foremost,—spontaneity is evident rather than intensity of message. And there is ever a sweet echoing cadence in deep brown of low strings:

BRAHMS' THIRD SYMPHONY

Everywhere is the frugal economy of highest art and soundest, purest thought.

In placid assurance of beauty the melody runs on with ever echoed cadence from resonant depths of the basses. With the finite quality of a tune, it yet spins along as in easy narrative, coming soon to climax of spontaneous though well-restrained fervor, an utterance that betrays as high a state of serene bliss as is known to mortal. The first strain of the lyric dwells and ends in the home tone, neighbor to that of the first *Allegro*. The second gently glides into the abutting key, the nearest resting-place. Thence it roams ever to farther limits, but suddenly swings through moving climax home again. Now the tune turns towards the region on the farther side with inverted answer, but quickly takes refuge once more in the main tone.

The melody now puts on a graceful ornament that enriches, but not disguises her individual beauty. To be sure, it is a mere phrase, a special glimpse of the first friendly strain that we catch here and there; then another, its answer, that looms up through the shifting tonal light in dim minor. The two strains, indeed, sing a duet of gloom and cheer until the former vanishes,

BRAHMS' THIRD SYMPHONY

and the sombre call is heard far down in basses, ever descending in darker depth. Whence emerges a song of the same fibre in clarinet and fagot, in plaintive appeal, taken up by horn and

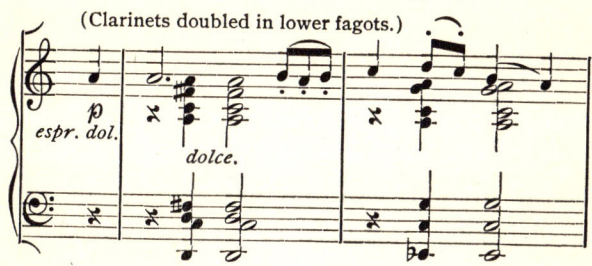

flute. As they end in mournful cadence, the neglected strings enter with new human note of soothing appeal:

With no outer relation, it is the meaning of essential, intrinsic contrast of answering solace. Taken up by wood, and carried on by strings with further answer in the wood, the whole is a melodic poem of its own, with just the quality lacking in the main verse, a touch of intimate romance gliding in hushed groping through dim changing tones to the first theme. But this has caught some of the personal quality as it moves in low strings, while the higher hover in wavering suit above.

The charm of placid pace, in Brahms, is greatly helped by a new cunning of richly varied rhythm. In the interweaving of two waving strains that differ in the pulse of smallest beat (where one has two, the other three) there is a gentle clash, a wealth of trembling motion, with all serenity of separate voices. The melody, too, is more of song; leaves the staid periods and soars freely through urgent, even passionate, sequence of the first phrase, losing in its romantic guise most of the earlier semblance; and so through fresh tonal scene:

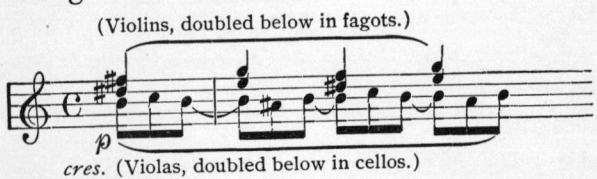

(Violins, doubled below in fagots.)

cres. (Violas, doubled below in cellos.)

But soon the answering motive appears as before and rears a strong climax, and brings us

BRAHMS' THIRD SYMPHONY

gradually to the impersonal humor of the first melody.

In the free play of initial motive, we notice the kinship even of this phrase with the former answer,* until it seems that Brahms is all built on the atomic plan, where the whole can be dissected to one bit or motive of central thought. This is wonderfully true of his Second Symphony.

Here the last-quoted phrase in its rhythmic and harmonic variations betrays this basic unity, —finally strikes the first melody, in whimsical rhythmic change of original motive:

(Woodwind, doubled above and below.)

espress. ma dolce.
(Chords in brass; obligato of $\frac{1}{16}$ notes in strings.)

Again the glorious classic grace of Melian Venus. Instead of the old echoes of low strings, the clarinets answer in spirited strain. Indeed, the whole has now a more glowing air of transfigured beauty and more fervent freedom of utterance. At the end of the tune comes the epilogue,—if that can come before the last verse or last act. Freed from staid pace, swinging aloft

---

* See page 339.

BRAHMS' THIRD SYMPHONY

on the last bit of cadence to bold Gothic heights, it seems to translate the cold classic grace to our warmer Teuton sense, and then commend to us a final verse of the poem.

Third Movement. The second movement is certainly the reflective,—that is, it has least of the dance. In this sense the second and the third are directly opposed. The third has a distinct dance swing,—not merely the rhythm of all music.

But what does this mean to us, if it is not merely a technical matter? It is this: all dances are national,—of here or there: Hungarian, Teutonic, Celtic, or Slavic. The dance is opposed to the pure lyric of Andante. It is necessarily ingenuous; in a sense, it lacks mood, or, at least, consciousness of mood. In a way, it has not the element of individuality for true mood,—the national sense prevents.

This element is a function of the third movement more than any other. It is naturally the usual channel of humor; but it need not be. A dance need not be merry. The sarabande is a type almost of pathos; the minuet, of stately grace. The most tender vein may steal into the Trio of dance, old or new, as of a Bach gavotte. A certain barcarolle feeling has here a

BRAHMS' THIRD SYMPHONY

special place. It must be unreflective, of folk or national rather than of individual hue.

If the third movement is looked to for humor, it is certainly not found here, in spite of the *tempo poco allegretto*. In this respect, of strict category of mood each in place, this symphony is out of the reckoning. It is possible we may find a humor elsewhere, and thus make good the apparent lack. We must not forget that the third movement was of old a dance, that the dance became the national channel for pure merriment or profounder mirth. Technically, the dance is ever in place.

It is possible that the scherzo is too rigidly an element of symphony. We have seen Mendelssohn miss a footing here. The scherzo was Beethoven's own typical creation. It suited his special humor far more than Schubert's. Indeed, there is no subjective humor of musician to compare with Beethoven's, save Schumann's, and even with the latter the profound sardonic element is wanting.

There is no doubt that, from the traditional point, humor is wanting in this symphony of Brahms, and not merely negatively. All but the Andante are overcast with sombre clouds. Serenity is confined to the second movement.

BRAHMS' THIRD SYMPHONY

Here in the *Allegretto*, with all lagging motion, the step of slow dance is somewhat strongly marked with a beat of the foot that has something of the German *Ländler*, again something of Slavonic in the late deferred accent:

But the gloom is thick overhead, and leaves but a shadow of the dance; even in the second melody, where for a moment we hope for a

BRAHMS' THIRD SYMPHONY

sunnier light, we have at most the odd shifting mood of first Allegro:

(With waving strings and sustaining woodwind.)

To be sure, after the friendly sequence there is suddenly a cheerful intimate descent in neighboring key of major, merely to be hurried again into the fatalism of first theme, now sung with more poignant feeling by all the treble voices. But in the third is a change of mood. Still in the old uncertain humor, there is much more of joy and trust, though of a timid kind, in the melody with its delicate hesitancy, with just a faint reminder of dance in the pace:

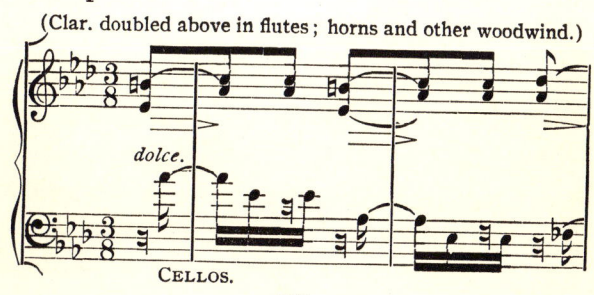

(Clar. doubled above in flutes; horns and other woodwind.)

BRAHMS' THIRD SYMPHONY

This vanishes completely in a kind of postscript of the tune, where all formality of swaying dance is dropped in direct tender appeal, crowned with fervent climax of trustfulness. To be sure, in the rehearsing it is all hushed by the nearing gloom of the first tune. We have heard of a Death's dance. Though there is nothing of the kind here, there is yet a clear tinge of doom, of dim Fate, about the main melody. Once more followed by the second, of uncertain hue, the subject ends in an extended appeal of moving pathos, like a last burst for deliverance, with a final resignation.

Last Movement. Our symphony is thus so burdened with stern gloom that we shall need a strong balance of cheer. Humor seems banished, dethroned from its abode. The only refuge is the *Andante*,—to be sure, of calm serene beauty and assurance. Even there we saw a stress of

BRAHMS' THIRD SYMPHONY

the one mournful bit of the main tune, and out of it grew the sad second. Though wavering long, it surely settled into sweet contentment. We are used to thinking of the Andante as the true key, its humor as the final mood, leaving to the Allegros a more tempestuous utterance, the first in achieving, the last in the triumph.

We must not forget, however, that in our first movement uncertain fitfulness was really conquered by a clear spirit; the minor yielded at last to the major. We must note, too, the meaning of the alternation in mood of the movements themselves, sombre *allegretto* succeeding serene *andante*.

What, then, shall we make of this barbarous war-tune, ruthless in rough minor, that is softly growling in low violins and bassoons with firm, rapid step:

(Unison theme, doubled in two lower 8ves.)
STRINGS AND FAGOTS.
Allegro.

p e sotto voce.

BRAHMS' THIRD SYMPHONY

answered in equally harsh mode and grim, halting pace?

It is certainly all o'ercast, ill-boding for final cheer. As the melody soars along in higher flight, among the woodwind, it wings a freer course, with chance pauses that give new and bolder rhythm,—again answered haltingly. Now follows, in strings and lower wood, a phrase in darkest hues of minor-major, with still a tinge of war-call as it is heralded and backed by hollow notes of low brass:

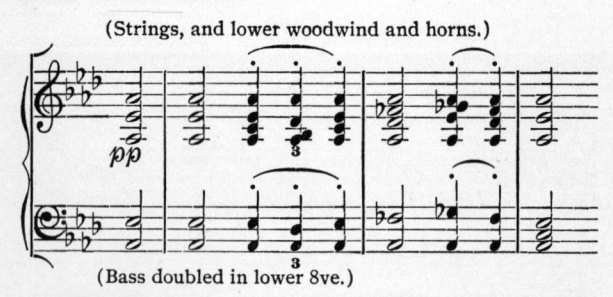

Full of temper as it is, it seems no integral element, a mere chance strain between verses of

BRAHMS' THIRD SYMPHONY

the theme, a certain disputation on the first, mainly on the second motive. Here, by a fine reversing of the answer, is reared upon the modest bass a powerful climax, where, to the halting but insistent inquiry, a broad conclusive response comes marching down in double file from the heights:

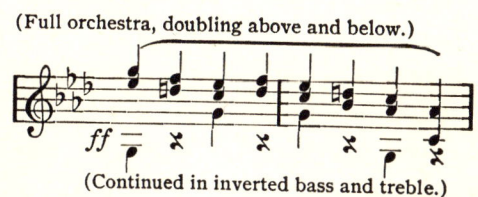

(Full orchestra, doubling above and below.)

(Continued in inverted bass and treble.)

And here is the heart of the movement, the spot where, conscious striving escaped, a direct thought brings best melody of utterance. Still as the march is kept in striding basses, and violins sound lightly

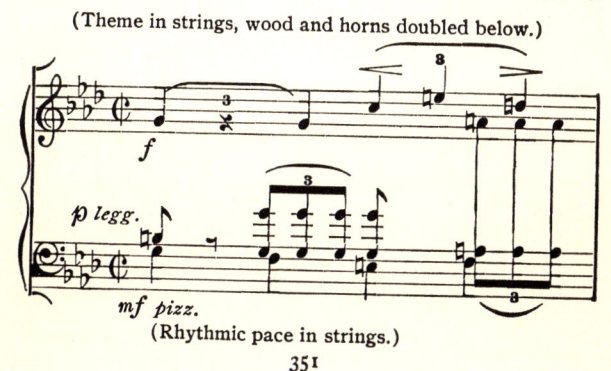

(Theme in strings, wood and horns doubled below.)

(Rhythmic pace in strings.)

BRAHMS' THIRD SYMPHONY

a constant tremulous call, cellos strike a cheery tune in curiously new swing, strongly and broadly crossing the strict stride of marching basses.

All in bright major it sings, and with no trace of sombre shadow. As the air now reaches high wood and strings, it is like brilliant sun glittering

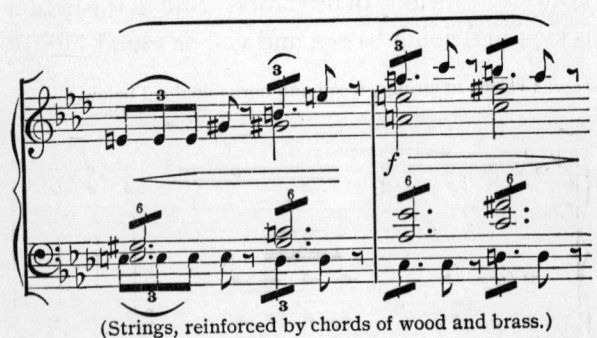

(Strings, reinforced by chords of wood and brass.)
(See page 353, line 6.)

on marching helmets and waving plumes, the

BRAHMS' THIRD SYMPHONY

vibrant call of trumpets still distantly blended in the war-song.

And the tune has a way of winding through indefinite turns, like constant thread of story or unending line of warriors. Presently a longer curve of cadence appears, and, recurring, soon presses all the verses into its unison strain in full acclaim, leading into a second big climax with similar hammer-thuds:

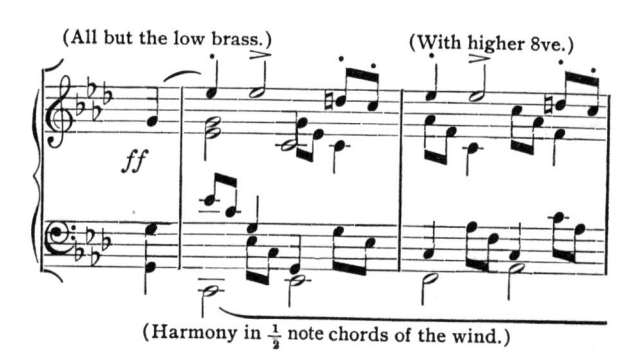

(All but the low brass.) (With higher 8ve.)

(Harmony in $\frac{1}{2}$ note chords of the wind.)

BRAHMS' THIRD SYMPHONY

that grew in earlier crisis out of the answer of main theme. Indeed, throughout, the first motive of the theme gives melodic fibre; the second or answer is bone of contention, meat of discussion. But in the last climax we seem to see the new-gotten phrase stealing over the bass in big broad notes. There is, to be sure, a new thud of accent on the second beat, 'mid richer

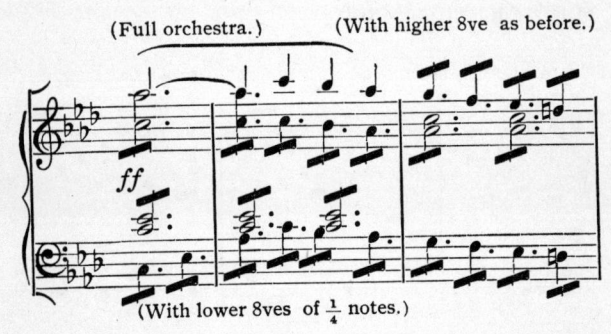

setting of low tonal background, with new swing of blows. But presently the old stress on first and third re-enters in response. At the height of battle a quick phrase of former bits, doubled in speed, relieves the strain.

Once again the battle rages to the inspiring height, and again, on quicker phrases, tempers down to a semblance of first theme in distant tonal quarter,—but merely for a moment, min-

BRAHMS' THIRD SYMPHONY

gled with other war-cries. Here, again, is a rough snatch of it; there, high in woodwind, a lengthened call of its first notes. At last the strife simmers down to the original tune in the wood, all in the hush of twilight; and now beautiful is the answer, transformed in gait, in speed, and in mood. Almost prayer-like the former trip now sounds in solemn choral notes with hopeful calls:

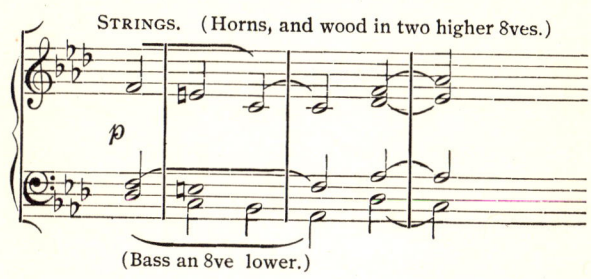

And the main tune goes playfully whispering on, with varying tricks of accompanying figures, that somehow take away the old sting and gloom. Again the solemn cheer of answer; now the latter sings as new song high in the wood, while low violins, like fire-flies, are darting here and there with chance snatches of the subject. The light is mysterious, flickering 'twixt gloom and cheer. Suddenly high strings loudly

BRAHMS' THIRD SYMPHONY

sound the solemn strain, and high wood ring out the quicker snatches:

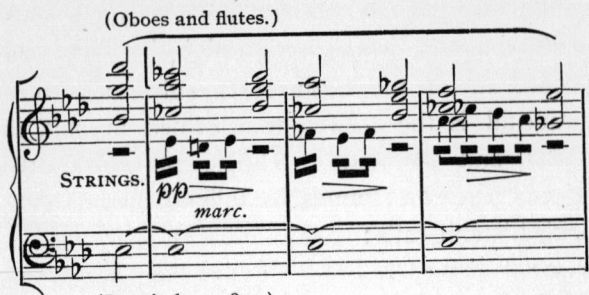

(Oboes and flutes.)

STRINGS. *pp marc.*

(Bass in lower 8ve.)

each alternating with lowest voices of opposite group. The hymn gains a new stride of march, with, too, the continuous turn of new sequence; the quick snatch becomes threatening blast of trumpet.

At this nodal point two sustained tones ring out alone of the hymn, dimly familiar, while, below, strings are coursing

f ben marc.   *ben marc.*   *ben marc.*   *f ben marc.*

BRAHMS' THIRD SYMPHONY

on a figure that seems a quick mockery of an earlier slower one. Then, broadly across the quick woof of their motion, here is the solemn second theme, which we thought to have dismissed. It is all a new poetic guise of ancient round of tunes.

Of significant charm is the comfortable conflict of these two paces, the quick triplet playing about the big broad skip of second tune, like a great mountain seen through the laced veil of fleeting mists. So slowly ponderous is the quaint jog of the tune that we do not at first feel the outline, which all recurs as long before, save more freely extended in rhythm and in sequence of tonal scenes, all brighter than before, finally transfigured with blazing halo of dazzling scene and crowned with all-cheering close.

Here is the same rearing of climax on the insistent inquiry of halting fragment, again with the broad conclusive response marching down in double file. Only it is all more assured and exulting. The main theme no longer steals softly into the midst, but boldly rings out on eminent heights. Besides, there is the reversing of tonal scenes, the clear return homeward towards the

BRAHMS' THIRD SYMPHONY

original regions. This is best marked by the swinging, brilliant war-song, which again comes marching past with the old glittering maze of movement and ever surer air of victory. It ends, as before, with a long curve of cadence, and leads again to the climax of hammer-blows. The whole battle is fought once more, and again, on reaching the heights with a fragment, simmers down to the whole of main melody in mysterious light, and, strangely, in the quaint jog of third tune. Soon it reaches a more familiar spot, and here, amid the same richer setting of background, is that freer flight of the melody, pausing at chance will, as of old.

But the setting is infinitely richer, of deep beauty of wood-sounds, and there is a sense, in the melodic flight, of work done and reward well earned. The strife is all o'er. From this point the whole mood is changed; the feeling is strong of fulfilment, of transfigured purpose. Quicker phrases are merely the placid, subdued company of nature-sounds attending the final conclusive refrain and assertion of theme, now past contention.

So the main melody now enters, losing its old

BRAHMS' THIRD SYMPHONY

speed, like chorale hymn, with soft tenderness, ending with a higher strain of new, serene confidence. As the theme mutters again in low bass,—now a little faster,—echoed in high wood, a strain of ancient melody

(Motto in oboes.)

STRINGS.

(Theme in horns and cellos.)

gives sweetly comforting answer. It is the motto of the big beginning of the symphony, cleared of turbid gloom, in simple soothing conclusion. The rest seems a mere dying away of the trembling nature-sounds, though there are pauses of solemn chords, and here is a strain in slow trip that soars aloft with strong appeal. We had not thought there was in our second melody of darkest hues such a potency of sweetness and light. Still the pausing chords come. And now the same strain descends from its lofty perch. Though full of solace, it somehow has in the

BRAHMS' THIRD SYMPHONY

very end a clear tinge of the same flickering mood we saw at the beginning of the whole work, and the same oscillation of light is kept as the basses still mutter the theme through the whispering branches, until all dies away in the clear brightness of original tone. The constant dual strife ends in serene rest.

BRAHMS' FOURTH SYM-PHONY

THE fourth of Brahms' symphonies stands opposed to the others. It has less of the subtle interweaving of basic motive. It seems more of a return to romanticism, freer in scheme and spirit; motion is an element more than intricate design. The harmony, or organic character, is less of visible figures, however obscure. After all, the reappearance of actual motto is not the only test of unity, however minute the phrase may be. There may be most intimate harmony by reason of the relation or contrast purely of the moods of the movement. In a way it is like chemical and mechanical structure. You may start any mechanical separation and approach the chemical solution in the sense of smallest particles; but you will never reach the final constituents. So it may be the best symphonic connection is an invisible one, an inner relation of mood-purpose.

We are struck with the pre-eminent motion

BRAHMS' FOURTH SYMPHONY

of the first *Allegro* (*non troppo*). It is like getting into a vehicle that instantly is going its delightful pace of speedy journey. The actual tune is secondary:

(Theme doubled in lower 8ves.)

(STRINGS, WOOD AND HORNS.

In fact, the tune lacks rhythmic variation, and leaves the motion supreme with mere tinge of air. It is, indeed, less tune than motion, a thread of movement that becomes more melodic as it proceeds, works itself into song,—a musical story with special episodes.

After the first period, the last cadence suggests the variation of theme in the second, with more fluent note throughout. Towards the end, a jerk of notes, from close of main tune, has much sway:

BRAHMS' FOURTH SYMPHONY

gets into the bass, goes jolting through the whole chorus, is softened by prettily rustling lower figure.

A firm, assuring conclusion:

moving in its fervor, leads suddenly to the startling second melody, of bold, broad, rhythmic curve, that we have a way of finding in Brahms:

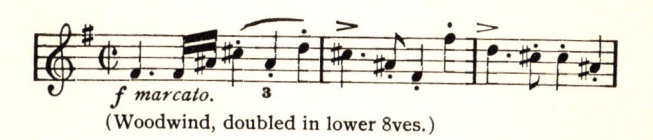

(Woodwind, doubled in lower 8ves.)

A breezy air of resolution is here, not the usual episode of feminine grace that is almost traditional in the second subject of *Allegro*, so that the beginning is but a setting in motion towards the more incisive theme. Again there is a sharp jerking motive, which goes driving along between the lines of the smoother, sustained an-

BRAHMS' FOURTH SYMPHONY

swer, that first sounds in cellos, then climbs to the heights and holds sway in treble violins:

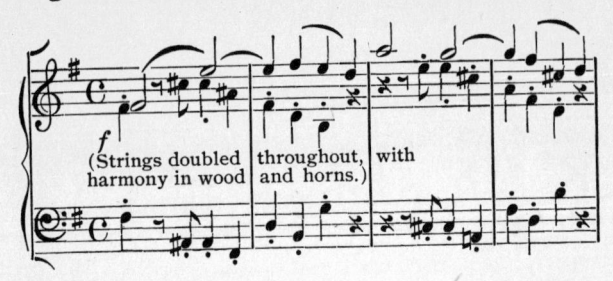

(Strings doubled harmony in wood throughout, with and horns.)

while the bouncing motive stirs the foam of the stream of song and returns to the bold swing of second melody, knocking its uncouth rhythm against the regular beat, and crashing its relentless harmonies against the prevailing basic scheme:

(Bass doubled below.)

all an utterance of resistless stress, seeking and needing obstacles for true progress.

BRAHMS' FOURTH SYMPHONY

The hostile tide exhausted, the stream runs pelting on in the current of the evener pace (answered between the choirs):

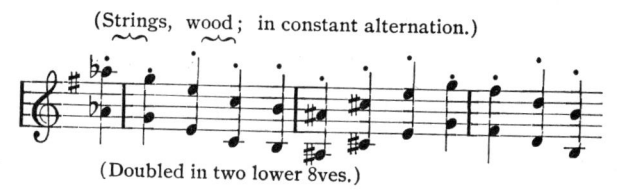

(Strings, wood; in constant alternation.)

(Doubled in two lower 8ves.)

which takes us back with strange reminder to the very beginning of the first tune, and knits all together in onward drive of action. Again, all is concluded in freer singing strain (built still on the jerking motion):

(Strings, wood and horns; tune and harmony in 8ves.)

(Bass an 8ve lower.)

but standing on the broad swinging rhythm in triple time that marks the boldness of second theme. It is answered by a strain of softer, more appealing hue of all, in more mincing

BRAHMS' FOURTH SYMPHONY

(Clar., doubled above in oboe, and below in horns.)

(Strings, *p legg.* sustained by fagots.)

pace; but, broken only for a moment, it resumes and leads to modest, idyllic bit of tune, like violet that is the hidden gem of the woods:

WOOD AND HORNS.

pp ma ben marc.

STRINGS.

BRAHMS' FOURTH SYMPHONY

somehow with more sweetness than all the prouder blossoms of song, introduced merely by solemn lull of wind, dim call of trumpets, and mystic swirl of strings. After the same ceremony it sings again bold and loud, now echoed by firm call of brass. Apart from our simile it has a flavor of woods in its haunting notes.

Now it rears overpowering climax, tune and call all sounding together, and in the bass the constant stride of even march, until, breaking again into the jerking pace, we return through gradually familiar sounds to main theme as at first. The woodland call has a beautiful way of coming nearer, stronger, and clearer at each new verse, and each time in a new light.

Now the first close (of main melody) has a peculiar charm as it refuses to stray again to

BRAHMS' FOURTH SYMPHONY

strange scene, nestling intimately about the home tone:

(Strings, with sustaining chords in horns and clarinets.)

(Doubled below in basses.)

Pretty variations of the subject sing on, which now gambol about and play together.

All the smaller derived phrases show more and more a likeness to original theme, which it were dry to point in detail, varying in speed or changed in outline. Again the sweet nestling in the bosom of the cadence, to be sure, of remoter tone.

The main theme now assumes the guise of first conclusive strain * in sombre minor, and presently rings out in hammer-blows the varied phrase (of main theme), all changed from mild grace to rude quarrel with lower voices in strings, that

---

* See page 363.

BRAHMS' FOURTH SYMPHONY

come up in contrary figures, all of brilliant countermarching manœuvre, hostile though ordered, while the jerking motive breaks in from above in high wood in rough contempt of other measure:

STRINGS, WOOD AND HORNS.

Now the parties in the strings exchange retorts. All the while the middle voices of violas, allied with fagots, have echoed on the heels of the theme, wherever they heard it. So the great altercation goes on, ever with new alignment of forces.

Suddenly a hushed semblance of second theme is whispered in strings, a mere playful phase, the voices in low strings fleeing in fugual chase across the scene. Others in high wood pass in similar view, now against deep background of swirling

BRAHMS' FOURTH SYMPHONY

strings with the former solemn pauses; vague bits of the subject are dropped in the wood, answering in new tonal scene. Again the playful hushed chase in the wood of strains of the second theme. Now, loud and fierce, strings and brass shout threatening cries in the tune of the gentle hunting call, but, through it, striving for the second theme, which they finally reach and answer now with more effective strain:

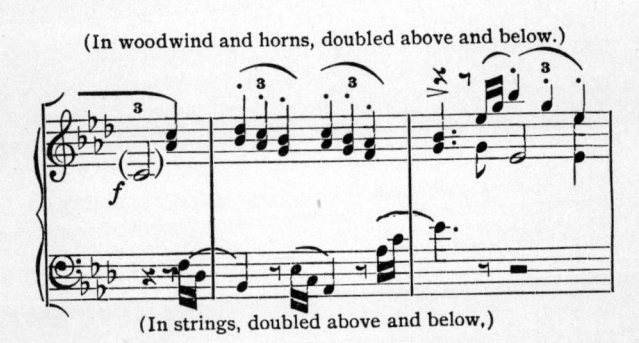

(In woodwind and horns, doubled above and below.)

(In strings, doubled above and below.)

with the broad freedom of triplet pace which is carried along in other voices and holds its rough course in spite of main subject, singing in obscure guise in even rhythm. The answer, with the quicker figure, is a series of tonal perches, alighting ever in a new quarter with the same hushed motive:

BRAHMS' FOURTH SYMPHONY

Reaching home at last, the little motive is lengthened and the main theme is heralded in long notes as of motto, interrupted again by long pauses of chords and rich swirling strings.

Brahms has a tendency to make us see bits of the theme even where it is not, like seeing the sun with closed eyes; you hardly know where to stop deriving.

The whole song of the themes begins now, as at first, save at the very beginning, where the first motives are clearly reversed,—as if to show again that the meat is in the movement, not in the tune. Conclusive strain comes as before, but of course the tonal journey is homewards, not afield. This must always be the difference of the first and last parts of the *Allegro*.

The design of the whole is new; we have lost our old order of themes restated and dis-

BRAHMS' FOURTH SYMPHONY

cussed in proper places. The main subject, we have seen, flows along in full course, doubling as it pleases, leading on in calm progress to the stormier second, where the motion of the first merely helps to mass the climax with episodes of bright soaring strain, with gentle appealing answer and hushed call of hunt, broken by solemn pauses with swirling strings. As the call sounds in strong blast, the main crisis is reached on the text of the virile second theme. As the first returns, its own special crisis now arrives on its own motives, followed by a lesser on the second. Hence a short blending of both subjects leads to the last statement, where the full climax of second melody is not allowed.

We cannot but note the difference between the Schumann method of broad, romantic lines, mere connection by contrast and intrinsic relation, and Brahms' minute but concrete kinship of contrapuntal fragments of one pattern. This seems like a new plan for a bigger design, of which, maybe, the poet is to come later.

The whole discussion is not formal, with duly repeated subjects. Rather it seethes in the wake of each, rising to a climax on one and then on the other. The first, instead of leader,

BRAHMS' FOURTH SYMPHONY

is often rather herald; or it forms placid lulls between the storms of the second, though to be sure it has its determined and overpowering triumph.

At the end, indeed, it rises after lesser crisis of second to a last word of magnetic virility and convincing power. But, before, the new answer of second melody* (the first has lost its function in the later stress) has a moment of absolute unanswerable sway.

The main melody then asserts dominance in lordly, stentorian bass. No greater musical symbol is there of complete conquest than melodic possession of bass. In the second line it breaks into uneven pace in insolent defiance. A new height is reached on the short jerk of motive. Twice the fine old conclusion tries its *envoi*. But still echoes and hallooes the first motive of main theme in a frenzy of assertion, and the battle is won.

Ever in kind of rondo fashion returns the first melody; never, as in sonata, is there a good cadence on the second. There is not the duality of the sonata. It is the monarchy of song or

---

*See page 370.

BRAHMS' FOURTH SYMPHONY

rondo, one prevailing idea,—εἰς κοῦρανος. The second theme, however powerful, is never enduring, has not even a foothold or close of its own, but falls back to the firmer footing of first; the stress of the former is ever resolved in the resistless, placid motion of the latter.

Second Movement. It is a frequent way of Brahms to come through gloom and desert to light and cheer. The best must come last; we must begin with the night to know the day; to fly the highest you must start the lowest. Here, in *andante moderato*, the strangest sense comes o'er us with the strain of horns:

enforced by woodwind. They take us back to darkest edge of doom-tempered world.

As curious fact the tones are of ancient mode, not merely of oldest church or catacomb, but of Stoic Greek song, Phrygian, or Doric.

When enter the clarinets, the gulf is suddenly bridged, the gentle strings sing the same tune, on the same bass, to be sure:

BRAHMS' FOURTH SYMPHONY

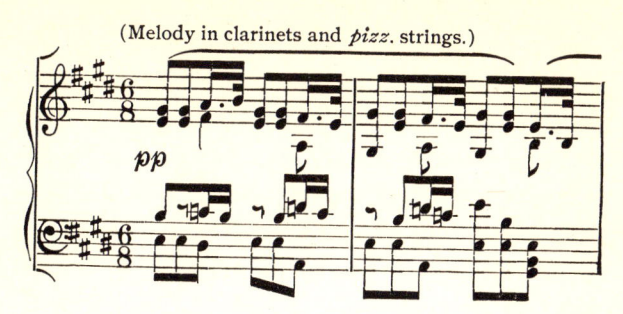

(Melody in clarinets and *pizz.* strings.)

but with all the human sweetness that since those ancient days mankind has learned to feel, and to utter mainly in obedient tones.

But ever the stern color steals across the harmonic scene. The answer, however, has all of the warmer glow of Teuton folk-song:

STRINGS AND WOOD.

Suddenly the old tones ring out in the woodwind, somehow less dismal, bolder, ascending in brighter tonal flight. From the height, descending uncertainly, the same sudden warmth of

BRAHMS' FOURTH SYMPHONY

modern cheer is felt again, as the strings again sing the true theme with a new, firmer touch. The answer now comes with more speaking appeal, with more intimate contrast, ending with complete assurance. The second verse is but a freer phase of the first, simple and childlike of humor:

(Strings, with more sustained figure in woodwind; horns.)

buoyant as it gently soars on waving motive in joyous wind, alighting soon with firm tread of sure content in exultant burst of all voices. An answer sings in piping wood:

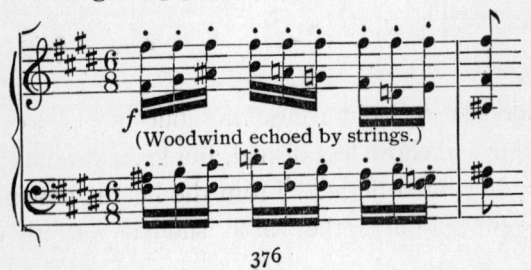

(Woodwind echoed by strings.)

BRAHMS' FOURTH SYMPHONY

in quaint, quick trip of tones, in shifting prism of colors, with something of brilliant triumph, almost of savage glee. It is echoed in strings and carried higher and stronger, but descends in solemn strides to the true second subject, all changed of mood, almost of simple pleading:

(Strings and fagot, with obligato in $\frac{1}{16}$ notes in high violins.)

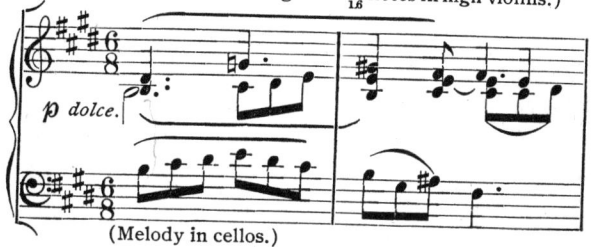

p dolce.

(Melody in cellos.)

which sounds in simplest lines in cellos.

But the accompanying strings lend the special touch, the high violins of gliding figure, the seconds of responsive and subordinate strain, all of richly changing harmonic color. The melody seems to have the Schumann trait of threading story, woven mainly in responsive voices, when the fagots enter as leaders. Strange how opposite the feeling in these succeeding themes, though really of the same fibre.

A speaking force has this latest theme, now in fagots and strings. At the close an expressive

BRAHMS' FOURTH SYMPHONY

phrase is handed from voice to voice midst the steps of the tune. But the brief motive soon expands and takes full possession, in echoing and answering voices of the leisurely dulcet cadence that leads back to first theme.

But now, out of the phrases of cadence, has blossomed a figure which lightly hovers, twining about the song of the melody, softening away the harsh lines. Through this contact, and also of its own change, the tune has thawed out its chillier harmonies in serener sunshine of modern experience, and glows with true Gothic love of kind. Striking how music in its modes and harmonies, ancient and recent, thus shows the increasing humanity, the diminishing spirit of destruction, so that the Hercules of to-day must exert his strenuous power all in work of greater blessing to the race, so that a Napoleon ideal of rise and power by destroying action is all fading out of fashion's glamour.

The wonderful magic of music is to reflect this, so that we feel instantly the change of spirit in the change of modes, and know in a

BRAHMS' FOURTH SYMPHONY

flash the inevitable intent of the poet.* Here the transition is absolutely convincing—from stern ancient gloom to modern genial sense of kind—in the poet's varying chords. True, later there is a return to some of the uncertainty, and here rings out the original rough blast of theme. Somehow it has less of chill gloom. It is all in the clear sunny atmosphere of high wood, and there is an electric pulse of accompanying motion above and below. So the sense is bold but hopeful, and soon the theme threads its sequence to clearer tonal light.

And now ring out the sharp clashes of eccentric figure on the quick jerk of the motive, now higher and ever bolder, in keener blasts of the rude theme and ever in brighter flashes of glinting light. The savagery is gone, but the vigor is all there and transfigured. And, finally, the former quaintly clattering phrase raises its war-shout once more at the loudest and brightest, suddenly hushing to most expressive verse of the second theme of appealing beauty. It sings first in rich timbre of sentient strings, answered then

---

* If scientific proof is needed, it is at hand in the recent confirmation of modern harmonies by their conformity to newly discovered laws, such as those of Helmholtz.

BRAHMS' FOURTH SYMPHONY

in full chorus with big sonorous double stride, the air ever a step behind the bass. Once more the strings sing it simply, and the wood answer in touching response from the first strain of main theme, and the clarinets send a sigh from the very heart of it, to which the close (of main subject) comes as truest and surest solace.

In the last word the theme once more sings out in full, as at first; the bitterness is cured in a new way, not softened to modern sense and rounded off, but in its ancient lines transfigured in a true light and verified as a true whole. For the old tones stand as before, but a new base is found for them, and thence a pervading (tonal) light, that justifies and harmonizes all.

Third Movement. A tinge of the old stern mode is in the breezy dash of scherzo song that bursts in big array of voices:

TUTTI.
Allegro giocoso.

(Horns in lower 8ves.)

(Bass doubled below.)

BRAHMS' FOURTH SYMPHONY

It is all vigor typified, idealized, the full sense of freedom, strong and withal a bubbling spring of quick action. In the very beginning there is a type of rock-like power, that gets its secret somehow in a turn of chord that again takes us back for the nonce to grim ancient mode, to the old plagal close, as the schoolmen have it, of the stern Amen, avoiding the soft cadence of modern dominant that slides easily and comfortably to the main tune. Nothing can exceed the bold contempt for all modern smooth trick of chord in the sweep of these primeval harmonies. Heavy fall the blocks of chords in the first phrase of theme, plunging sheer into the resounding deep. Light of spring the answer dances off in chords of curious ponderous grace, where one playful motive is eminent:

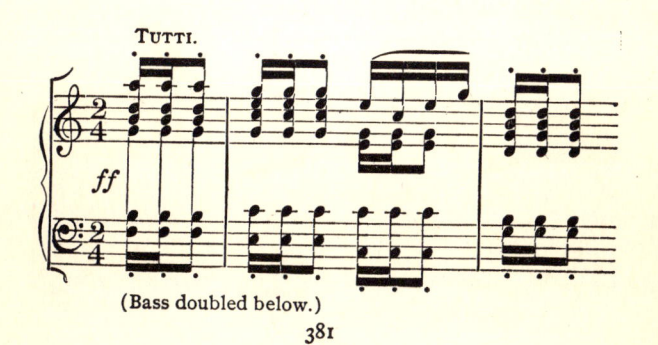

(Bass doubled below.)

BRAHMS' FOURTH SYMPHONY

On sweeps the song with surging figure of after-phrase, in bass:

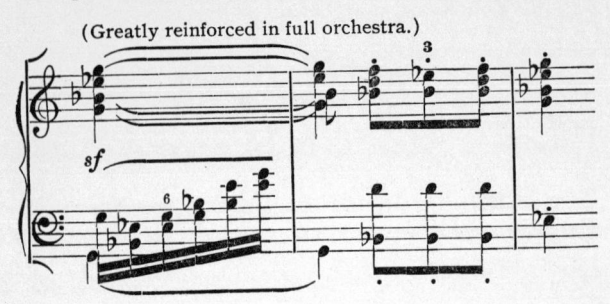

then united in all; repeated with some basic change. In childlike sport the answer now glides along with no heavy chords, mere skipping steps of strings. Another jolly retort is rung between low strings and higher, on simplest phrase from text of main theme, while highest violins are singing merrily on in a skipping answer, and finally draw all the strings in a scampering run back to the main theme, but reversed.

Topsy-turvy it is, basses have the air, the old tune is bass, and it sounds as fine, even merrier. The answer, too, is jolly, upside down. The outer line of tune has, after all, less to do with it; somewhere between the rhythm and har-

BRAHMS' FOURTH SYMPHONY

mony lies the magic of the melody. On the
answer trips softly now through shades, halting

Strings, Wood and Horns.

(See page 382, line 10.)

and groping, when in bursts the cheery song of
second theme:

Strings.

p grazioso.

pizz, Basses.

like an old dance or *rigaudon*, where, by way of
answer, the wood run mockingly off the scene.
The glee goes unbroken; the wood come run-

BRAHMS' FOURTH SYMPHONY

ning back with the same silly laughter. Then the dance changes step in mincing pace, demurely hushing and slowing with eccentric skip. Very prettily it is softened down to solemn glide of pious suppliant, and the tune is hymn.

soon even stern chant, suddenly clashing, vigorous main theme again; but with a new sting and fire in the dancing retort, finally rollicking off with a magnificent mocking stride of first theme in the bass:

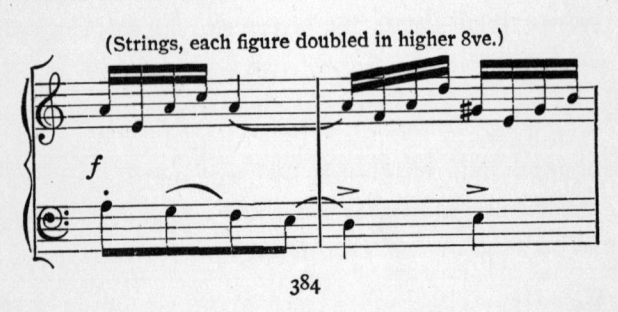

BRAHMS' FOURTH SYMPHONY

But the answer holds the main flow with slight departure in pace and tonal mood. Indeed, the rollicking motive

saucily rises to learned fugue with real stirring effect, but soon dances off on empty trip.

In bursts on high the first theme, reversed, in full blast, with strange turn of tune and bass; it is answered in loudest strings, all in hollow themal tones. After all, it is mere pranks, playing with the idea of the tune in many phases, fast and slow, and both together; and a little of the answer returns with inverted figure and the bass striding mockingly as before, hushing to softest whisper.

There is ever, even here, that magnificent relevance of all detail, the wonderful logic peculiar to Brahms.

High in woodwind the main theme now pipes timidly as in choir-loft of cathedral; follow the solemn lulls of chords oft repeated. Out of them emerges what seems a new tune of soothing air in simplest lines, ascending and descending:

BRAHMS' FOURTH SYMPHONY

It has, to be sure, a sense of harking back, but it has all a verse here of its own, a new color of mood. And the further thread is, perhaps, the best as the melody glides simply, far down in murmuring strings,—singing drowsily its answer on high, descending in the wood. So the plan of question and solacing answers continues the discourse, when, on rude blast, breaks in the old after-phrase,* roughly showing kinship with this new strain, the very same tune with some slight changes of pace. Triumphantly it moves out of the moment of confidence and lightly back to the merry tripping of the answer, again with the retorts between high strings and low, on text of theme with all the old scampering back to the full main tune. But this is now inverted, nay, much extended before the answer comes merrily

---

* See page 382.

BRAHMS' FOURTH SYMPHONY

tumbling with quivering, prancing step, in full, heavy cohorts.

Just as before it hushes again to a lull and again the gay old dance of second theme sings its saucy tune. Instead of pious hymn, however, we are soon lashed (on the figure of a former retort*) into a sort of war-cry, which, mounting in its frenzy, does, at the very top, take on something of the former festive solemnity.

There is the most real simulation in music of actual dispute or discussion. It is, to be sure, reached only in symphony or sonata; and it seems to have been conceived mainly by the German mind. It is one of the highest touches in the art for power, not so much in itself alone as for accumulation and architecture. A real debate goes on here between motion of first theme in bass and a second on high, soon exchanging, of course. It seems to have the seed of unceasing flow. Indeed, it is in the nature of all debate that it must be stopped by force.

A new and firmer assurance is struck when horns take a hand; the tone is friendlier, too, though ever growing in strength. Presently this

---

*See page 385.

BRAHMS' FOURTH SYMPHONY

works into a hurly-burly on the quick motive, while, above, the wood slowly and definitely affirm the main theme of debate.

And at least one more festive refrain of all the first melody,—big swelling after-phrase, too, all freer now than ever, extending and varying without bondage of mere restatement, ending with conclusive strain of first phrase of main theme.

Finale. A wonderful drive, impetus, has this *passacaglia*,* a close thread of connection; everything of beauty is there; the one question still lingers: is it symphonic, at one with the rest? The fragmental working up in short-breathed spurts, almost gasps, like a doomed demon, a Sisyphus, is unlike the symphonic spirit so far as it leads nowhere, to no big climax, cannot in the nature of things, is, in a way, asthmatic, cannot accumulate energy, comes to a height too soon. The whole, indeed, is Titanic; Brahms is ever a Titan. Still, we begin to have glimpses of a form within a form.

It is not the slavish succession of theme or

---

* An ancient contrapuntal form, originally a dance, where the theme recurs in unbroken iteration.

BRAHMS' FOURTH SYMPHONY

bass that we must keep our curious eyes upon; it is rather the same drive that must come ever in different ways, like the historic attempt of the persistent Scot. To enjoy, you must get away from the idea of ground-bass.

The difference of *passacaglia* and mere variations lies here: in the latter there is no form but constant repetition; in the other there is room for a larger form, within which the lesser can ply its unceasing round. In a sense, the whole is in the first eight bars:

Allegro energico e passionato.

f
(All the wind.)
(Bass doubled below.)

But, again, you must look as much at the bass as at the melody; if you had to choose, the former is the more typical. Strangely, the theme is really no tune. Successions of notes are not all tunes. There is nothing of symmetry, or responsive balance. It is a mere series of blasts,

BRAHMS' FOURTH SYMPHONY

all in the wind, too; more an invocation, a kind of " Hear, O Israel!", a herald figure of more to come: " The Lord your God . . ." But see what happens. In sharp double thuds, this is, after all, the same strain, though more vehement, with the strings in strange, slamming, tardy ascent, on the heels of sturdy calls of the horns on the same note, clashing with the chords of the theme.

At last something like natural melody seems to flow in answer:

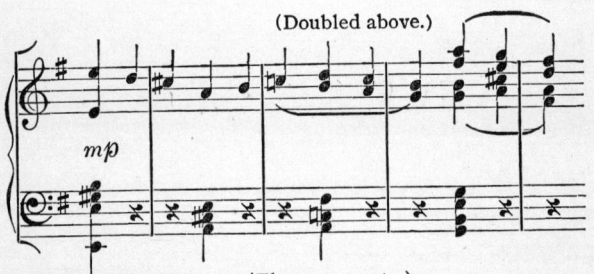

STRINGS AND HORNS. (Theme marcato.)

But it is curiously like fugal theme, repeated before it might blossom into a tune, coming to a certain climax, too, which, though brief, is fitting. Before its close, our sense is awake to a dim din from below. We feel rather than hear the actual course of the tune in steadily unsteady, eccentric pace, through all the new fabric above.

BRAHMS' FOURTH SYMPHONY

Then, in full band, sounds the unmistakable line of the theme high in treble of all the choirs, brass, wood, and strings.

So far is a clear alternation of subject in bass and treble. Now a livelier figure with vigorous, jolting gait sings above the tenor of the theme:

(The theme strengthened by fagots.)

and now a smooth one, very like the last, varied. As the strings surge upward, marking the latest phrase, the wood flow downward, some prettily breaking the even stream with smaller ripples. The persistent bass sings away on the old sonorous text, and still a new motive starts from the last word of cadence, but holds the same flowing pace.

So, on goes this strange progress. Like a stream it is, incessant, unexhausted, unchanging and ever-changing, ever and never the same, gain-

BRAHMS' FOURTH SYMPHONY

ing, too, and growing in its rough vigor. Only, it has one trait of the sea, as it rises in the climax

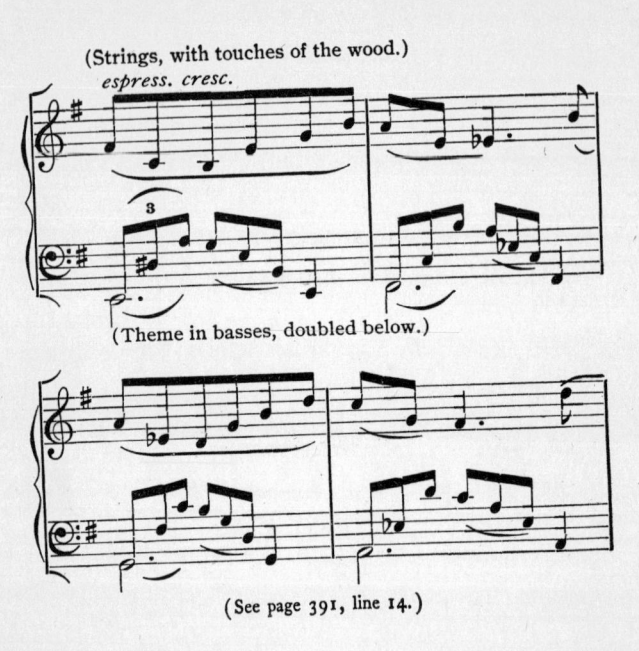

(Strings, with touches of the wood.)
espress. cresc.

(Theme in basses, doubled below.)

(See page 391, line 14.)

of each periodic pulse, like the waves advancing in groups.

As each wave has its crest, so there is a slow surging and massing through the series to a fierce height, and soon a lull, where low chords in strings are answered high in the hushed wood:

BRAHMS' FOURTH SYMPHONY

And still, with all disguise, the same essence of tonal idea, rising to its own climax.

After minor strains of gentle plaint and of playful longing, the *dolce* major has a great

(Melody *espressivo* in clarinets, then oboes.)

soothing charm. The melody plays daintily in snatches, tossed back and forth in pretty response between clarinet and oboe, while the viola has started with the foregoing phrase; the waving of low strings is important part, and the

BRAHMS' FOURTH SYMPHONY

pace is still kept from the previous verse. But where is our motive? See the top of every wave-beat (rising in each bar); the crests form the theme. Somewhere in the process you will see it; but never be too literal in its pursuit.

It may lie invisible in mere possible consonance. In other words, its spirit is present,—a wonderful quality, here, of the variation, where room is left as for invisible, sacred guest, as in ancient custom. You feel the presence in the air largely because you have made room for it. And in so far it is present, too, in your thought, which is all that counts.

Here comes the golden spot, as rich horns sound a deep-toned legend still in quaint halting pace:

(Trombones and fagots with arpeggio figure in low strings.)

The pace throughout changes but in infinitesimal step; the sense of high solemnity forbids. But the melody is warm and full of sympathy. There is still the tinge of the theme in the bass and

BRAHMS' FOURTH SYMPHONY

broken waves in low strings. Again the same melody sings; but more voices enter; all the brass sound the legend, topped by the woodwind, and the melody has greater sweetness and even passion.

Now the first stern chant sounds as at the beginning in full wind; but in the midst a more articulate phrase comes coursing down from high strings as if to give its own terser conclusion.

There is now a new nervous force in the strings trembling with action, as cellos hold the *cantus*, while aloft the woodwind play a melodious countertheme, rising ever more anxiously on ragged, eccentric rhythm, nearer the sun.

Now in lowest basses a new quarrel begins between low strings and high wood. This is the question:

(Strings, wood and brass, doubled above and below.)

(Trembling strings throughout.)

BRAHMS' FOURTH SYMPHONY

It is so interesting, vital, mastering, that we do not care to look for the undercurrent motive, though it must be somewhere in low violas. That matter settled, comes a further playful retort between the same groups. You would not guess in this game of hide-and-seek that the theme was staring at you in the first notes of every phrase; but it surely is not good to look too closely for this one literal element—you lose the whole scene. Disputation now merges in the vigorous onward drive, mainly of strings, in nervous triple action, where the wood merely give a clearer tinge to the outer line of theme. The motive is all implied.

Now the motion becomes the most rapid possible under sure control. In coursing streaks, strings and flutes tear up the scale, and the motive clearly stands out on the tip end of the figure. It is not possible more than faintly to suggest the fresh vigor of these succeeding chords, surprising, each time, in their bold completeness. At the end, in sudden whispering, the strings dart in lowest depths like frightened shadows, while the high wood break into clear chord above the rumbling below. Solemn, ominous it is in the blending light and shadow of

BRAHMS' FOURTH SYMPHONY

high pitch of choir of wood, singing in strange odd bits of rhythm against the steady wave of rumbling bass. But the two groups approach; at the end they exchange places and figures.

After the lull, of course, the storm breaks loose the more. Contrary figures start together from the midst of strings, the upper accenting the cantus. High in wood the waving motion continues. Great is the force of these figures, starting their impetus in phrases of two bars, each in magnificent clash, too, of differing rhythm, like companies of horse and foot, countermarching to one big tune or swing. At the end of the verse the motion is more tumultuous, the triplet canter dominates. Here is the phrase which has a familiar sound and surely carries us back to first verse after original statement, with its steady calls of trumpets answered in eccentric notes of theme. Only here the whole force of the band is in action, and the answering notes quiver in nervous triple rhythm.

And still the next verse comes as before, but with much greater force and power of motion. As before, there is a new melody above, answered fugally, and fitting to the lower cantus. We recognize the former course of tunes and phases;

BRAHMS' FOURTH SYMPHONY

but there is ever newer beauty, richer and fuller grace of motion, the lines of melody are more rounded, the harmonic color is warmer. Indeed, the added wealth of melody so prevails that you cannot swear it is the same verse recurring. The former sequence now grows shadowy. Here, in a beautiful duet in the tree-tops of the wood, seems an inversion of the first hushed verse,* in slow melodious answering calls, while below a former tuneful figure is flowing in the strings. And then this very duet is extended in mellow, speaking song of pervading beauty:

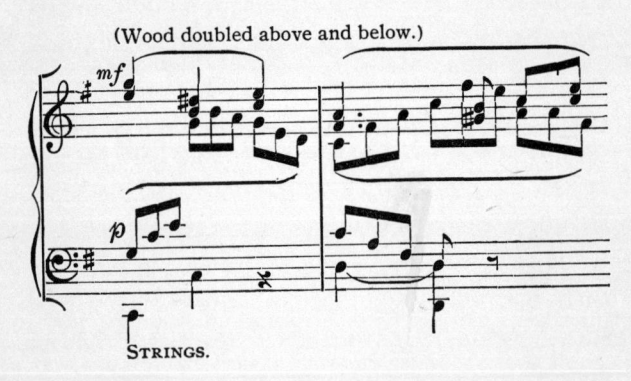

(Wood doubled above and below.)

STRINGS.

Follows a gentle verse of new naïve turn in short phrases, each sounding before it seems due,

---

* See page 392.

BRAHMS' FOURTH SYMPHONY

while strings stride softly downward in intervening beats:

(Woodwind, strengthened below.)

p dolce.

(*Pizz*, strings doubled above and below.)

In the next the striding strings, in loudest unison, take the lead in time and dignity, and are followed on their heels in canon fashion, while ringing groups shout the chords in the ragged intervals.

The storm has one more verse and breaks out at wildest in overwhelming chords of the brass, shouting the notes of the theme to the heavens, while the strings are coursing down the range of their harmonies like torrents from ever higher leaps. Soon even the waves meet from above and below in the stirred and flooded depths.

And we have said nothing of the Titanic force of these natural harmonies. At the height, for once, we halt in the basic course of theme,—at

BRAHMS' FOURTH SYMPHONY

the highest note but one; we halt like a brave horse pausing to leap into the abyss. Then instead of final descent comes still a new fugal chase on the last four notes of the theme, ever rising higher, reckless now of regular rut. Clashing on the heels of ascending treble comes the bass furiously pursuing in blind loyalty. The strings are ever coursing as before, and the big harmonies make the heavens ring. The ambitious climb of Titans heavenward must stop, in broken chords.

Suddenly in comes an old phrase of the Scherzo, of retorts on bits of its theme, moving with perfect fitness in the course of the motive, and so binding the two cantos together in letter and spirit. The end is in final firm song of theme, though in proud contempt of the strict rhythm, closing in revel of dance on the quickened trip of the cadence.

XIII
LISZT, TSCHAIKOWSKY, STRAUSS

THERE is a danger of impertinence in a survey of contemporary art, in an assured acclaim of the coming classic. So often have the favorites of their day vanished from the lists that it almost seems the master is never hailed in his time. Ever more eminent stands the art of the man whose masterpiece, his great completed symphony, lay buried unknown for ten years after his death. So to-day it were idlest vanity to find in the newly applauded name the latest of the immortals. We cannot know that the work of a modest poet who is now singing, or of one whose song is hushed, may not loom in great dimensions through the sobering years.

All we can do is to note the signs and tendencies and to wonder at the outcome. In the realm of instrumental art a wealth of new traditions must come into the reckoning. Their effect on the symphony (taken as rough type) falls indirectly from another field, of the musical drama. A history of all music would take cognizance of this school. Side by side the new tradition has run with the purer art of absolute tones. The sharp contrast in outer form has delayed a mutual merging of the lines. So in the days of Bach was the riotous revel of Italian monody out of all plane with the sublime architecture of the Church school. Almost never have the symphony and the musical drama had points of contact in later centuries. Indeed, the *Lied* is more closely akin to the former. With one great exception, the composers of the drama and those who wrote for instruments alone worked and thought in separate lines, as of different arts.

Of the opera there is here no room for basic discussion. But we cannot ignore the new growth that has flowered on the field of the music drama.

In the middle of the past century came a wave of recoil, not from the mere spirit,—from the very foundations of classical masters. A group of radicals, in various lines of the art, made common cause of a general revolt from the traditions that stood, broadly, for order or sequence, —in the creation of rhythmic melody, in the achievement of genuine harmony, in the coherent process that fashions a perfect whole. They were impatient artisans in eager pursuit of striking effect. They craved a sensational element in their emotion. They lost heed of the utterance of truest feeling in the quieter process, the "still small voice" of purest art. Yet in their irregular course they lit on sporadic ideas of alluring beauty; they took the world by a storm that almost overthrew a saner balance.

Outer traits of their iconoclasm might be numbered. Melody was sung in fragments; the very name was abolished with the true type. Harmony was largely exploited in bold splurges of strange and sudden group of tones,—harmony that before was viewed as the achieved result of the independent paths of concerted voices. Thus the harmony of Bach was no aim in itself, was ever an incident of a greater polyphony; yet it had an infinite variety that flowed from the vital process of infinite change in the separate movement of voices. Here lies the secret of the inexhaustible harmony of Bach.

A result of the conscious striving for harmonic effect was a certain trait of stereotype, a special almost mechanical mode in the fashioning. Fads and devices have been many in the history of music, and probably of most art. In oldest days was the discovered cipher for setting all words in tones. Later the scheme of false bass, the parallel motion of voices, started in a certain way, relieved the composer of all need of harmonic toil, until the Church stemmed its riotous course by special decree.

Of like nature is the modern use of the extended grace note.* Delay the integral sound by a neighboring whole tone or half, from above or from below, and you may give the simplest chord a new sense of romantic desire. Write it in more of the voices, and you have transformed a primitive chord to strangest harmony. There is no doubt of the real beauty. The harm to art lies merely in the overdoing. So it is, too, with the trick of false bass.† And then, to be sure, the first discoverer has special credit; so it is, too, with the *faux bourdon*.

Striking is the number of modern motives where the whole point lies just in this stress of deferring tone.‡ No doubt, the greater poets de-

---

* The *appoggiatura*.

† Beethoven uses it in the main subject of the Finale of his Piano Sonata, op. 2 No. 3,

‡ Most of the motives, including the expressive main theme

pended least on the artifice.   Many of Wagner's themes are free from it.   Brahms disdained its use.

The brevity of the new *motif*, displacing the full cycle of the older melody, gave a tempting scope to this new harmonic manner. Indeed, it may be said, the smaller the separate effect, independent of its place in the whole, the more danger is there of mechanical means. So Monteverde produced a marvellous *furore* with his new *tremolo* and *pizzicato* of strings; and they have remained, though the works have departed.

It was in the lyric drama of Richard Wagner that some of the elements of an ultra-romantic music had their rise; to its exigencies they are expressly fitted. This drama has no place here, save in its bearing upon symphonic writing. Whatever be its outline, from the dramatic point, —of pure musical structure or form there is none beyond the limits of the separate lyrics. And here is involved another of these special traits of this spirit of recoil, that is far the subtlest to perceive.

---

of Wagner's "Tristan and Isolde," are examples; and almost all the themes of Liszt's "Faust" Symphony and of Tschaikowsky's *Pathétique*. See *infra*.

LISZT, TSCHAIKOWSKY, STRAUSS

The freedom from form, from the strict coherence of thought in absolute tones, gave the strongest vent for a newer polyphony, a so-called counterpoint, much vaunted as the redeeming symptom of profoundest art,—a thickest mazing of concerted themes.* This is in the natural course. The supreme element of high art, with the frigid name of form, whereby the tonal ideas grow and merge to significant whole, so that in the form of music lies its true meaning, acts as a fetter of other elements. The theme of pure music cannot have the freedom of the song. It must be fitted to the stress of discussion and structural growth, just as the fugal subject is not a tune. The mystic quality of counterpoint, of true polyphony, is in its real condition obedient to the sway of this other highest trait of organic wholeness. When that is withdrawn, the ease of such a massing of simultaneous strains is infinitely increased. If you may wander endlessly, and may stop when you list, you can add another line of tune above, below, in the middle,

---

* It was reinforced by boldest exploits of the limits of dissonance, based mainly on the extended license of *appoggiatura* This is seen most strikingly in Richard Strauss's "Heldenleben." See *infra*.

LISZT, TSCHAIKOWSKY, STRAUSS

and so write your "counterpoint" by the yard. But when you must round all in a true cycle of crystal growth and cogent sequence, reaffirmed by the united agreement of all the ideas, you have the testing conditions for true polyphony. Thus it is that the so-called counterpoint of Wagner has so very different a taste from that of Bach or of Beethoven.

Again, we must not forget that these terms *counterpoint* and *form* are not concrete things that you can point to and label by the page; they are qualities that constitute true poetry. There is no guarantee of true form in the outline of sonata or rondo. These are merely types that have served to utter the profound sense of this quality of tonal coherence. It is no mystery. A child will understand whether the parts of a story hang together. The idea is familiar in architecture. Music, that has no directing words nor familiar figures like other arts, needs the test of this pervading sequence of organic structure. There the tonal art reaches its highest. Elsewhere it delights, thrills, startles; there, in the overwhelming consent from all the corners of the document, it tells its resistless message, as of sacred oracle.

LISZT, TSCHAIKOWSKY, STRAUSS

It goes without saying that you cannot see form in individual spots. It must come in glinting glimpses of the whole. No matter how beautiful the separate touches, they do not affect the real beauty and meaning of the whole.

Still following our original plan, we will take a direct view of certain works that show the new spirit each in their way, beginning with one of the earliest, Liszt's "Faust" Symphony.

The only clue to a composer's intent, aside from the notes themselves, lies in the title. In this work, accounted by many the greatest that Liszt wrote, the exact title-page is most to the point. For it is all there is of verbal titulation, where, yet, the temptation is constant to find precise correspondence and label of musical phrase,—where, too, it seems that the composer himself must have felt a special meaning in certain motives that recur throughout.

"A Faust Symphony," runs the title (in German), "in three pictures,—in the spirit of Goethe. I, Faust. II, Margarete. III, Mephistopheles, and Final Chorus 'All of earth is but symbol'; for full orchestra and male chorus."

The chorus is not an indispensable part; for, before its beginning, there is an alternate ending

LISZT, TSCHAIKOWSKY, STRAUSS

of twelve closing bars, in case the chorus is omitted.

Throughout the work certain brief motives form the common text of all the movements. Thus, one is tempted to think of three psychological phases rather than of individual rôles. The German is "*in drei Charakterbildern.*" The meaning of the word *Charakter* is so broad that the title certainly does not forbid our construction. Indeed, it seems very clear, that in *Charakterbild* the stress is laid on the psychological view, as against the mere picture, or *tableau*, as some have translated.

The best test is the music itself. It is evident, however, that we are here in a new kind of writing, with the discursive freedom of opera in pure instrumental music; with the symbolic motive, in place of full-fledged melody; with vehement massive strokes of bold harmonies, instead of the blended song of many voices, of classic art. Without regard to the merits of the newer plan, there is no doubt that Liszt's orchestral works are startling in their likeness to much later music that makes greater pretence of original thought. There is no doubt that Liszt, with all the brilliancy of his *virtuoso* life, is very late in finding recognition for his composition. There are increasing signs that Liszt was the true author of much of modern vein that has been ascribed to others who merely followed in his wake. To-day, a performance of the "Faust" Symphony, so rarely heard, must, by the intrinsic music as well as the impetuous spontaneity, bring striking proof of a certain prophetic quality.

Where brief motives recur throughout, in opera or in unsung music, it is impossible not to ascribe a definite intent of meaning. Where a strain from a remote movement enters later, here and there, instead of any other chance phrase, there must be intended the association of a certain idea that becomes an intimate element of the poetic content. Once for all,—not to discuss the underlying principle,—the idea of the *motif* is bound up with that of programme music. Liszt chose to give no verbal clues. It may seem impertinent to attempt to suggest them. The answer is that a chance name that may be given to a symbol may serve no more than as designation, for better study of the music itself. There need be no intent definitely to translate the themes.

It is, however, surely urgent for the listener to

LISZT, TSCHAIKOWSKY, STRAUSS

mark well these integral elements on which the whole is joined in poetic significance. Their recurrence here must convince us of the subjective nature of the work,—must refute the notion of three objective "pictures," such as the title might seem to mean.

The first of the motives begins the "Faust" movement, *lento assai:*

It seems to utter the mood of the restless scholar (as we read in Goethe), wondering and dreaming of the true life without the limits of his cloistered cell,—the life that his own narrow quest has all but closed to his view.

Immediately after the motive of wondering follows a second that has the more human impulse of *longing:*

LISZT, TSCHAIKOWSKY, STRAUSS

The two alternate, with clear significance, the first growing more restless, the second ever calming with a sense of answered question. The halting sadness is broken by a quicker, active pulse, *allegro impetuoso*, on lesser phrases that are no part of symbolic plan. Rushing to big climax, it is vented in the irresistible drive of first motive. But the following tempest breaks off, sheer, in sudden pause. In the original *lento assai*, the second theme (of longing) appears, for a single strain, to burst with passionate rage into a third motive, *allegro agitato ed appassionato*,—one of those phrases of vehement desire that mark the sadness of latest Russian symphony:

3. *Allegro agitato, ed appassionato assai, molto piu forzando.*

STRINGS.

It drives along, in much freer and more extended course than the others, to a height of brilliant joy, where all gloomy tinge is dissolved. But presently, in changed hue of tonal light, above trembling strings, sings our fourth symbol, the most sustained *motif* of all we have so far heard, *espressivo ed appassionato molto.*

LISZT, TSCHAIKOWSKY, STRAUSS

It has not quite the serenity of true andante. But there is a trace of contentment,—rather of

achievement. In the second part is still the sense of longing. Voice after voice follows as in relentless fugue, and soon the furious (*agitato*) theme is mingled in its career. Now an entirely new scene moves before us. *Meno mosso, misterioso e molto tranquillo*, are heard soothing sounds of strings very like the forest notes of the *Waldweben*. Under their shelter, in mellow mood, the first symbol of longing sings, all transformed to clear happiness of major, winding along in entrancing voyage of tonal light, though it never shifts to the dim gloom of its original mood. Soon comes another joyous phase of older theme,

LISZT, TSCHAIKOWSKY, STRAUSS

when our second symbol sounds in glad major, *affettuoso, poco andante*, in chorus and lower woodwind, ever answered by delicate strain of strings, *dolce con grazia*. The heart of the movement is here, the true *andante* note is reached of contained bliss, and a little further, a triumphant height, *allegro con fuoco*, that is affirmed with conclusive finality in the big march, *grandioso* (*poco meno mosso*), where the theme is wonderfully changed to an opposite mood of assurance:

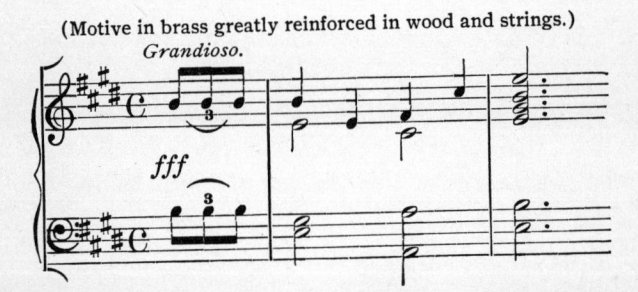

The first two symbols now sound in responsive duet with martial vigor, crowned with re-entrance of the march. The various motives are woven in rich blending of a canon on the first in the brass, and of the fourth in strings. The masterful pace soon dies down to a lull, when the fourth motive breaks out as at first with the old passionate agitation. This leads to the mood of the beginning, with the themes in their original guise. But, here in the *reprise*, there is more of wealth of interwoven phrase, there is less of anxious gloom in the strife that once again reaches the height of triumphant march.

The close, where the first four motives prevail, begins *andante maestoso assai*, the woodwind and brass singing the first theme over trembling of low strings. Indeed, this very figure of accompaniment seems to mark the return of the old mood of uncertain striving. The theme quickly hurries in pace and darkens in discordant tone, the second hovering about with ominous answer. The serenity is gone, though the strife still rises to big height. The end has the dim feeling of the beginning.

In the second picture, "*Gretchen*," a prelude of melodic duet between flute and clarinet leads to the central theme of the work announced in strings: the unmistakable symbol of the Eternal Feminine, of the words of the closing chorus.

For some kind of understanding of this difficult conception, we must remember several things. For one, this central and crowning melody does not appear in the "Faust" picture, has no part therein. Clearly, then, that canto of the poem (so to speak) is not final; it stops, at

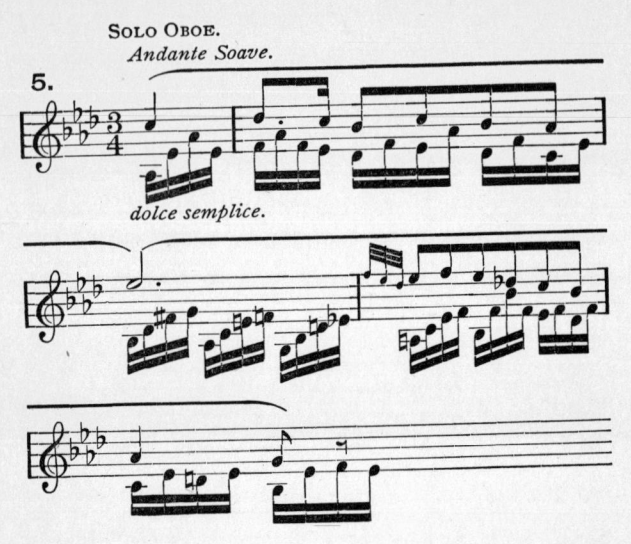

[musical notation: Solo Oboe. Andante Soave. dolce semplice.]

the very least, within the first part of Goethe's drama. Again, the "Gretchen" music seems clearly, like the "Mephistopheles," after all, a mere succeeding phase of *Faust* himself. There is nothing of individual characterization; it is all a subjective drama of a single hero. Thus, there is no trace, in Liszt's setting, of the famous song of Margarete's "*Meine Ruh' ist hin*," that Schubert has made musically familiar. With Liszt, we do not think of "Gretchen" individually. The whole is a beautiful idyl in two veins. But in the first, with its supreme symbolic theme, there is interwoven the third of the motives of the first movement, which had the first sense of contentment. The second verse of the "Gretchen" idyl begins with a new melody *dolce amoroso*, in strings,—that does not recur as symbolic motive,—that seems sufficient in the meaning of its own beauty:

But in the midst of the movement is a dramatic moment, in heightened pace, where the play of early motives must be of highest significance for the perception of the composer's intent. And here is the final point that must not be forgotten: all the motives recur here save the first of all. Thus clearly is that theme confirmed as the restless stirring and vague wondering that is free of the thought of woman.

The second motive—of longing—does play a striking rôle, sounded in brass, against ominous quivering of strings and of harp. Our third symbol—with its more contained sense of hope—now enters in soothing response, *espressivo con intimo sentimento*, in cellos, below muted violins and lightly dropping chords of flutes. Lastly, the fourth passionate symbol sounds in softest strings, *soave con amore*. The interplay of these three themes is ended by the final song of the two verses of the movement, with lesser interweaving of casual motive.

In the third picture, "*Mephistopheles*," after prelude of demonic phrases, the first motive appears in constantly spurring *allegro*. Soon the fourth symbol sounds in new step of dance that has a touch of Satanic mirth.

The second appears, distorted, too, in sardonic trip. But the fourth seems to hold the main sway. It has, too, a more joyous air, and runs to the same triumphant climax as in the first movement, where the "common" time alternates with the dance of six-eighths.

LISZT, TSCHAIKOWSKY, STRAUSS

The second symbol has another stranger disguise, in united hurried pace, where all of the original longing seems to have vanished. Indeed, the whole masquerade of motives is most bewildering, and can be caught only by a tense concentration. Throughout, there is a grim playfulness of perversion. It is to be well noted that all four of the symbolic themes recur, and another new melody appears. A most spirited verse of the former march returns, too, where the new figure, of high wood and strings, is marked *fortissimo giocoso*.

In the midst of the whirl suddenly sounds the "Gretchen" melody, symbol of the "Eternal Feminine." Though the stormy strife breaks loose again, the demon element has vanished,— as before a sacred symbol. Once more the original cycle of themes leads to triumphant march, and the end comes with unbroken ring of joy,—the end, that is, of instrumental symphony. But this is, after all, a mere substitute for the bigger ending with male chorus, who sing, *Andante mistico*, to the accompanying "Gretchen" motto, the closing verse of Goethe's "Faust":

LISZT, TSCHAIKOWSKY, STRAUSS

> " All passing things
> Are symbols sent:
> Here the Inadequate
> Grows to event.
> The Indescribable,
> Here 'tis done,
> Th' Eternal Feminine
> Leads us on."

Thus we see that in Liszt the close coherence and sequence of musical ideas, and the resulting structure and form, give way to a highly thoughtful play of brief symbolic motives, in a plot of external conception. The whole work becomes a tonal drama, lacking only words and the visible scene.

It is perhaps curious that among classic symphonies—the highest form of music, that may correspond to the drama in poetry, and that may be said to present a kind of view of life of the composer—there are no tragedies. In poetry the tragic seems the native element for the boldest flights and the deepest questions. Now either there is no such analogy between music and poetry, or composers have been strangely conventional. One difference in the art is this:

LISZT, TSCHAIKOWSKY, STRAUSS

dramas, like "Hamlet," even "Œdipus," are tragedies in outer event. Music has none of these,—that is, pure music. It deals only with the moral state, the sentient, or emotional condition; in other words, it is purely subjective (though there are varying degrees of objective association). Now music in this sense cannot afford to be tragic, though in a wider view the word might be applied. The Fifth Symphony is quite as tragic as the Book of Job, and very like it in intrinsic content. Here, as in almost all the great tragedies, there is a moral recoil from the "arrows of outrageous fortune." This, in the symphony, is typified in the triumphant *finale*. In the tragic drama the worst physical ill that can befall is not the real end, after all. Death, not even fate, can touch a man's soul. A symphony that ended in the tragic note would be darker than any plot of poets. So of this kind of tragedy that mean complete surrender to despair, there are in art few, if any,—none among the classics. Goethe's "Faust," in the first part, is perhaps the nearest approach. *Macbeth* suggests it. But the hero of the drama is, after all, not the real *ego* of the poet; the view is never purely subjective, certainly not in the same degree as in the pure lyric, or as in music. The tragedy of the drama, once more, is largely external, not moral. But in music, where there are no events, the hopeless tragic note means a surrender, and, in so far, it is, in a certain sense, immoral. Even the Sonata Pathétique ends in a frolic. All the classic symphonies end merrily. There is ever a scherzo after the funeral march in sonata and symphony. It is, therefore, not strange, after all, that there has never been a tragic ending before Tschaikowsky's *Symphonie Pathétique*.

It is significant, not merely as a philosophy in itself, but as the burden of art. The emotional content of art is limited to the feelings which make for a better state. Murder cannot be the theme. There are no patriotic songs save of self-defence. "*Böse Menschen*," say the Germans, "*haben keine Lieder.*" So the gospel of despair is surely very near the limit of the musical realm of subjects. Still, truth is the highest object of all, so Tschaikowsky would certainly answer.

There is a consistent sadness blended with tense passion throughout the symphony. In Adagio the bassoons begin an expressive characteristic motive:

LISZT, TSCHAIKOWSKY, STRAUSS

against a hollow chord of the basses. Later in a chord of low strings, *Allegro non troppo*, echoed by woodwind, it has not lost its sadness; it returns in various haunting guises. An episode follows in light flitting figures, catching each other in alternate chase in a kind of strained gayety, dropping, after a climax, by vanishing steps into *Andante* song of speaking pathos:

LISZT, TSCHAIKOWSKY, STRAUSS

The first motive, repeated, is answered by a phrase highly typical of the new spirit in its passionate quality.

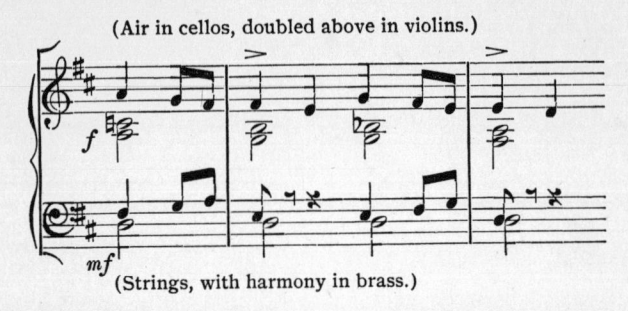

(Air in cellos, doubled above in violins.)

(Strings, with harmony in brass.)

There is no mistaking the blended beauty and desire. This leads into a responsive duet between flute and bassoon, on a new motive:

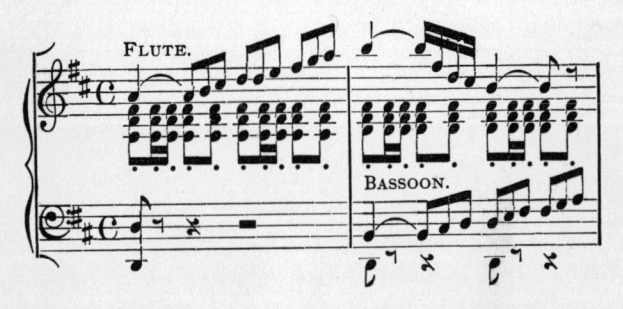

with a *saltando* rhythm in the strings, other voices joining with more sustained answering figure, suggesting the song into which they lead, again

LISZT, TSCHAIKOWSKY, STRAUSS

in *Andante*, now with enriched quiver of rhythmic setting. The song, too, comes to a climax in the pure lyric manner. Indeed, the drama is, as it were, full of monologue. The action halts, the other characters disappear, leaving the hero ever alone to pour out his griefs (all in the *Allegro* chapter, too); anon the drama is forced into renewed action. After one of these climaxes the melancholy motive of the introduction enters in *Allegro* on the G string of the violin with a fierce obligato (*feroce*) of violas, working up with great animation, though always in sombre mood in the quicker extension of theme sustained in tempestuous sequence:

In the midst of the storm, redoubled voices in high wood and brass peal forth a mournful blast, a varied line of the passionate answer of second theme. When the paroxysm has abated, a solemn fateful chorale sounds in the brass that soon rises into a new tempest of lament, that dies away in the wail of first theme. In this final song of main theme is none of the lesser motive.

LISZT, TSCHAIKOWSKY, STRAUSS

Instead, insistent reiteration of the motto alternates with the broad fateful strain, descending in

(Full orchestra, theme redoubled in 8ves.)
(See page 425, line 18.)

the brass. The two meet in a blended song of deep tragedy. A purely lyric plaint of the second theme ends the movement.

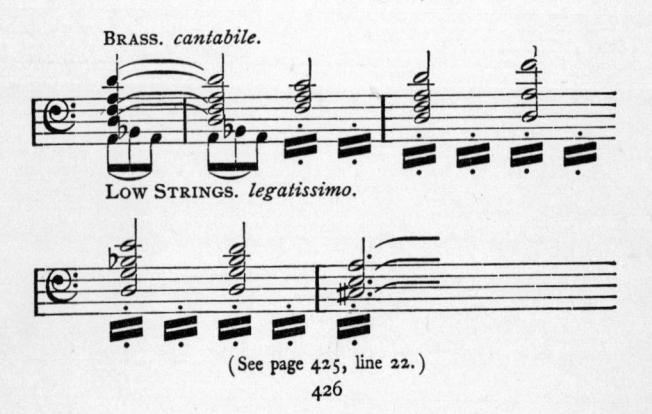

BRASS. *cantabile.*

LOW STRINGS. *legatissimo.*

(See page 425, line 22.)

LISZT, TSCHAIKOWSKY, STRAUSS

The second movement, *Allegro con grazia*, is on a dance-like theme of whimsical rhythm in 5-4 time:

(Cello theme with chords of *pizz.* strings, horns and wood.)

introduced by cellos and taken up by chorus of woodwind. The second melody is but a counterpart of the first, all in simple song form:

The middle verse—*con dolcezza e flebile*—is a quaint blending of the strange dance with a tearful strain.

The third movement is most spirited, almost feverish in the tonal scene that first greets us. To a fitful, elfish play (of alternate strings and woods) —like will-o'-the-wisp in indistinct laughter and

LISZT, TSCHAIKOWSKY, STRAUSS

con dolcezza e flebile.

(STRINGS, WOOD AND HORNS.)
(See page 427, line 9.)

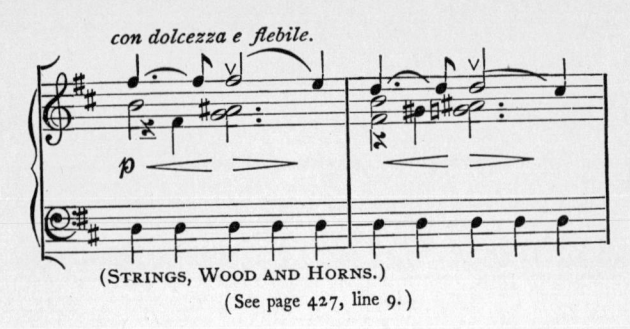

mockery—there is presently added a call as of a bugle, in simplest outline, but ending in a strange barbaric turn, new to us of western culture, of mingled defiance and fatalism:

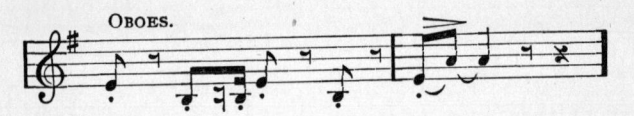

OBOES.

With all the wildness there is no note of joy. At first it sounds more hopeless than frank lamentation,—a kind of sardonic laugh at personal damnation. The first approach to relief, to a sense of *terra firma*, is where related melody works its way to the major, followed by brilliant flashes of modulating chords. Though wild to savagery, they have lost the uncertain, unsane feeling. They come near to exultation and seem

LISZT, TSCHAIKOWSKY, STRAUSS

(See page 428, line 9.)

the true (though not the intended) high point of the symphony. And, strikingly, on its return the first flickering play has a more hopeful tone.

Bright melodic snatches now spring up and illumine the purpose, all to the original murmuring background, though now with lighter hue. And rougher, ruder strokes come in brutal unison, and yet they are looking towards the

LISZT, TSCHAIKOWSKY, STRAUSS

light with fine glimpses of it. We are tense as to the outcome. Through hushed murmuring of woodnotes comes to the ears gradually the old call, and still the turn at the end is terrible and barbaric, though with much softened surroundings, which soon affect the whole. Above all chime high solemn tones of the wood, and all rises to a big climax—not of despair. And now comes the fruit of it. The strange ominous turn of the call has blossomed into a graceful, human melody:

LISZT, TSCHAIKOWSKY, STRAUSS

And so all is well with the world as yet. Presently, after a stern call in united chords, comes an answer of light witchery, from playful siren figures in the woodwind against low droning of strings. We must beware of the too sensuously beautiful, which is always closely akin to fatalism and despair.

Thence we return to the melody which has developed from the trumpet call. Now the figures re-enter, as at first (by good old sonata rule); but the herald call has lost much of its ominous sting, for we know where it led to; we cannot be frightened again by the cry of wolf. At the end, through all its hues and shades, we fall into a clashing strife, as the call, in its worst phase, is hurled from all sides in hardest clangor. If it is not demonic, it is certainly barbaric. What is joyous to one, shocks and frights another. Barbaric it is; for presently it leads to a triumphant pæan on the full-blown melody with all the accoutrement of victory.

To some it may seem, for inherent elements of highest purpose, that the composer ought to have stopped here, or at least to have closed with this as final word.

Adagio lamentoso is the mood of the last move-

LISZT, TSCHAIKOWSKY, STRAUSS

ment. It is all a recurrence to one cry of grief, in the strings, followed by a dull note in the wind:

Adagio lamentoso.

There are extensions of this theme (especially one, where the last note is delayed from above), and other melodies, all of great beauty, especially one in *Andante* (in strings), ever closely echoed below in the basses:

(Each part doubled in 8ves.)

while the horns throb in constant time and tone. And yet it is a mere foil to the other. Nothing can exceed the terrible beauty of its anguish of re-

LISZT, TSCHAIKOWSKY, STRAUSS

gret, which grows fiercer at each refrain. We can now see why it must come last, for its own fullest self-expression. It could not be consoled nor tempered; the tears would not run into smiles.

A reason there must be for a choice, for final word, of a work that is not a symphony. The music of Richard Strauss, so richly charged with the influence of the school of Wagner and Liszt, offers too tempting a significance to resist. The manner and process are here that must sooner or later enter the symphony in its broad sense. Even if Strauss himself does not fulfil an obvious promise to advance to an instrumental work of poetic breadth and profound art, his striking exploits must affect every coming work of value. Moreover, his peculiar merit, as we shall see, is that Strauss is clearly leading towards a reconciliation of warring tendencies. As Brahms, by the temper of his inevitable attitude, firmly eschewed all contact with a contemporary school, his work is in separate lines,—which will in no wise disparage its greatness. The younger writer shoulders all Wagner traditions that may be digested in the art of absolute music, and cheerfully sets himself the task of forging the fitting mould, of fashioning bottles to hold the newer wine.

All the overtures and other orchestral tone-poems of Strauss may justly and broadly be viewed as essays in the wider plan of form and structure. How great is the need of such change does not belong to the present book to discuss. It must depend on the proven worth of these newer elements: in the main, of the brief motif-symbol; of a certain luxuriance of massed themes; of a special device of harmonic and melodic effect. They have been already discussed; they must vary in value; some are clearly ephemeral. Least of all doubt there will be of the permanence of Wagner's masterful strokes of orchestral color. One thing is absolute. True coherence of the tonal thought, a pervading sequence, that make the complete structure, will never be lost so long as there is a vital art of instrumental music.

It will be well, then, to take a glance at the last work of the most radical composer of the day, who, whatever be his merit, has somehow centred the expectation of much of the musical world for the latest idea in tones. Our simple plan will be at once the most direct approach

LISZT, TSCHAIKOWSKY, STRAUSS

and at the same time its own severest test. For all is new, the very A B C; the nature of themes; the process of their treatment; a vast field of undreamt clashes of tones; so that, at first, pure cacophony seems to be an equal means with true harmony. There need be no prejudice towards a final verdict; for opinions are bitterly divided, and, moreover, the startled world can have as yet no estimate of so youthful a living poet.

"A Hero's Life" is the title,—tone-poem for full orchestra. The word *symphonic* is not used. Forthwith, in lively swing, the heroic theme is announced in free declamation, with a mere stray strum of chord, as of old troubadour:

It is all rhapsody more than melody, where three parts are striking: the first for a broad, graceful

LISZT, TSCHAIKOWSKY, STRAUSS

sweep; the second for a most bizarre, quick turn of notes, where the lack of smooth sequence jars the ear; the third, where from on high the motive descends big-stressed in whole steps, reckless of the natural tone. When the final height is reached, we seem to see the second phrase, of strange run, in constant sequence, with response, to triumphant end:

Scarce has the theme started anew with resounding suit of rhythmic vassals, when a new scene sweeps all heroics aside in a trice, and amid rich languor of soft murmurs of whispering harps and strings the high voices sing a dulcet plaint of vague phrase, while lower voices start the more fervent song of second theme. Quickly even this light has changed to another hue, as a third melody, of brighter spring, rises like answer to its forerunner.

The woof of languishing song winds its sweet tenor, ever with new flashes of tonal light.

LISZT, TSCHAIKOWSKY, STRAUSS

STRINGS.

(Reinforced and accompanied in wood and harps.)

(3d theme, with added horns.)
(See page 436, line 15.)

Here is one difference from older poetry. You do not wander into slow changes; they come upon you as by sudden shift of total scene. There seems here less of infinite art, more of the rut of recurring device.

As all but the fervent theme remains, there is almost the strife of fugue, the voices rising in higher curves towards a bright empyrean, where the heroic theme now rings a blast. But again the later melodies interfere, first the brighter answer that seems to fit either mood. Here is a clear struggle of languorous beauty with heroic resolve; unmistakable is the quick chase of expressive strain and the spring of action. When the former has almost conquered, the heroic drive, that was lulled, breaks into lusty strife with the siren song, that seems itself to grow fierce in the fight. We feel the growing triumph of the virile theme, in succeeding burst of great beauty. And yet at the height is not the original type of pure vigor; it is the bright answer of later tune, that seems the tonal idea of joy against the earlier action,—Apollo or Balder against Mars or Wotan. The lesser figures play about in a verse of exquisite delight, that has merely deferred the full course of first motive, ending on high in trembling pause of chord that strongly leads towards the main tone.

Here is one of the main surprises of this youngest music, where mere boldness seems alone to capture our approval. It is really, for all purposes of first hearing, a rough and scraping war of noises; nothing like it has ever been called music. Indeed, the very directions for the players show the intent, borrowed as they are from hostile sounds of nature. And yet we cannot condemn. After the first rebellion we do feel the subtle *rationale;* it is like a demon mockery of playful harmonies, grim spectres of sweet gambols. Clearly the intent is symbolic, by a certain objective figure. It is not the mere wail of despair. The figures are a mere foil.

It is not the idea of such cacophony that is new, as its actual and abundant use. In earlier days Scarlatti wrote a "cat's fugue" on the theme of scampering chase across the keys. Theory sets no limits to the tones of a phrase to safeguard the beauty. It is again from a subtle point that form is seen to do this, to hold the right balance. Any theme will do; and in combination the laws are few and negative; even they are shaking on their ancient base. In contrary motion of clashing strains there is no rule that one need fear. But, of course, there may be no gain of beauty. The mere freedom from theoretic fault insures no progress. Complaint will all come from an absence of beauty, not from trespass of rule. Art cannot be mastered by a criminal code.

The sense of beauty is so much in the intent, the hidden sequence of idea, that in apparent chaos lie the greatest resources for novel strokes, where the final solution of harmony proves the aim and the striving. All the progress of the art has been gained by such raids on hostile sound. Order and reason have redeemed the wilderness.

LISZT, TSCHAIKOWSKY, STRAUSS

It is not that the end justifies the means; but the dissonance, type of evil, is seen as a mere temporary departure from the harmony, type of good, to which it ever tends.

In so far as cacophony slowly gains the hue of tonal color, does it find a basis of beauty. Is there such an intent here? The desert runs on for long stretches of wildest waste. The only reason, it almost seems, can be such as is found in the drama, where music is often used as external, mechanical means. Demoniacal humor shines in the grisly perversion of that strange run in original theme.

One thing is certain. It would not be fair or true art to have a whole scene of chaos and ugliness as a foil to a following scene of beauty. Such an end of cacophony does not count. But there is here, it must be admitted, a slow-growing undertone of clear color. The more we hear, the less we rebel,—a strong redeeming sign. And so the sense of boldness takes captive our remaining remonstrance.

The resulting peace sounds in the expressive flow, instead of heroic drive, in minor of main theme, blended with a varied phrase of yearning song of the second, poised over harmonies of

LISZT, TSCHAIKOWSKY, STRAUSS

gorgeous, languorous beauty. A phase of the quick motive comes to give a new spring and a fervid crisis with cadence of pathos. The demon perversion of heroic idea returns for a brief shadow. Then the first theme slowly lifts itself from the passive glamour, and throws off the languor and the demon pursuit in desperate bursts of the strange run of quick notes.

Suddenly a little tune of childlike joy (that gets its cheery jingle from the end of third theme) rings out, clear of all strange humors and modern hues.

(Redoubled in full orchestra.)

From this point is a long reign of fantastic monody. There is a sharp succession (in unaccompanied solo violin) of short melodic outbursts, in all kinds of swiftly changing humors. They seem like whims, or shadows of moods, that come as tempting visitations, and so stand out from the main text of subjective emotion. Again, the mere directions help to enlighten the place. The lively joy we last saw, is followed by a sentimental phrase *much quieter*, that later turns

LISZT, TSCHAIKOWSKY, STRAUSS

to one of *hypocritical yearning*, then glides into a jolly fling. Ever and again in the midst of these fleeting visions sounds a motive as of peace and solace in full choir of hushed chorus, that slowly

unfolds a growing sequence of lyric song, in various ways. One of these impish phrases was *flippant*; then after the reassuring word comes a strain, *tender, somewhat sentimental*, then an *insolent* turn. So, with the quieting phrase between, they run a rich gamut of humors, *sedate, playful, amiable, jolly again, faster and more raging, suddenly quieter and full of feeling, insistent* and

LISZT, TSCHAIKOWSKY, STRAUSS

soothing, angry, scolding, tenderly expressive. The quieter motive hovers throughout and finally ends the strange chase of elfish moods in full harmony of trembling strings and harps that softly glide or boldly twang. The song has grown to the full length almost of traditional tune. The monodic strains were not all different, some recurring. Of these, several are now treated with much fulness. You might safely say, in the rough, that it is all the heroic spirit proving itself through a chain of experience.

The languishing motive (last quoted) now in turn grows to enchanting bloom of melody, and still the soothing strain plays about. The episode ends in the passive phase of heroic theme, again in minor, again followed by the brief demon play of mocking sprites, with an expressive farewell.

A new figure enters, a fanfare of treble trumpets, in rough and vague harmonic call, that seems very slowly to waken the sleep of the hero. In a long struggle, various of the older chance strains are flitting in teasing chase, in uncertain light. Roughly the martial mood breaks on the sentimental,—at each big rhythmic beat, relentless. Neither can be said to prevail; but

LISZT, TSCHAIKOWSKY, STRAUSS

the mere strife is a triumph of the martial idea. The languor has vanished.

Still a new phase, heralded by strum of low basses, following the roll of drum, in firm step and liveliest pace. There is no missing the demon theme. But the old bedlam is not here. The theme has the order of rhythmic pace. The sounds are drawn out in the semblance of tune. There is no chorus of imps, each to out-din the other. Though the sense of unearthly tones remains, there is an agreeing harmony, but for one terrible blank at the height of the tempest. Here in a quick chase of chords the pursuer (in the woodwind) has caught his lingering foe (in the strings), in a horrid clash, where the beauty and reason of each is all destroyed. On goes the rough ride of eerie phrase, ever haunting the border of strained sense.

What is this mystic symbol, of shrill and ominous mirth? Whatever be the meaning of the poet, we know that there is here a certain rescue from chaos, a redemption from the furies. Elsewhere in Strauss is the haunting of this goblin humor. The line is here crossed from mania, however wild the riot. There is in latest music, markedly in Strauss, ever this element.

LISZT, TSCHAIKOWSKY, STRAUSS

It is a modern vein of Scherzo. A rough line of descent is here from the sardonic fancy of Beethoven. In his Fifth Symphony was a like mood in its place in the general plot.*

The gnome-like phrase has given the main theme a new fillip, though still coursing in sombre minor. When the mocking phrase stops, the wild strain of treble trumpets enter the din. Suddenly all is resolved in the sweet song of the languishing tune, that now soars on new and prouder wing. Recurs the chase of grim sprite and conquering beauty, while the main theme is master in the bass.

With all the joyous spring, the strife is not over. Indeed, in this, the glory of heroic idea, the phase of stress must be present, the very native breath.

The earlier discord of treble trumpets seems somehow more grateful with the sense of brightening triumph; even the mocking phrase grows less inharmonious. That third motive of principal theme, in steady masterful stride of even whole tones, is now eminent, in antiphonal chorus of horns and of lowest brass. But the hero

---

* See Vol. I., 3d ed., pp. 166–169, 226.

LISZT, TSCHAIKOWSKY, STRAUSS

gains no easy dominance. Once more the demon plays his impish gambols, now in canon of several voices, while still the struggle continues of masterful stride, and of the first heroic strain; ever the graceful theme comes to shed the peace of its beauty.

Once again that jolly jingle breaks in, close woven with an extended line of the graceful phrase, and is answered with irresistible power by the return of soothing legend,—wonder of wonders—in simplest cadence of original tone. Indeed, the eternal maze of motives, without clear tone or rhythm, gives a new sanction of contented delight to the firm ring of clear chord. It seems a type, this refreshing return to order, of a like triumph in the whole art, in tune, tone, and rhythm.

A sharp line is thus drawn to the long conflict; a new turn is marked. We are sure of the survival of heroic phrase, as it now sounds out in full career. When we await a like return of the second melody, we are met by the beauty of a new idea,—new, yet most fitting. A greater relevance may thus lie in a strange figure. We have seen in Schumann the *envoi* of melody that sums the foregoing in new beauty. Recurrence

LISZT, TSCHAIKOWSKY, STRAUSS

(Very expressive.)

(Part of 2d theme, out of a mass of combined motives.)
(See page 446, line 23.)

of themes is not the only means. Indeed, it is in the nature of true coherence that it can never be said to lie in this prescription or that. Its subtle magic is never assured by mere conventions.

The whole texture is woven with crossing skeins of this expressive phrase in a song of moving fervor, closed by a verse of main theme. At this late point a mazing wealth of new melody keeps rising to baffle the quest of themal plan and meaning. One new pathetic strain grows out of another, as if eager of a single hearing before the end.

We seem to see in Strauss, to be just, a vein whereby melodies are developed in separate phases, out of mere earlier germs. The beautiful line that begins the farewell, is a striking type. There seems here a thought of a new plan of inner coherence, with its chain of blossoming tunes, each growing out of the other.

LISZT, TSCHAIKOWSKY, STRAUSS

STRINGS. (Slowly.)

Molto espressivo.

(Harmony in horns and trombones.)

(See page 447, line 16.)

Again there seems less stress on actual theme than on a whole group, singing together or in close suit. So the old theme of joy is surrounded by a thick clustering bevy of newest song. Later, in closest twining, of old and strange phrases, we seem to have but a richer vein of the second phase, that before was cut off. And there is still a return to a mad fury, revelling in the thickest fray and fugue of the harsh run (of

LISZT, TSCHAIKOWSKY, STRAUSS

main theme), where one turn of chord is like the last drop of bitterness.

Final peace comes in a purified mood of heroic idea, in soft pastoral guise. The soothing and the languishing motives sing once more before the last word, of profound pathos.

We have seen that Liszt yielded to the full sway of the fragmental theme. Tschaikowsky, too, made here a strong though not a complete concession. We shall see how Strauss wonderfully links the new and the old idea, and by the plan of melodic growing from germs points a way back to normal art. Of all three, however, the Russian shows in these motives the highest creative power.

The lack of strong-knit musical structure in Liszt (as well as in Strauss) is explained, it cannot be justified, by the special title or purport. All three poets are essentially lyric, though in the symphony the profoundest temper ought to come in play. Series of scenes flash upon us,—lyric plaints, with intervening tempests on themes that have often nothing to do with the plot. Of all three, Tschaikowsky has most sense of outer form. But of close cogency he has almost none;

a sensational riot of passion forbids. With him fluency takes the place of coherence. But mere fluency is no surety of clear structure. The Russian symphony is really an impassioned, impetuous rhapsody. Only there is so easy an abuse of words. For, the ferocity of passion is not a measure of depth of true feeling, of a real intensity. That is a truth the age needs most to learn. The frenzy can come as well with shallower themes as with the great,—it will come in improvisation as soon as in the quiet retreat. We must not seek in unpremeditated art the supreme mood or mode. Rather is meditation the surer channel of lofty and lasting truth.

Perhaps the most eminent trait of Strauss is a freest use of discordant sound, so that he might almost be dubbed the Poet of Dissonance.*
In the boldness of harmonic touches, whether in the single motive † or in the group of themes, he carries the use of delayed note to an undreamt degree; yet both he and Wagner are

---

* We have spoken above, in the course of the *Heldenlied*, of a rational view of dissonant tones.

† A good example is the languishing motive of the monody, quoted on page 442. The delay is by double note, that gives an eerie clash of dual harmony.

LISZT, TSCHAIKOWSKY, STRAUSS

here free from mere slavish dependence. In varied flashes of rich harmony Wagner must stand alone of all his school. In his noblest moments of polyphonic climax Strauss completely recalls, if he does not surpass, the older poet.

Indeed, the more the harmony is earned, the less it comes by sensational (and often mechanical) flashes, the truer the art and the beauty. To speak boldly, harmony is not a primary aim; it is the mere dress of a tune, or the single vertical view of the polyphonic woof. It is, in truth, impertinent to make of harmony the chief display. We have spoken above of a rational view of dissonant tunes. Strauss may be said to have carried the harmonic manner of his school to the limits of entrancing beauty and of harshest bedlam. Yet, in all truth, we must instantly add,—a mere figure of speech and the kind of figure that easily lies. For bedlam is just what these clashes are not. It is not a mob of fortuitous sound. An harmonic basis is ever present, however faint. There is hardly need of saying that Strauss has never crossed the bounds of ordered sound.

The boldness of Strauss here lies in the strained extension of older harmonic idea. Yet it is this

LISZT, TSCHAIKOWSKY, STRAUSS

the path of each new tonal conception. There is no chord that has not a reason rooted in purest science. But the poet dreams the chord first; the reason is afterwards seen. It is in the lines of adornment, delay (of true note), elision, and even subtler feat that the future field is without limit.* Each newer idea begets a fresh group. So Strauss has found his own vein of the romance and humor of a quasi-cacophonous sound. The one danger of the question with Strauss, from a broad view of art, is how far he may lose the whole beauty and meaning in a conscious stress on special effect.

Of high promise is Strauss's own way of

---

* This, to be sure, is to speak of mere harmonic tinkering. For, the infinite ideal lies rather by the true polyphony, that needs no special device. In the boundless crossings of many concerted voices, it finds a natural path of endless new delights. Purest algebra will show that where all the voices sing in independent lines, the harmonic permutations must vary far more rapidly than where one voice holds the melody and all the rest move in a single mass. As elsewhere in the world, the conscious pursuit is barren. In counterpoint the abundant harmony comes of itself, unsought. So counterpoint has ever found the chords; harmony has merely recorded and repeated them.

LISZT, TSCHAIKOWSKY, STRAUSS

having the motives grow, in separate phases, to slowly extended melody. Here he not only transcends the limitations of his school, but he points an original line in the growth of pure musical form. We must never forget that true form is a quality, not a prescription. It is not at all needful to write like Mozart or Schumann. The special value of Strauss is here a true and original sense of intrinsic musical structure. If he would go a step farther, would extend his budding themes in pervading sequence, would restrain an enamoured delight in single sporadic flashes, would eschew the extravagant massing of motives that are not thematic, he would utter a true poetic meaning, in clear homogeneous beauty.

The genius and temper of this radical group all inclined to single effects. Where these are fragmental and often mechanical, the danger is that they will live without the works themselves, like the tremolo of Monteverde, and so the poet be cheated of his immortality. And there is, somehow, no patent of smaller exploits. Even Wagner's harmonies he did not really invent; they are all to be found in Bach. But he did combine them with wonderful lyric touch in fragmental strains of exquisite beauty. This harmonic process Strauss has even extended. But alas! the jumble of pretty effects is like the display of toys in the window.

We have spoken before of the wild error: that sounds might be massed in irrational chaos. But the principle holds quite as true of the rearing of phrase in the whole. It is all the same need of irresistible sequence. Once for all we must never yield to the rough cry for unbridled license to please the mob. There is always a mutinous band in art that mutter for the abandon of all law,—that want the sweetness without the light. There art suddenly tumbles from highest worship to lowest orgy,—a farther fall than Satan's; from light to darkness; from clear vision to chaos; from reason to madness; from true feeling to bestial passion. One who could thus profane the highest temple were a traitor to art.

It is here that our modern world suffers the lack of courage of critic, who has ever an eye for the time of surrender. It is here there is need of true watch-dog, who will boldly assail the false prophet,—who knows the weakness of his own people. Even if they scoff, he must

LISZT, TSCHAIKOWSKY, STRAUSS

stand his ground. One great German figure still towers to show the reality of type.

Finally in the broad view there is no room for complaint. Art will run its zigzag course, of new experiment. Genius is not a matter of schools. It will break out in varying utterance. There is no need to disparage the individual poet, in pointing mistaken directions. We saw, before the beginning of secular tonal art, how a new plane had to be started. The ground was broken with artisan toil and rude trial. A great descent there was from the high style of Bach to his son's graceful pieces of *salon*. We can hardly imagine the exploits of the modern school embodied in the sonata. As, of old, the pure traditions were never lost, were carried on in concurrent lines, so the ideals of form and cogent sequence were preserved in the later phase by a Schumann and Brahms. Thus we may view the Radicals of our own day as a group who have widely enlarged the resources to be embodied in future works of art.

APPENDIX

BERLIOZ'S FANTASTIC SYMPHONY

AN account of the programme idea, alone in the field of the symphony, would begin with Beethoven's Pastoral. Next in time, and very like in plan is Berlioz's Fantastic Symphony. The whole design, in both these works, appears most clearly in the light of those graphic touches, of thunder and rain, of shepherd notes and funeral march, besides the full list of titles for each scene. By the side-path of such association, the mimicry of nature-sounds and other chance convention, Beethoven led and Berlioz followed to a lower level, that does not lack its lyric beauties, though they do not make the beauty of the whole. If the true base of symphony is of pure tonal meaning, there is no avoiding a surrender in the resort to nature-sounds.

A very different, indeed the highest kind of programmatic art we have seen in the works of Raff, where, with less pretence, a simple poetic subject is treated with main stress on the feeling.* And so in Mendelssohn's symphonies there is an aim to utter a national idea by purely musical means.

The "Faust" symphony of Liszt has the new device of brief motif. To discuss its value as pure tonal symbol would lead us far astray into the whole question of modern music-drama But, granting the full symbolic power of the motif,

---

* See chapter on Raff and Mendelssohn.

APPENDIX

without a kind of special courtesy of agreement, we have seen an inevitable clash of basic plan, as the play of motives bars the true inner structure. The real meaning of music lies in its form by natural growth; the dramatic play of symbolic fragments, telling the tale in the literal sense of the ideas for which they stand, cannot agree with the former plan. It were like telling an epic in two languages at once.

The Berlioz Symphony, in some ways, to be sure, the forerunner of the later Radical school, does not use the strict *leit-motif*, though it has the leading melody of special association.

Interesting, of course, is the preface, with the titles:

1. REVERIES; PASSIONS. (*Largo*; *Allegro agitato ed appassionato assai.*)
2. A BALL. (VALSE. *Allegro, non troppo.*)
3. IN THE COUNTRY. (*Adagio.*)
4. MARCH TO THE SCAFFOLD. (*Allegretto non troppo.*)
5. WITCHES' SABBATH. DIES IRÆ; WITCHES' ROUND DANCE. (*Larghetto; Allegro assai; Allegro.*)

Most significant is the foreword that precedes a full account of *An Episode in the Life of an Artist*, which is the burden of the symphony:

"The following programme must be distributed whenever the symphony is performed dramatically, and followed by the monodrama 'Lelio,' that ends and completes the story. In this case the whole orchestra is disposed on the stage behind the lowered curtain.

"If the symphony alone is played, this arrangement is not needed; in fact, the programme may even be dispensed with, the titles of the five movements alone being retained. The author hopes that the symphony may offer in itself a musical interest independent of all dramatic intent."

The composer shows here exactly the right perception. In so far as his symphony tells its own story, in pure musical

APPENDIX

process, it stands on a higher plane than Beethoven's "Pastoral." But again we must not forget that genius is not a mere matter of school or method. Even with a stray lapse in general plan, smaller lyric beauties of the greater poet may transcend the pervading process of the lesser.

To test the Berlioz symphony in this high purpose, we must, in hearing the work, ask the one question: Does the music tell the story, or merely heighten the effect? Therefore, the full account of small incident, in our "episode," must fairly be reserved to the end, there to test the message of the music.

A dreamy melody begins, *Largo*, followed by more feverish strains, and a more fervent burst of the first tune, in full melodic career, with free play of lesser phrases. The whispered close is broken by bright chords, *Allegro agitato appassionato assai*, that heralds a song of sweeping beauty. It is not a mere theme, though its essence is most centred in the first phrase. The middle verse stresses the passion; the

whole needs no words for the clear stamp of a lyric of love. On the first phrase in low strings rises a fiery dialogue of profound beauty, against a new answer in high wood. Then

APPENDIX

the sovereign beauty of the song reigns alone. Later a second climax is reared in fevered response of lower strains of first phrase, topped by a higher course of the passionate motive, ending in crowning verse of the pure melody. The close comes *religiosamente* in softest solemn strokes of united chords. The first strain has not recurred.

Sounds of glad expectancy soon usher the clear notes of expressive waltz, that flows in its repeated course, with intermittent vaguer play. But in the midst the love-lyric sings a verse right through the gayety of dance,—and once more, before the bright close, alone in softest confidence.

Bucolic reeds betray the scene, of mournful (English) horn and cheering oboe, echoing a chance tune in lonely duet. The quaint simplicity, the impromptu song of the *Ranz des vaches*, all mark the rustic spot. The oboe, too, has moved his distant notes to clearer foreground. And now, in gathering of all the accompanying sounds, low strings sing the main rustic theme. But it is not all a placid pastoral. A tremulous pulse pervades. A passionate phrase now strikes in romantic depths of strings. Suddenly answers on high—the soothing love-song. The bitter, jealous theme wars with its own solace. Peace comes with a return of the first idyl.

The march to the scaffold hardly needs the title, with the solemn doom of funeral tramp, the fatal ring of death-song, with the sad terror of overwhelming chorus, that gives a more poignant sense to the single gentlest strain of impassioned love, just before the end that has somehow a sudden rift of hope.

APPENDIX

The last scene is, once more, clearly pointed by the title Witches' Sabbath, that begins a stormy revel in mad medley of restless discord and vague cries. First of defined strains is the old love-motive, now piping dimly distant in merry mockery, over the dull dance of low drums. Now bursts a tempest of warring cries. Then the full course of love-song dances as before, where the cheer is blighted by uncanny trip of basses and the nearing rage of mad cries. Symbols of doom abound in the clang of bells and ring of fateful *Dies Iræ*, that is itself distorted in mocking rhythm. The Witches' Round Dance starts a grim orgy; later the pitiless chant mingles with the dance to crown the hopeless terror that ends the dream.

For, a dream it is, and we have little need to read the story of young artist, whose ineffectual draught brings, not death, but strangest visions of desires, of his love in varying scenes. He kills her and is condemned, and dreams the full cup of last agonies.

Most of the tragic tale is told without the words of programme. So far we must yield. But first are the titles that give, themselves, a strongest clue. Finally, to waive the old question of former pages,* and even the need of these verbal hints, the mystery soon vanishes of this magic of musical narrative. Though we bar all telltale names that the poet offers, and though we grant the graphic touch of main line of picture, the means are not pure musical resources. A confusion is here that is rarely solved. In the art of the master there is no room for nature-sounds and like conventions.

---

* See the chapters on Schumann in Vol. I., and on the Pastoral Symphony, on Raff, on Liszt, in Vol. II.

APPENDIX

Even with lowest minstrel, the shepherd's reed pipes of rustic scene,—the waltz is ever its own symbol of light gayety ; a funeral march needs no master hand to make its meaning clear. The pure beauty of the melodies, in the hue and contrast of their humors, may justly spin their thread of epic sentiment.*
And here the main recurring song is a true symbol in the story. Again, as in the "Pastoral" of Beethoven, and in the "Faust" of Liszt, the intrusion of extraneous signs, of tempest, of the chance clang of bells, even of the song for mere dramatic, for no musical reason, must break the pure woof of tunes.

The true meaning of music lies still in the play of mere tonal thoughts in the vital essence of their growth to fulness of organic art.

---

* Schumann's *Noveletten*, for the piano, have a striking sense and fragrance of narrative, without the least aid of words.

GADE'S SYMPHONY No. 4, IN B FLAT

Andantino. Allegro vivace é gracioso.
Andante con moto.
Scherzo. Allegro ma non troppo é tranquillamente.
Finale. Allegro molto vivace.

GADE has been likened to a landscape-painter. The simile is true in so far as his melodic figures do not stand out in sharp relief. Instead, by a true artistic process, by close continuity of treatment, by intuitive grasp of form, by a fine sense of orchestral color, he gives the whole a poetic tone, where it is difficult to choose salient phrases. Of course, this is equivalent to saying that Gade has genuine mastery, without the periodic strain and labored method of composers of higher lyric power. So he must stand as a true tonal poet, though of a lesser message. Gade seems to have the trait of naïve unconsciousness which strives for no special effects, does not seek to astonish by clever originality; and so the inner feeling is most perfectly expressed. He has been called a composer for musicians; rather he is for the true music lover, who feels sincerity of sentiment. Then Gade's temper is one of quiet, unpretending contentment, a certain repose that is strange to us Americans; but, once caught, it is the more keenly welcome. The only way to understand Gade, however, is to take his works each as a whole, consecutively, not in melodic snatches. Hence, in suggest-

APPENDIX

ing his musical thought, the mere quoting of "themes," of itself, is of slight use. Where we are accustomed to look for melodic subjects, we find a disappointing simplicity until we see that the essence of the theme lies in some harmonic or rhythmic trait of the setting; or, again, the true beauty does not appear until the discussion of one theme with another. Gade seems to drift along into his episodes in utter disregard of the approved way of ceremonious introduction. The only help is to listen sharply for the whole story as it develops.

Throughout the Fourth Symphony there is the simple, clear mood of joy, in different phases, now noisy, now quiet, exultant or reflective, here in lightest fancy, there in quaintest utterance.

The first movement begins with the *sostenuto* introduction, which is not part of the principal melody. Even on entering the *Allegro*, the *sostenuto* feeling lingers before it bursts into the leading theme

in woodwind and strings, repeated by the full orchestra. This is followed closely by a sweeping, soothing phrase:

first in the cellos, gradually pervading all the strings and the

APPENDIX

woodwind. The second melody is a flight from the noisy shout into the realm of lightest fancy, all in the strings. The subject

depends for its effect on the dancing rhythm and full harmony of the lower strings. Most beautiful of all is the binding together of the two melodies before the *reprise*, where the real feeling, elusive as a fire-fly, is often expressed independent of actual subjects, in a responsive and harmonic play of them all, or in motives that subtly and almost invisibly grow out of the principal themes. After the repetition appears an inversion of the second melody, leading into a brilliantly fanciful development, out of which the first theme steals with surprising stillness, again re-echoed by the whole orchestra. Again follows the second melody with the same beautiful passage as before. At the end there is another lull in the strings before the principal subject is sung in triumphant canonic stretto.

The *Andante* begins in a characteristic idyl. Throughout there is an unbroken stream of melody, yet not reiterated nor diluted. The first theme seems almost ended when it leads into one of such beauty that the former sounds like introduction. The melodic texture is so close that it is difficult to

APPENDIX

separate first from second theme; nor does it matter where all is melody. There is no purpose in quoting each distinct from the beautiful intertwining of all, nor in whole, nor in part.

The *Scherzo* returns to the vein of light fancy of the second tune of *Allegro*. It lies, of course, largely in the strings. The subject

again depends for its beauty upon the rhythm and harmony of the accompaniment. The first Trio is in sharp contrast, with its simple diatonic theme, though still in dancing rhythm:

The second, equally poetic, abandons the dance. Simplicity itself, the melody is sung in strict *legato* by the violins:

while the violas sway in graceful rhythm.

The *Finale* is the climax: one continuous, infectious frolic. The opening melody, less impressive in its first

APPENDIX

statement, gradually carries all before it by an insistent swing and spirit; the second has a more quiet, contained happiness.

The whole is complete sonata-form without the repetition.

GOETZ'S SYMPHONY IN F MAJOR

BETWEEN title-page and score is given a motto:

> "In des Herzens stille Räume
> Musst du fliehen aus des Lebens Drang."
>
> SCHILLER.

> Into the quiet chambers of the soul
> Flee for refuge from the stress of life.

Hermann Goetz has something of the strange charm that clings to the figure of Chatterton, though it lies not in the precocity of his work, but in the keen regret for the loss to music from his untimely death. Somehow this feeling is almost greater than in the cases of Mozart and Schubert, whose work seemed to grow in natural career to complete fulfilment. That of Goetz, it is clear, had merely begun. His was not the early day of rapid outpouring of melody. The romantic message, of German folk-song, of rebellion against classic formalism, had been uttered. Goetz was born to the later time when the better vein of tonal poetry sought the blending of classic art with modern feeling, the quality of form, rather than the barren stereotype.

A near contemporary of Brahms, Goetz would, in almost certain probability, have joined that master in the neo-classic period of German symphony. They might have been the Mozart and Beethoven or the Mendelssohn and Schumann of the latest age of masters.

APPENDIX

The symphony of Goetz is scored quite simply, with four horns, two trumpets, and three trombones.

Through chords of horns and clarinets, and waving strings, the theme of *Allegro* steals in, in lowest basses and cellos

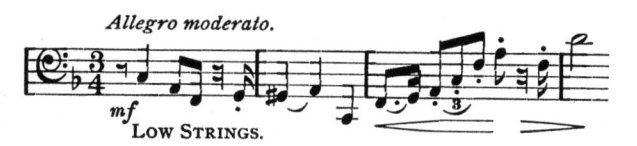

topped with melodious answer of violins and wood. The melody has the secret of endless thread, though of its own special strain. An embodiment there seems here, in clearest crystal of pure tones, of a spirit that found other utterance in a setting of actual legend and drama. A most spirited climax breaks sheer before the expressive motive, the true second subject:

an idyl in the heart of the fervent song of the main text, whence it soon gains a new spring that leads to a concluding phrase, that sums the joyous sense of the whole:

APPENDIX

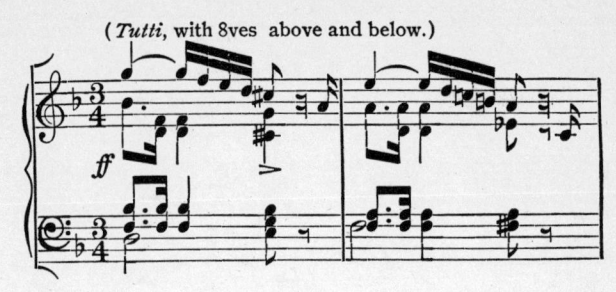

(*Tutti*, with 8ves above and below.)

Very beautifully the first melody comes coursing into the bass of the end of the third, pursued in turn by another entrance in high treble. Before the repeat, this free canon on main theme dies to a sombre lull.

The discussion begins much like the prelude, then it is given o'er to a placid, dulcet guise of the first strain, where a most expressive countertheme is more and more eminent, at first below in cellos, later in high solo flute. In the discussion no theme enters but the fervent flow of the dominant song. And so, the idyllic episode recurs at the end, just as in the beginning, though there is a last special verse on the thread of main melody.

The brief themes of the *Intermezzo* do not, in themselves, seem the full text. It is in their commingling and interplay that the true purpose appears and the humor of the whole is shown. The first, a mere call of horns:

HORNS.
Allegretto.

APPENDIX

is answered almost jestingly by high wood. Soon the second runs right on the heels of the first:

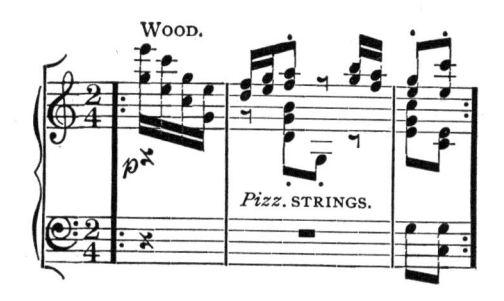

and thus the relevant beauty of both is most clear, though there are verses of the separate tunes. An entirely new color comes with a third one, in minor strings:

sombrely playful, stealing anon into sunnier light (of major),— finding its own thread of weaving song without the need of

APPENDIX

other text, until far on, where the first sings anew in horns, and, somehow, a kinship of tune now appears. Then, again, the third makes playful answer, much like the former second. One more verse follows of the third alone.

The ending is altogether naïve. The minor hue of the third is broken by a new hymnal tune,—*un poco meno moto:*

in strings, with sustaining notes of wood and horns. Its solemnity leads most temptingly to the merriness of the second melody, that now gambols about in all kinds of light, with answering strain now and then from the first theme. After a big, coursing climax, a new response comes to the purling song of second theme,—building a new, expressive tune on the simple call of the first, growing finally to full melody, out of all the original lines. The very end is in duet of the first call, and of a simple, major strain of third theme.

The slow movement of symphony is probably the final test of the composer. No pomp or tricks of scoring can fill the want. Pure melody there must be, in quiet, contained flow, without the nervous throb, the quick rising storms of the *Allegro.* So the slow movement is the final essence of the

APPENDIX

poet's thought; its utterance is the end of all the earlier stress.

By this high test, Goetz is not wanting. Beginning in low strings, the noble song winds a graceful curve of solemn beauty:

There is, again, a striking quality here that marks a difference from the style of the great romantic masters and from any of their successors. A certain lyric strain, of modern sense and feeling, here was finding highest expression in the symphony. With the death of the poet, the spring seems to have dried; or it may have found a less pure channel in other forms. In certain ways, Goetz reminds us of Gade, mainly in weaving small themes of lesser import to a beautiful tonal scene. Gade has been called the landscape-painter of music. The *Intermezzo*, here, shows some of this art and method. But the *Adagio* is, all, spontaneous flowing song. In the midst, in complete change of tone, is an episode of simpler lines of tune and of quieter humor. The mode, too, is in serene major, leaving tne romantic color of the first.

APPENDIX

(Horns, with obligato strings.)

dolce.

CELLOS AND BASSES.

With the art of a master, the horns, that first sing the theme, are answered, in unguarded moments, by clarinets, with exquisite touch of dissonance. A speaking climax leads to a varied verse of first melody, *un poco piu largo*,—really a free song of first violins, with *pizzicato* of lower strings. Soon the cellos are drawn into the melody. Then, above the later, flowing course of all the strings breaks the chorus of wood in the original melody, *tempo primo*.

The second theme returns briefly, and is followed by a still bolder verse of main tune, *molto agitato*, where tumultuous waves of responsive phrase play in eager canon. The final verse has the theme transfigured in placid song of serene major without the dross of the earlier passion.

In the *Finale, Allegro con fuoco*, joyousness is clearly stamped on the swing and line of the theme. Again the sense of ever-winding thread is there, as of unending dance. The bright motive that begins, plays a large part in the digressions between the verses of tune. In the simple phrases of second subject, woven in canon of three voices, in strings and wood, we seem to see again the art that paints in minute touches,—that can rear a great work on small figures. With

APPENDIX

Allegro con fuoco.

(Tutti, reinforced in 8ves.)

(See page 469, line 14.)

all the melodious beauty there is a festive interplay of phrase (where, too, the answers of themes have no small share) that gives a richness of polyphonic life and harmony, and makes, perhaps, the main charm. The lyric beauty of the second theme is clearer in a later appearance:

where the melodic flow is freer than in the first fugual statement. With all the wealth of contrapuntal art, there is a

APPENDIX

gay freedom in the informal entrance of voices in unexpected response, and a blithe discourse of lesser strains, where, anon, the main theme strikes in with the highest note of festal glee. In the midst is quite a disputation, as phrases, from second theme and its answer, meet from above and below,—all sustained in long sequence. At each meeting they reach a final concord by narrowest pinch of dissonance. Then the controversy is repeated with changed positions of the parties.

In the final return to the first array of disputant strains, a high point is reached of dramatic feeling,—though the word seems a mockery of the real beauty.

From here the pure note of high delight reigns, first in the mere dancing swing of main theme, then in the full play of both subjects. There is a fine ring in the joyous pranks that end the symphony.

GILCHRIST'S SYMPHONY IN C MAJOR

THE symphony begins with a spirited unison attack on the motive:

Vivace impetuoso.

(In unison of full orchestra.)

presently falling into soft, sliding chords in united band, and broken whispers of sighing melody before the entrance, *molto allegro*, in strings, of the main theme, in strong, swinging rhythm:

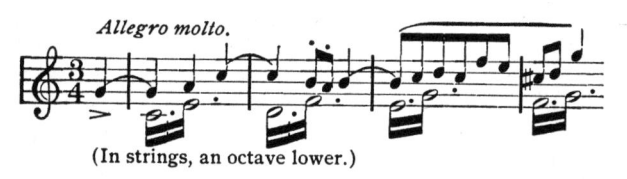

Allegro molto.

(In strings, an octave lower.)

followed by a vigorous answer. The theme presently varies its song in saucy humor and dashes into a *ff* cadence, whence emerges the gentle second melody, mostly in woodwind, of which the answer glides into a flow of tender song, one of those phrases which with the composer we feel we cannot have without rehearing and rehearsing. The second theme now re-enters in more heroic guise, in full orchestra, with added noisy coursing of violins.

APPENDIX

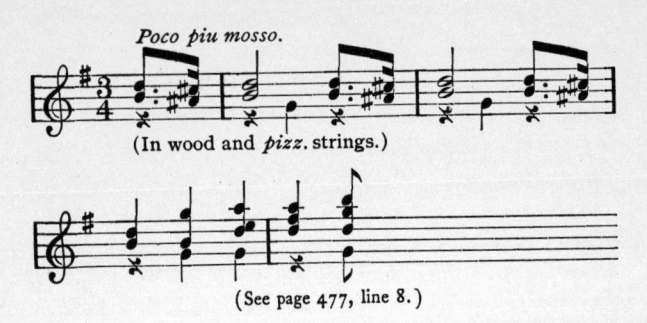

Poco piu mosso.

(In wood and *pizz.* strings.)

(See page 477, line 8.)

After a triumphant climax and cadence the discussion begins, briskly, on odd ends of the second theme. Through misty changes of color echoes a more subdued strain, in playful duet of strings and wood, from the old, repeated phrase. Out of it emerges, very simply, a new song, in strings and clarinet:

Espressivo.

pp

(In clarinet and strings.)

This, with the preceding strain, is led through fresh and moving changes of tonal scene, with answering bits rising anon to a climax, so that the whole discussion is a woof of clear, running melody rather than a mass of complex tones.

APPENDIX

At the end of this idyllic dialogue, the spirited attack of the second theme breaks the spell and rushes in noisy ascent into the introduction, whence, through the whole of its varied course, we enter again on the simple, joyful song of the first melody, followed by the second, with the strain which we like to repeat, ending in triumphant blast of second theme.

The *Adagio*, in prelude, foreshadows the main tune in sombre, descending chords and chanting clarinet. Here, where all is lyric song, we do not know whether most to enjoy the first melody, sung by solo clarinet in naïve rhythm and a sort of Phrygian mode, softened by the murmuring hum of strings:

(In solo clarinet with accompanying strings.)

or the more speaking later theme in low cellos, with rhythmic woodwind:

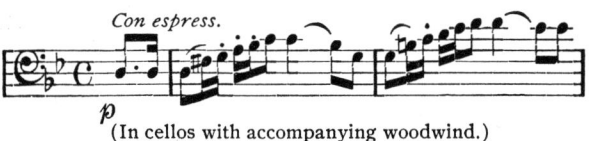

(In cellos with accompanying woodwind.)

But it is not quite all lyric song. Out of the second melody grows a phrase that proves the bone of contention, with a distinct sense of altercation between basses and trebles, in pure counterpoint, after which the main melody, with a new breath of pastoral freshness, returns to close.

APPENDIX

The *Scherzo Bacchanale* is perhaps truest of all to its own humor. There is no escaping the rollicking dash of the theme, in violins:

(In violins with *pizz.* strings.)

carried along in flowing merriment on the motive of the first three notes. The second theme, growing directly out of the other, appears first in minor on strings, later in major in comic cellos, with a special abandon of drollery:

mocked lightly by the high woodwind.

APPENDIX

But most of all has the *Trio* the Bacchanale flavor, as the strings, in clumsy gait, stumble along, falling and picking themselves up :

A brilliant extension of the dance, with contrary figures joining in, leads through the repeated Trio back to the original Scherzo.

The *Finale* is based on two very opposite themes, one a true *fanfare*, in spirit and in function, with its electric motive :

the bass descending in diatonic steps, followed in sequence. The second, in spite of a quicker pace, has distinctly more sentiment, and is marked *legato espressivo*:

Singing mainly in strings, it draws on most of the band, though seldom in *tutti*, working in profuse polyphony on its

APPENDIX

smallest motives. Though the movement is rather rondo than sonata, it has more of discussion than any of the others, ever on the second melody, and, in mood, hovering between sparkling fun and gentler feeling, until an answering kind of melody is suddenly evolved, like the wings of a chrysalis:

(Melody in clarinets and flutes.)

in clear retort to the original (second) tune, and the more welcome and relevant for the waiting.

Here follows the greatest polyphonic revel of all, around the (second) melody, part and whole, in changing tonal settings, with a new and quicker counter-phrase in strings: the kind of passage where, in the glow of the story, a composer will do all the feats of counterpoint without knowing it—the only true way. But we must hold fast to the outline of the theme, even in small fragments, else we lose all bearings in the dizzy whirl, though here and there the new-fledged tune does appear clear in a placid calm. The whole shows how a lesser melody (in official rank) will assume control, and from its small compass give full resources for varied and spirited discussion, leaving to the principal theme little more than the formality of introduction and finally of a triumphant ending.

GOLDMARK'S LÄNDLICHE HOCHZEIT (COUNTRY WEDDING) SYMPHONY

THE title ought not to suggest a peasant wedding, This would surely have been called *Bauernhochzeit*, —a well-known term and a most characteristic event of German village life. This is evidently not what the composer meant. The title means the typical wedding, which must, of course, have the simple surroundings of the country for full course of festivity. The fourth number, "Im Garten," is clearest proof. For the peasant has no garden; that is quite a special mark of social difference. A peasant wedding is a most picturesque festival, expressive of true folk tradition. No one, if he were in the neighborhood, would miss a sight of the highly-colored costumes, richly worked, nor the jolly scenes at the tavern. And a peasant wedding were unmistakable in music. We should not fail to find the rollicking Ländler, the peasant waltz, towards the end.

The country wedding of Goldmark is altogether another sort of celebration. The difference were not worth noting, save that it has so sharp a meaning in Germany itself, the land of the composer, and, therefore, in his mind.

The symphony is all written in simple lyric manner, is "symphony" merely in a very general sense. It were a mistake to read into it too many scenes and situations, too much detailed meaning, however tempting this may be. For, it is the sentiment that finds fullest play, with no more of special labelling than the titles themselves of the five parts:

APPENDIX

1. Wedding March (Variations). 2. Bridal Song (*Intermezzo*). 3. Serenade (*Scherzo*). 4. In the Garden (*Andante*). 5. Dance (*Finale*).

Under the big name of "March" in the variations, a sense of expectancy in different phases is poetically uttered. First, the pretty rollicking theme alone:

Moderato molto.

then contrasted moods, where the melody is woven in subtle beauty, seeking often to elude all sense of march, while keeping the essence of festive idea ever prominent. Thus, after first simple accent of march comes a dreamily flowing canon of strings, *poco animato*, that plays into a suggestion of the melody; then the march breaks in full tread in basses, with acclaim of all the band. Third is a gently swinging, almost sad *Andante con moto*, beginning in strings, horns, and fagots,—restless often in seeking new tones, reaching the tune in clear light, or ending in quaint cadence. The flowing *obligato* of lower strings is strengthened in fagots; the chorus in swing of slow dance just escapes the sense of dragging; then a smart trip,—*Allegro scherzando*,—the violins leading the motion, the solo horn holding the tune. In delicate confidence flute and violin start the duet, *Allegretto poco andantino*, where only cellos guard a reminder of the theme. *Molto vivace* breaks in a most charming verse of the tune, in

APPENDIX

three time. Before the final refrain of the simple march is a very extended verse, beginning, we are sure, in church, as the solemn organ tones (of the wood) drone out a fugal play about the simple *chorale* that is first given out by oboes:

Later the flutes and clarinets join in the hymnal song. Between its lines an intimate strain is played in soft trio of solo violins and viola,—that reminds us of *Walther* behind the church pillar, in the *Meistersinger*. The sacred and secular strains are richly blended in the close.

The *Bridal Song* stands out in the clear beauty of sense and song, throughout all the verse, and has no need of cumbering words.

The *Serenade* is like dainty madrigal in several verses. The themes, to be sure, have with all lightness a serious grace and feeling. But between them are flashes of fine humor in lesser phrase and in tne interpiay of motive. So the whole is beautifully blended of bubbling humor and tender sentiment,

APPENDIX

where each runs into the other, and each is pressing for main utterance. The first verse is on the pretty vein of main theme, whose mirth and lightness is not free from sentiment. In the second there is a new tinge of pathos in the graceful melody:

But its own answer has a true humor of well-marked primitive bass, as of bagpipe. Before the last rehearsing of verses is the full interweaving in big polyphonic climax, all in the ancient manner of stately madrigal.

The scene "In the Garden" has the most intimate shade of beauty, where the clarinet tenderly and dreamily begins its appealing song in rarest harmonies of wood and lower strings. Later it is heard in high violins.

Two distinct melodic elements there are in this romance. Against the rare delicacy of the first is the ardent tone of the second, in cellos echoed by violins.

Though beginning *poco piu lento*, there is ever a rising to passionate climax, where question of lower voices spurs the answer of higher,—and then a subsiding to the timid first phrase. As the *Andante* may be called the epitome of a symphony, so this idyl is clearly the heart of the work.

APPENDIX

(See page 486, line 16.)

The *Dance Allegro molto,* is all on big scale. In polyphonic design, it is profoundest of all the movements. For after a brief *fanfare,* violins lead off a fugue in four voices, on the dance of theme.

(Dance theme.)

(Later counter-theme.)

APPENDIX

Later, as the woodwind take up the tune, a jolly countertheme runs in cellos and fagots, that adds a jogging pace, so that the whole gets a rich charm of cheery bustle. The fugue, somehow, has not the least smell of the lamp. The more complete it is the more we think of a gay reel, with varying figures and freedom of individual motion. Soon the polyphonic maze gives way to a second tune of united simple dance:

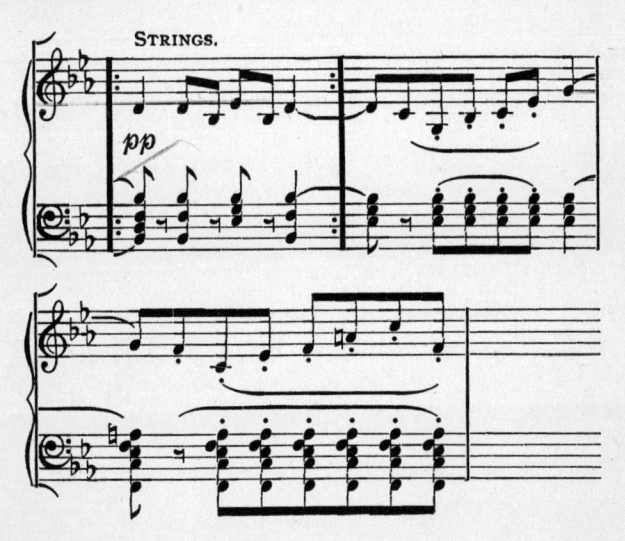

started gently in strings, waxing lustier with added woodwind, finally bursting into big march-like fling in loudest chorus. Whimsically the soft tread and the heavy stamp of jig alternate, and there are sudden lulls broken by frightening volume. Then back to the comfortable swing of first round dance.

APPENDIX

For a moment we steal out of doors, and are again lost in the rare strain of the garden scene. Of surprising beauty is the epilogue, where the simple second tune (of dance) broadens into true, moving song, like festive hymn, rising to height of fervent appeal, that is too intimate for mere trip of foot. As the original swing steals into the midst, the end is in climax that is much more than frolic of dance.

INDEX

Ambros, von, 13

American symphony, an, 477–482

Andante : Melody, 42, 69, 284, 299 ; movement, 84, 99, 111, 262–3, 344, 472 (see Lyric); in Mozart and Beethoven, 22 *et seq.*, 46, 49, 69; of G minor symphony, 45, 49

Aristophanes, 101

Art, 160, 175, 323, 455 (see Preface); and nature, 141

Arts, basic purpose of the various, 137 *et seq.*, 324, 421 *et seq.*

Bach, 40, 241, 326, 403, 407, 453, 455

Ballad, 218 (See Folk-Song ; "Lenore.")

Beauty in art, 144, 439 (See Art.)

Beethoven, 13–14, 16, 18, 22, 24, 31, 34–194, 230, 247, 282, 284, 286, 295, 299, 326, 331, 407, 457; disciple of Mozart and Haydn, 53–58, 69 *et seq.*, 79 ; humor of, 49 *et seq.*, 76–7, 97 *et seq.*, 305–6; poet of fraternity, 98–101, 323, 378 ; of humor, 101–3, 111 *et seq.*; first symphony, 34–58 ; second symphony, 59–86; third symphony, 41, 113; fourth symphony, 87–110; fifth symphony, 37, 39, 97, 111, 113, 149, 445; sixth (pastoral) symphony, 111, 133–152, 230, 242, 457; seventh symphony, 111, 113; eighth symphony, 111–132; ninth (choral) symphony, 99, 153–194

INDEX

Berlioz, Fantastic Symphony, 457–462
Brahms, 282–400, 405, 433, 455, 468; first symphony, 282–322; second symphony, 313; third symphony, 323–360; fourth symphony, 361–400; humor of, 305–10; greatness, 318; and Beethoven compared, 323
Bürger, "Lenore" ballad translated by Scott, 257–267

Cacophony, 141, 143–4, 435 *et seq.*, 438 *et seq.*, 451–2
Canon, 25, 190
Chadwick. (See Preface.)
Chorale, 485 (See Hymn.)
Cimarosa, 17
Coherence in music. (See Sequence, Form.)
Content, emotional, in pure art, 13 *et seq.*, 263 (See Feeling.)
Counterpoint (see Polyphony), 279, 406–7, 451–2
Criticism, 178–9, 454–5

Dance, 344 *et seq.*, 346 (See Scherzo.)
Definite utterance in music, 153, 171, 189; in art, 324
Depiction. (See Descriptive, Programme.)
Descriptive music, 136–140, 145 *et seq.*, 148–9, 230–1, 241–3, 267 *et seq.*, 408, 457 *et seq.*, 461 *et seq.* (See, generally, Chaps. VI. and IX.)
Development, themal, 315 *et seq.*, 317, 320, 361, 464 (see Discussion), 371, 372 *et seq.*, 447–8
Discussion, themal, 84, 135, 160, 171–2, 180–1, 208–9, 217, 223, 226–7, 335, 386, 387, 406, 464
Disputation. (See Discussion.)
Dogma, 323

INDEX

Dominant, 37
Drama (see Opera), 178, 420, 422
Duality in the sonata and symphony, 36, 38

Emotional element (see Content, Feeling), 403
Ethical element, 323, 378 (See Moral.)

Fairies, 213, 249–50
"Fantastic" Symphony. (See Berlioz.)
Feeling, in music and in the other arts, 136, 137, 149, 152–3, 242, 257–267, 262
Finale, 125; in Beethoven, Mozart, and Haydn, 53–8, 81, 103–4; of "Jupiter" symphony, 53–5, 81, 104
Folk-Lore, 323–5
Folk-Song, 68, 92, 124, 218, 275, 299, 375, 468 (See Lyric.)
"Forest" Symphony. (See Raff.)
Form (see Meaning) 15–16, 160 (see Development, 403, 405–8, 420, 433, 447 *et seq.*, 458)
Fugue (see Preface), 36, 483

Gade, 463–467, 473; fourth symphony, 464–7
German humor and fancy, 336 *et seq.*; mythology, 251–253; folk-song. (See Folk-Song.)
Gilchrist, 477–487
Gluck, 17–18, 116
Goethe, 421
Goetz, 468–476; symphony in F, 469–476. (See Appendix.)
Goldmark, 483–489; country wedding symphony, 483–485

493

INDEX

Haendel, 178

Harmony, basis of, 37, 402–3, 409

Haydn, 13, 17, 18, 24, 34, 55–8, 79, 87, 112–3, 116, 196, 282, 285, 325, 451–2; finale of E flat symphony, 55–9

Hebrides overture. (See Mendelssohn.)

Helmholtz, 379

Homer, 77

Humor, 67, 76, 97 *et seq.*, 344 *et seq.*, 486; poets of, 101 *et seq.*, 112, 119 *et seq.*, 305 *et seq.* (See "Scotch," "German"); an epic of, 111–132

Hymn (see Chorale), 275, 489

"Im Walde" Symphony. (See Raff.)
"Italian" Symphony. (See Mendelsshon.)

Jean Paul, 101
"Joy," ode to. (See Schiller.)
"Jupiter" Symphony. (See Mozart.)

Key. (See Tonal scene, 37, 378 *et seq.*)

Legend. (See Folk-lore, 324)

Liszt, 408 *et seq.*, 449 *et seq.*; "Faust" symphony, 408–420, 433

Leit-motif, 404 *et seq.*, 409 *et seq.*

"Lenore" symphony and ballad. (See Raff.)

Lied, 402

Logic (in music). (See Sequence, 385)

Lyric element in music, 149, 168, 273, 344, 405, 422, 449, 457, 459, 479, 483 (See Andante.)

INDEX

Meaning (see Sequence, Form), 145, 180–1, 361, 406, 421, 454–5, 457–8, 462   (See Preface.)

Melody, 45, 403

Mendelssohn, 230–241, 299, 345, 457, 468; "Italian" symphony, 231–2; "Scotch" symphony, 231–241; "Hebrides" overture, 233

Minuet, 27, 49, 76, 102, 122

Mode (see Key), 378 *et seq.*; Phrygian, 479

Modulation.   (See Tonal, Preface.)

Monteverde, 405, 453

Moral element in music, 323, 378 *et seq.*, 421 *et seq.*

Motif.   (See Leit-motif.)

Mozart, 13–33, 36, 45, 46, 53, 323, 331, 335; andante of G minor symphony, 45, 49; finale of "Jupiter" symphony, 53–5, 81, 104; Mozart and Beethoven, 13, 17, 53–9, 69, 79; symphony in E Flat, 13–33 (See Beethoven.)

Music, absolute, 175, 180, 185, 409; dignity and purpose of, 324, 378, 407, 421 *et seq.*   (See Preface.)

Mythology, German, 251–3

Narrative element in music, 197–8, 201, 377

National element in music, 232 *st seq.*, 344 *et seq.*, 398, 457

Nature-sounds, 141–5, 147–9, 359, 457, 461–2

Ode to Joy.   (See Schiller.)

Opera, 178, 231, 402, 405, 457, 469

Overture, 231–2

Paer, 17

Paine.   (See Preface.)

495

INDEX

Passacaglia, 388 *et seq.*

Pastoral symphony (see Beethoven) music, 457, 459

Pathos 112, 119

Phrygian mode, 374, 479

Poetry and music, 175, 177, 179–80, 189, 421 *et seq.* (See Words.)

Polyphony, 172, 186, 403, 406, 482, 487 *et seq.* (See Counterpoint, 451–2)

Prelude of symphony, 17–18, 34–5, 60 *et seq.*, 79–80, 87–9, 313, 325

Programme music, 230 *et seq.*, 288 *et seq.*, 267, 457 *et seq.* (See Descriptive.)

Prose and music, 324

Radical school, 401 *et seq.*, 433 *et seq.*, 449–455

Raff, 230–1, 241–281; "Forest" symphony, 241–257; "Lenore" symphony, 257–267; "Winter" symphony, 258–281

Realism in music, 148–9, 257–267 (See Descriptive.)

Reflective phase of music, 207, 209, 213, 218–9

Rhythm, 171–2, 278, 342 *et seq.*, 362, 40

Romanticism, 230, 295, 323, 331, 361, 468, 473

Rondo, 30, 86

Scherzo, 49, 76–7, 81, 84, 91 *et seq.*, 102, 344, 380 *et seq.*, 445, 480

Schiller, Ode to Joy, 99; translated, 173–5, 176–7, 179

Schubert, 87, 177, 181, 331, 468

INDEX

Schumann, 87, 138, 195–229, 323, 331, 372, 377, 446, 455; "Rhine" symphony, 227, 230; first symphony, 195–209; second symphony, 210–229

Scotch humor and romance, 236–240; "Scotch" symphony. (See Mendelssohn.)

Scott, "Lenore" ballad, 257–267

Sequence, 168, 180, 216, 331, 385–407, 449–50, 453–4, 458 (See Development.)

Shakespeare, 101, 102, 421

Slow movement. (See Andante.)

Sonata, 36, 431

Strauss, Richard, 406, 433–455; Heldenleben, 406, 435–449

Structure. (See Form, 458)

Symbolism, musical, 41, 268, 313, 320, 321, 322, 408–20, 438, 441, 457–8 (See Preface.)

Symphony, basic purpose of, 112, 232–3, 420 *et seq.*, 433, 483; moral force of, 59–60, 98–102; entitled, 230 *et seq.*, 241–2, 483. (See Titles.)

Theory in art, 143–4, 153, 177–8, 438–9

Theme. (See Development.)

Titles, 135–40, 148, 180, 189, 230 *et seq.*, 408, 438 *et seq.*, 449 (See Symphony.)

Tonal scene, residence, or light, 164, 193 (See Preface. See Tone, Key.)

Tonality. (See Tonal.)

Tone, various meanings of, 37, 108, 334. (See Key, Preface), 378 *et seq.*

Tonic, 37.

INDEX

Trio, 51, 98, 221, 223
Truth in art, 144, 161, 179, 324
Tschaikowsky, 449, *et seq.*; *Symphonie Pathétique*, 412, 422-433

Wagner, 243, 403, 407, 433, 451, 453, 474
"Winter" Symphony. (See Raff.)
Words, need of, in music, Preface, Chap. VII., 153, 172, 173, 175-6, 179-80, 185

THE END